Reminiscences of the
Russian Ballet

DA CAPO SERIES IN

DANCE

GENERAL EDITOR: DALE HARRIS

SARAH LAWRENCE COLLEGE

Reminiscences of the Russian Ballet

By
ALEXANDRE BENOIS

Translated by
Mary Britnieva

DA CAPO PRESS • NEW YORK • 1977

Library of Congress Cataloging in Publication Data

Benois, Alexandre, 1870-1960.
  Reminiscences of the Russian ballet.

  (Da Capo series in dance)
  Translation of Vospominaniia o balete.
  Reprint of the 1941 ed. published by Putnam, London.
  1. Benois, Alexandre, 1870-1960. 2. Artists—
Russia — Biography. 3. Ballets russes de Serge de
Diaghilew. 4. Dancing — Russia — History. 5. Ballet —
History. I. Title.
GV1785.B39A3813   792.8'0947   77-7791
ISBN 0-306-77426-7

This Da Capo Press edition of *Reminiscences of
The Russian Ballet* is an unabridged republication
of the first edition published in London in 1941.

Published by Da Capo Press, Inc.
A Subsidiary of Plenum Publishing Corporation
227 West 17th Street, New York, N.Y. 10011

THE BOLSHOY THEATRE, ST. PETERSBURG, 1885

From a water-colour by Alexandre Benois

Frontispiece

Reminiscences of the Russian Ballet

By
ALEXANDRE BENOIS

Translated by
Mary Britnieva

PUTNAM ∾ LONDON
42 Great Russell Street, W.C.1

First published, September, 1941

Printed in Great Britain by
Wyman & Sons, Ltd., London, Fakenham and Reading.

INTRODUCTION

IT is with particular pleasure that I have accepted the suggestion that I should write my reminiscences of the ballet; yet I am not, strictly speaking, a devotee of the ballet, or even a *balletomane*. It so happened that at a certain period of my life my creative activities were devoted to the theatre, and mainly to the choreographic branch of that art; but even to-day my knowledge of the classic dance and its theory does not go very far and I have never really taken much interest in the past history of the ballet. Nevertheless, it is true that the ballet has played a tremendous part in my life, from my earliest years onward, and has been for me the source of inimitable delights. Finally, fate seems to have decreed that I, together with some of my nearest friends, should have helped to create the "world success" of the ballet. It was in 1909 that the ballet appeared on the world stage, so that this year it can celebrate its thirtieth anniversary, and celebrate it throughout almost the whole universe.

It is remarkable too, in a sense, that, in spite of the great variety of my activities—I can claim a not inconsiderable output as a painter and as an author of works on the history of art, and have been, among other things, curator of one of the most celebrated museums of Europe, the Hermitage—I am nevertheless chiefly known abroad as "Diaghilev's collaborator," and this mainly in the ballet. Yet how surprised even Diaghilev would have been had he been told at the beginning of his career that he was

to become famous throughout the world as an apostle
of the ballet, and that all he had created before
would count for nothing.

Let me say again that the way it all happened was
quite unexpected; nevertheless it all did happen. So
now I am asked just as unexpectedly for my reminiscences of the ballet. Those who ask for them evidently
take a very slight interest in my past life, in the
delightful atmosphere in which I grew up, in my
artistic development, or in the story of how, though
belonging to a past world, I have outlived its collapse
and find myself in utterly new surroundings. But I
still cherish the hope that I may yet have time to
write the complete story of my life. What I have
written here about the ballet is, to a certain extent, a
part of my general memoirs.

My reminiscences of the ballet naturally fall into
two parts. For a considerable time I was but a
spectator in the theatre. It was only in 1901, at
the age of thirty-one, that I began to take an active
part in theatrical work, and only in 1907 that I
fulfilled a dream and turned my attention to the
ballet—that is to say, I created ballets and directed
their production. It seems to me, nevertheless, that
the first part of my theatrical life is not less interesting,
from the point of view of the ballet-lover, than the
second.

It was indeed my extraordinary engagement as a
spectator, that stimulated the next stage of my
development, and made me devote myself seriously
to theatrical work. And of all the joys the theatre
has brought me, those that I have experienced from
the ballet have certainly been the most thrilling; and
in my work for the stage it is again the ballet that
has fired me with the greatest enthusiasm. I would
even say that the most successful of my other work
has had some connection with the ballet. Such are
the doctor's dedication in *Le Malade Imaginaire,* the

Turkish ceremony in *Le Bourgeois Gentilhomme*, the short ballet in Gounod's *Le Médecin Malgré Lui*, the ballets in *Manon* and *La Dame de Pique* and the interludes in *Il Servitore di due Padroni* of Goldoni, which I consider to be my masterpiece.

Wherever and whenever it has been possible I have always gone back to the "language of the ballet" and I must confess that when I expressed myself in this language I felt a greater freedom and inspiration. The ballet has, so to speak, its own mysteries, its own spell; one feels in the ballet "the presence of a ruling spirit of its own."

But I am anticipating what I have set out to tell, so let me now begin my tale.

As is usual to every story-teller, I feel a certain timidity, for it may be that the facts that I consider interesting and important will not be so regarded by the reader. In any case I must warn him not to expect any philosophical reflections, any sort of treatise on the ballet. These are purely *personal* reminiscences. It is *the human document of a personal character* that interests me more than anything else. Among those who will read this book there may be some who share this preference.

To them I dedicate this book.

A. B.

Paris,
     December, 1939.

CONTENTS

PART ONE

SPECTATOR OF THE BALLET

PART TWO

WORKER FOR THE BALLET

A*

PART THREE
THE BALLETS RUSSES

CONTENTS

ILLUSTRATIONS

PART ONE

SPECTATOR OF THE BALLET

Chapter I

THE BENOIS FAMILY

OUR name is not Russian, and its French spelling is somewhat peculiar, for, although deriving from the name of St. Benedict, it is written neither *Benoit* nor *Benoist*, as is usually the case, but *Benois* with an S at the end. It is impossible to know which of my ancestors is to be blamed for this lapse, but our family is by now, after 200 years, rather fond of this illiteracy, which distinguishes us from the innumerable other people who respond to the sound "Benua." The fact that the error is comparatively ancient is proved by different family papers that were preserved by my father and other relatives. It is also poetically confirmed by an acrostic dedicated by my grandfather to his father—my great-grandfather—every verse of which begins with the successive letters of his name and christian name, Nicolas Benois. This acrostic strictly follows the rules of ornamental eighteenth-century calligraphy and used to hang in the exact centre of one of the walls of my father's study, which was entirely lined with old family portraits.

Just above the framed acrostic hung the portrait of my great-grandfather to whom it had been dedicated. It was the picture of an old man, blind in one eye, wearing a modest grey coat. It was this Nicolas Benois who caused his family to break away from the old bonds of peasant life and led them, and the generations that followed, into the broad realms of culture. It was this great-grandfather who first abandoned his plough and harrow to become a village schoolmaster, and so was able to give his own children an education and a good start in life. His three sons, however, left their country during the Revolutionary terror, as quite young men, and began their lives again outside France. Two of them came to England and one even got as far as India. My grandfather, the fourth son, found himself in Russia, where in quest of his daily bread he learned the art of cooking. There can be no doubt that my grandfather had real talent and calling for this difficult art, because, though still quite young, he became *maître d'hôtel* to the stern Emperor Paul. After the tragic death of the Tsar he remained *officier de bouche* to his consort, the Empress Marie Feodorovna, who seems to have been especially gracious to him.

The supposition that my grandfather was not a quite ordinary character is confirmed by his memoirs, which are written in the rather frank manner of a Restif de la Bretonne, and also by a copy-book of verses which include the acrostic mentioned above. It is also remarkable that grandfather Benois was a lover of art. After his death he left his heirs plenty of good furniture and porcelain and a portrait gallery, which, although it does not extend beyond the time of his father, still contains excellent examples of painting. Many of these portraits used to hang in my father's study, others were left as legacies to his brothers and nephews. Among the most successful portraits I must mention those of my great-uncle Anne François Benois—the one who had lived many years in England—and of his attractive wife dressed in the fashion of 1810. Both are the work of a forgotten but excellent French artist, Boileau.

The portrait of my grandfather and grandmother painted in Petersburg at the same period by the *émigré* artist Courteuil are equally good. My grandfather looks pleasant though imposing; his white powdered hair contrasting with his very dark eyebrows gives him great charm. My father had two other portraits of my grandfather, one of which was a miniature by the famous Ritt, framed in the lid of a snuff-box. The other, a very curious composition, was the work of an amateur and showed my grandfather surrounded by his family—and this family was very numerous. My grandmother bore him seventeen children. Six died in infancy and one while still young, but all the others reached more or less extreme old age. My uncle Louis lived to celebrate his golden wedding, my father died at the age of eighty-five. All the descendants of my grandfather, the St. Petersburg Benois, married and had children, so the number of people calling themselves Benois—with an S at the end—who were living in Russia was more than a hundred.

My grandfather Louis Benois died comparatively young and was deeply mourned by his family. He perished in the smallpox epidemic of 1822, leaving his wife to bring up the numerous children, the youngest of whom was three years old. It is true she was provided for and helped materially by the Dowager Empress, but there still remained the spiritual side.

My grandmother, who was an extremely energetic woman, proved herself quite equal to the task. All her children made their fortunes and one of them— my father—very early began to distinguish himself as an artist. At the age of twelve he was awarded a full scholarship at the Academy of Arts, and there he soon showed a distinct leaning towards architecture. He was awarded, out of his turn, the large gold medal which enabled him to continue his studies abroad, and in 1840 he left for Italy. He remained there for six years, living chiefly in Rome and in Orvieto. During his return journey he visited the chief centres of art and stayed some time in England, where he was deeply impressed by the English Gothic. He followed this style for one of his best works in Russia, the gigantic Imperial Stables in Peterhof, which look like a small town, and are perhaps larger than the famous ones at Chantilly.

My father's artistic and architectural career seemed to promise great and glorious possibilities during the lifetime of Nicolas I, who singled him out for quite special attention; but the Emperor died in 1855, and his successor, Alexander II, did not share his father's enthusiasm for art. Material conditions in Russia were considerably shaken after the Crimean War, and all great enterprises were cancelled; my father's career as architect was cut short. Luckily my father had a deeply artistic nature, and the fact that he was deprived of the happiness of creating anything else of outstanding importance did not deter him from devoting himself to art in all his free time. This was art of a purely "domestic" nature in connection with our family life. The chief object was to amuse and entertain his children and much of it was dedicated to the Benjamin of the family—myself.

It is heart-breaking to think that all those wonderful, spontaneous, fairy-tale illustrations in pencil and water-colour and the charming, artistically made toys—sleighs, houses and furnished flats—were barbarically destroyed by us children, and that only scraps have been saved of all those treasures. I am happy to say that a number of my father's water-colours have remained intact, most of them depicting scenes of our family life, and a whole series of interiors, some of which are enlivened by delightful figures. In style and character these drawings closely resemble those of the German Romantics. My father was in fact a typical romantic of that charming school which one could hardly expect to find now in the country of Schubert, Schumann, Schwind and L. Richter.

THE EMPEROR NICOLAS I. VISITING THE NEW ARCHITECTURAL WORKS AT PETERHOF
The figures marked x and xx are the two Court Architects Stakenschneider and N. Benois
From a water-colour by Michel Zichy

Facing page 6

CAMILLE BENOIS, NÉE CAVOS, MOTHER OF THE
AUTHOR

*From the portrait by Kapkov, c. 1850, in the collection of
Albert Benois*

Facing page 7

The reader has now some idea of my father, who played so great a part in my life and in my artistic development. But it was my mother, whom I worshipped, who played a still greater part in my upbringing, being more intimately concerned in it than my father. In fact, she was the good angel of our extremely patriarchal house.

In spite of their difference in age (my father was thirty-four when he married Camille, the eighteen-year-old daughter of the Court Architect, Albert Cavos) my parents were an ideally matched couple. I cannot imagine them ever quarrelling or causing each other the least unhappiness. At the same time they were totally different in character. To begin with, my father was half French and half German, whereas my mother was a pure Venetian. The difference in race corresponded to the difference in character and outlook. My father was deeply religious and a practising Catholic who attended church regularly; he was engrossed in art and had little interest in business and affairs. In spite of his intelligence and education and his deep sense of duty, there was a strain of childishness in his nature, a kind of charming, whimsical waywardness amounting at times to inoffensive fractiousness.

The Church practically did not exist in my mother's life—but this did not prevent her from closely supervising her children's religious education. Except for music, she was indifferent to art. In her hands lay all the housekeeping and the family budget. She was absolutely without caprice and always followed a set purpose, which common-sense dictated to her, and never allowed herself to be diverted from her chosen line of action.

The chief link between my parents was an enduring kindness of heart and an honesty amounting to saintliness. They stood out in the society around them as a kind of miracle, whose light attracted innumerable

friends and relations, and made of our home an extraordinary centre of interest, without any deliberate effort
on the part of my parents. Our house was always
full of guests, mostly uninvited, and from my earliest
years I was accustomed to seeing a continual stream
of new faces. It is remarkable that nearly everybody
who was drawn into the orbit of our family circle
would discover in themselves some new quality; they
became, by adapting themselves to the atmosphere of
the house, kinder, brighter, more interesting and more
gentle. Of course, as I was only a child, I could not
take in this metamorphosis, but that is what has been
told me by those who had kept alive in their hearts
their admiration for my parents' home, an admiration
that I believe to have been well justified and deserved.

If asked what was the special quality of this
atmosphere, I would reply without hesitation: "It
was artistic." It was artistic not only because our
house was hung with many excellent pictures and
contained some beautiful things in the way of furniture
and *objets d'art,* and not only because my father was
a professional artist and laid great store by everything
artistic; nor again was it because most of my brothers
and sisters drew or painted, and one sister married a
famous sculptor; nor because most of our friends were
interested in some form of art and were continually
arranging amateur theatricals and concerts. It was
because the very air of our house was saturated with
art, so that there one breathed differently from the
houses of other people.

My parents' home was a poetic home—utterly
different from the usual conventional home. Our
house was quite unlike the homes of our nearest
relations, both on my father's and mother's side. As
a child I felt this very strongly, although I did not
recognise it as a special attribute of ours. Our
relations, like ourselves, usually had a household of
young folk who danced, arranged theatricals and

enjoyed themselves, and their houses, too, were full
of handsome furniture and pictures inherited from
both of my grandfathers' collections, but their very
gaiety had a touch of something ordinary and all
the beautiful things looked as if they were there by
mistake and were profoundly bored.

I loved it when people came to us—and there were
plenty of excuses for us to have guests with all the
innumerable birthdays, namedays and the annual
feasts. But similar parties given by my relations used
to bore me terribly, and I could rarely be persuaded
to sit through a family dinner or stay to the end of
a party. There was one exception—the parties at my
Uncle Caesar Cavos's. His house was far more
luxurious than ours. The rooms were filled with
beautiful silk-covered furniture and lovely flowers;
quantities of interesting things embellished his study.
But what attracted me to his house was my affection
for my two charming cousins, who were three and
four years older than myself and whose affection for
me I exploited despotically.

The reader may well ask what such purely family
matters have in common with what I promised to
tell—my ballet memoirs. But, after all, it is *my own*
ballet reminiscences that I am out to relate and
therefore it is important to make clear what was
the origin of the precocious taste which led the small
boy that I was, to fall literally in love with the theatre
and to do so in this rather peculiar way. If my
childhood had not been spent in the special atmosphere I have described, I surely would not have
developed the intense æsthetic sensibility which later
infected my friends and gave a particular *cachet* to
every theatrical enterprise, but especially ballet, in
whose creation we took part.

The atmosphere of our house did not affect all of
us in the same way. Two of my brothers dedicated
themselves to artistic activities; one of them became

a remarkable musician and the other an enthusiastic admirer of the theatre. But they remained
"spectators" and never took a creative part in the
theatre. My dream, from earliest childhood, had
been to create, and I had always been drawn from
the audience on to the stage and into the wings.

My elder brother Albert—Berta or Bertusha, as we
used to call him—had for me an extraordinary charm,
not merely because he could convey any landscape,
in water-colour or pencil, quickly, faithfully and
vividly, but rather because this gifted and enthusiastic
artist was also a wonderful musician. It seems to me
that his gift for music was even greater than his
talent for painting. That he did not follow in the
footsteps of our great-great-grandfather, Catarino
Cavos (who is considered to be the founder of the
Russian National Opera), was due, perhaps, to his
incapacity to realise and appreciate his own talents.
Everything came too easily to Albert, and this
typically Italian trait prevented him from taking
himself seriously. He was of a rather flighty disposition, charmingly so; inclined, perhaps, to take
things entirely as they came, without troubling to
react against them.

Following in our father's footsteps, he chose architecture as his career and was entirely successful. It
was only after many years of work in this profession
that he abandoned it for painting. At first he had
treated painting as a recreation, but later devoted
more and more time to it—encouraged by a fair
measure of success.

Precisely the same psychological causes which
prevented Albert from "finding" himself at once in
plastic art deterred him from serious devotion to
music. For serious application to music he lacked
personal initiative; his attitude was that of a dilettante.
He was entirely self-taught on the violin and piano
and even in the theory of music, and perfectly content

to delight himself and those nearest to him with his improvisations—which he would instantly forget. It did not enter his head to work out what he improvised, and if he ever wrote anything down he promptly lost or destroyed it, never considering it of the least significance.

Everybody in our house played the piano. My father played by ear the old quadrilles and marches of the time of Alexander I and Napoleon. I loved marching to them armed with sword or gun and wearing a hussar's shako or a knight's helmet; my mother could read music, and when she played a special little examination piece she had learnt when she was still a boarder at the Smolny Institute, it moved me to tears; my aunt and my godmother, who often came to see us, played too, and so did my two sisters, whose repertoire consisted of Italian classical music and some modern pieces *à quatre mains*; my brother Louis played arias from favourite Italian operas. My cousin Sasha Benois used to accompany Albert on the piano, violin or harmonium. I must mention my cousin Antoinette Khrabro-Vassilevskaya, who was a magnificent pianist and who excelled in dance music. All this, however, seemed quite insignificant compared to Albert's playing, which one could only call inspired.

Every time he sat down at the piano he seemed to compose a whole suite, gay and sad and even terrifying episodes skilfully interwoven. All this he would play with amazing *brio* and passionate expression.

Whenever I heard these magic sounds, I used to dash out of my nursery into the drawing-room and start prancing about and acting all sorts of things to the music, in front of the large mirror which stood between the windows. This was my first attempt at creative work as far as ballet and pantomime are concerned. The emotions I expressed had to follow the changing music, to modulate from the gentleness

of a woman to the defiance of a warrior, from sentimental tenderness to mortal terror. Other characters,
and the setting—which changed from a luxurious
palace to a humble hut, from a gorge in the mountains
to the sea-shore—had to be left to the imagination.
I actually pictured all this to myself at an age when
my ideas about nature and life in general were still
extremely vague, and when I had had no sentimental
experience whatever. There can be no doubt that
this music in my home acted on my half-conscious
being in the same way as the lyre of the ancient Orpheus
acted on the wild beasts.

As a matter of fact, it was Albert who taught me
to interpret music, to construct a definite programme
which could be expressed in movements. Sometimes,
as a special favour, he would tell me fairy-tales to
the accompaniment of his own improvisations—or
perhaps it was the inspiration of his own improvisations
which produced the tale in him.

Does the reader know a feeling which I can only
describe as a sort of nervous vibration? It is stimulated in its lowest form by scratching the head or any
part of the body. Some animals must certainly be
acquainted with it—cats, for instance, who close their
eyes and allow themselves to be stroked or tickled
behind the ears until, overcome by bliss, they fall into
a sort of irritation and begin to scratch or bite the
hand that is caressing them. It must be well-known
to primitive people—whether they be Neapolitan
lazzaroni, natives from Central Africa, or Russian
peasant louts. Russian peasants, apparently, never
cease scratching their heads. I have often thought
that it would be extremely difficult to train them to
the hygiene of the hair as it would deprive them of
the peculiar and agreeable sensation that is produced
by scratching.

Now it is a curious fact that this same sensation,
in a higher form, can be experienced during moments

of strong æsthetic emotion. I used myself to experience it when I watched my father or my brothers Albert, Louis, or Jules drawing something for me, or when Albert (and he alone) played something special for me on the piano, accompanying it with his stories. I, like the cats, would give way to a feeling of almost physical ecstasy. It would reach gradually a climax of unbearable torment—then I would begin to cry and run away to the nursery, overwhelmed by utter happiness and delight.

Oh, how unspeakably sweet were those moments when I used to listen to Bertusha's stories, and watch them being brought to life by the magic of his music! The subjects of his tales were rather primitive. One of them I still remember. It was about a little boy called Petia. "He was exactly like you," Albert would add, "and though it was forbidden by his parents he used to run away alone into the garden." (I would at once picture to myself the garden surrounding the Cathedral of St. Nicolas opposite our house.) Petia used to approach a hole in the ground and peer into it. Oh, horror! The hole led straight into the underworld . . . and suddenly from this evil-smelling abyss, through clouds of black smoke, a huge claw stretched out and clutched the boy, pulling him down into the depths. Salvation came at the most critical moment; Nannie arrives just in time and pulls him out by the scruff of the neck. . . . The end of the "tale of horror" was the safe return of the thoroughly repentant and reformed little boy, to the great joy of his parents, brothers and sisters.

Now imagine to yourself that all this nonsense is being listened to by a small boy of four or five, in a half-darkened room, lit only by the street-lamps and the feeble gleam of the lamp in the distant dining-room. Albert loved to tell his fantastic stories at dusk, and never allowed the lamp to be brought into the room. I too adored the twilight, because it only enhanced the vividness of the pictures flitting through my mind.

One must try to remember or imagine the simple mode of life of those days. Even the appearance of Albert's "devils" in the Nikolsky Gardens was considered as a perfectly normal event—in fact something domestic and homely. In the nightmares which our servants often told us, devils played an important part. Our maid Stepanida was frequently strangled in her dreams by the *domovoi*, a spirit which dwells in houses, and we used to hear her weird cries. Russian children were, in fact, familiar with the aspect of devils because they were quite a usual thing to see. For instance, the walls of our kitchen were hung with popular religious pictures. One represented the Day of Judgment with all the sinners being tortured by devils in separate little compartments. Another related the story of Lazarus, and the devils dragging the wicked rich man to hell. All were pictured in great detail—so one could easily study the devils with their bright red tongues hanging out of their mouths, their tails, their horns and cloven feet.

Chapter II

A RUSSIAN TOWN

NOW that I have lifted a corner of the curtain and given the reader a glimpse of our family life in those days, I should like to raise it further and show a more comprehensive view of the manner in which people of our class lived in those days. At the same time I do not mean to digress from my subject— my reminiscences of the ballet. The fact is that our mode of life has penetrated not only all *my* creative work, but also that of my friends and collaborators in the *World of Art*: Somov, Lanceray, Bakst, Dobuzhinsky, who have all in one way or another joined hands in the development of the art of the theatre. In the same way it is essential to have some knowledge of this mode of life in order to understand more fully Tchaikovsky, Rimsky-Korsakov, Mussorgsky, not to speak of Pushkin, Dostoievsky and Tolstoy. And where is the source and inspiration of the Russian stage to be found if not among these creators and poets of word and music? They taught the Russian people to understand themselves and to have a clearer vision of Russian life, of the life which must surely be fundamental even to the modern Russia, in spite of the devastating experiments of the Bolsheviks.

But the vastness of the subject is such that I shall have to limit myself to describing my immediate surroundings—in other words, the town life, and especially the life that was characteristic of St.

Petersburg. But even in this limited sphere—itself sufficiently vast—I shall not write about all I have seen and taken part in but shall describe only those happenings which, in one way or another, may have influenced me and made of me a "man of the theatre." As to my general reminiscences, I have been preparing them for quite a long time, and if I succeed in representing all I have seen and lived through, as vividly as I remember it, the result may possibly be a rather curious memorial, valuable in the history of culture, something in the style of Samuel Pepys, Mannlich or Bolotov, who have always been my favourites.

There is an idea—and it has taken fairly firm roots—that St. Petersburg stood apart from Russia and was not a typical Russian town. The fact that this town of the Great Peter—which was given, in 1924, a new and perfectly irrelevant name—was founded on the very outskirts of the empire, on land which, though ancient Russian territory, had first to be reconquered from the Swedes, and—most of all—that this town represented a challenge which the great reformer had thrown at the feet of venerable Moscow, the stronghold of traditionalism, had created a very unfavourable reputation for it in the eyes of the majority of Russians. In their eyes St. Petersburg was a *parvenu*, and this view has survived more or less to the present day. The very act of the Bolsheviks in transferring the capital back to Moscow can be regarded in a way as a "settling of accounts," a long-awaited revenge. It is also natural that foreigners who visited St. Petersburg, while they regarded it as a sort of miracle (since then America and Australia have produced many similar miracles, in the shape of cities grown over-night), readily believed the whispered aspersions of the Russians against their new capital; and they too would emphasise that St. Petersburg was *not* a Russian town—and was *not* to be compared with Moscow, which was so "full of colour and Asiatic originality."

This view was strengthened in the nineteenth century by the general triumph of nationalist theories and the glorification of all things original. But it has no foundation whatever. It is true that St. Petersburg emerged from marshes, that this "fantastic whim" of Peter cost the lives of thousands who had been driven there to build the town from all parts of the country; it is true that St. Petersburg is surrounded by villages whose inhabitants, to this day, speak faulty or practically no Russian, and that Finland lies only twenty kilometres to the north; it is true that one cannot find in St. Petersburg any relics of the epoch previous to Peter, and that all the buildings (with the exception of a few very unsuccessful attempts to return to the "national style") were designed according to the æsthetic principles prevailing in Western Europe in the eighteenth and nineteenth centuries. Yet, in spite of all this, St. Petersburg is essentially a *Russian City*, and even a characteristic Russian City. Its population is predominantly Russian. It is true that it consists of a mixture of all the races which form the Russian Empire, but the majority are Great Russians—the fundamental Russian tribe. The bulk of the inhabitants—the servants, the majority of artisans and workpeople, almost all the small bourgeoisie and most of the merchant class, the clergy and the civil service—were and are Russian. In the streets one heard Russian spoken; it was an exception to hear a foreign language. Similarly, the customs and habits of St. Petersburg, whether in the street or in the home, were Russian.

Finally, the very appearance of St. Petersburg, in spite of the "western" architecture of its buildings, was characteristically Russian, and not only in the winter when the wide thoroughfares, the classical colonnades, cupolas and spires were covered with snow, but even when the stormy, fitful Russian spring had given place to the hot summer, and the immensely broad Neva, freed from ice, flowed swiftly between her low banks, reflecting the northern sky. The very architects who created St. Petersburg—both the foreign ones and their Russian pupils—seem to have been inspired by something from the soil. Neither the splendid Rastrelli, the learned Quarenghi, the somewhat theatrical Rossi nor the Russians, Zakharov, Voronikhin, Starov, could have erected in France or in Italy the architectural compositions that so characteristically adorn St. Petersburg. They took advantage of the great spaces, and submitted themselves to the will of the Emperors who were obsessed by the mania for grandeur. The most beautiful and also the most typical building of St. Petersburg is the Smolny Convent. But its numerous towers and turrets, its curiously charming and harmonious cupolas, can never be classified as foreign; their outline is reminiscent of a Russian fairy story—like the famous Kremlin that rises above Moscow.

If we were to contemplate a street in St. Petersburg at the period of my childhood, when tramways and stage-coaches were few in number, it would be obvious that we were not looking at a street in Paris, Berlin or London. We Petersburgers lived in a world essentially our own, governed by its own laws and deeply rooted traditions. The masses of common folk wearing Russian dress, and the numerous pedlars, gave the St. Petersburg street a unique "national" appearance. This was emphasised by certain peculiarities of the vehicles, the harnesses and costumes of the various drivers. The well-to-do public walking on the main streets of St. Petersburg could be mistaken for those whom they strove to copy—that is, western Europeans—because they dressed and behaved in conformity with them. But one had only to glance away from the pavement to the middle of the street and the western-European illusion disappeared entirely, for here was a surging stream of the most extraordinary vehicles—sleighs in winter, *droshkis* in summer, harnessed in a strange way and driven by bearded coachmen, all wearing wide great-coats and headgear of fantastic shape. The coachmen of the nobility, foreign Embassies, and even those of the Emperor himself, were dressed in similar *zipouns*, with the sole difference that their clothes were made of more expensive material, their hair carefully oiled and combed, their beards tidily trimmed.

Innumerable carts—in winter, sleighs—loaded with every kind of goods, gave the streets of St. Petersburg a curious picturesqueness. This was enhanced by the special harness, by the gaily-coloured *dougas* rising over the heads of the massive cart-horses, by the drivers who walked alongside wearing, in summer, smart red shirts, in winter, extravagant sheep-skin coats. Another characteristic detail in this general picture was the number of drunkards progressing along the street, some with arms round each other, singing loudly, or drinking their bottles dry as they came out of the public-houses. The keepers of the peace—the policemen—eyed those rowdies with leniency and only when their behaviour really reached the limits of decency did they apprehend them, throw them into a cab, and lock them up for the night to get sober.

In my childhood, of all street spectacles, I was chiefly attracted by three kinds: marching soldiers, funerals and processions of condemned criminals taken in special "chariots of infamy" to the pillory —depicting three stages of social life with vivid symbolism. Our street was a privileged one in this respect, for it was along the Nikolsky Street (later changed to Glinka Street) that most of the Guards regiments used to march on their way to parades or to the

B

camps in the spring-time. It was along our street
too that most of the sumptuous funeral processions
usually passed, and, on special carts, the criminals
bound for the Semenovsky Place to be publicly
degraded before being deported to Siberia.

To tell the truth, I saw not more than three such
chariots in my early childhood, but they made a
shattering impression on me and even to this day—
after more than sixty years!—I can remember the
full horror of the picture: the deadly white faces of
the sentenced prisoners placed on a sort of elevated
bench and chained to a post. Our apartment was
on the first floor and the benches passed almost on
a level with the windows; thus I could see everything
in detail.

It was from the same windows, or better still from
the balcony, that one could admire the wonderfully
matched horses and shining helmets and glittering
cuirasses of the Horseguards, or the infantry with
their black and white plumes and smart red-breasted
uniforms, forming a dense wall as they marched
along on their way to change the guard at the Winter
Palace. But it was the bands that delighted me
most, preceded by the huge Drum-major performing
various antics with his golden bâton. There were
two kinds of military bands: one consisted only of
fifes and drums, the other had a full complement of
brass instruments. Sometimes those two bands played
in turn. The pipe band, with its rumbling drums
and squeaking fifes, always disappointed me. But
how triumphant I felt, and what a general, at the
joyous sounds of the approaching brass band—
especially if it were playing the traditional marches
I had so often heard from my father, who had himself
learned them in his own childhood.

There would be more music in our street when
the funeral of some important person progressed along
it, but music of a kind that used to terrify me. When,

ALEXANDRE BENOIS (SHOURA) AT THE AGE OF FIVE
From a photograph, 1875

Facing page 20

NIKOLSKY STREET WITH THE BOLSHOY THEATRE ON THE RIGHT
From a window of the Benois house. *From a water-colour by Catherine Benois, c.* 1868

Facing page 21

from a distance, the sad strains of a funeral march penetrated the quiet winter day, I used to run away to one of the back rooms overlooking the yard, and bury my head in the pillows. Usually, however, the temptation to have a look at the magnificent ceremonies would prove too strong for me, and, conquering my dread, I would join my brothers, already firmly stationed at the window. Together we would watch the procession with an interest that was perhaps even keener than what we experienced when looking at the soldiers.

It was indeed an interesting sight! If the funeral were a notable one, the procession would be headed by rows of black torch-bearers. They walked on either side of the street, carrying lighted lanterns; then came men bearing cushions on which lay the medals, the orders and other signs of distinction of the deceased; then the long-robed and long-bearded clergy, preceded by a choir in gold-braided cassocks; finally appeared the hearse itself, drawn by horses. It was these horses that particularly terrified me. They were covered from head to foot by black cloths, painted with coats-of-arms. The actual hearse, if the deceased was of the Orthodox faith, would be resplendent with gilt. If it was the funeral of a Lutheran or a Roman Catholic, the hearse and all the equipment would be completely black. This kind of funeral I found more profoundly awe-inspiring; it corresponded more exactly with the idea of Death that was gradually shaping in my mind.

The processions were followed by a dense crowd of mourners and a string of carriages—the longer the string, the more important the deceased appeared to be. I remember one procession which took up the full length of our Nikolsky Street across the Théâtre Square. The hearse had already rounded the corner by our house before the last coaches, which barely entered my range of vision, arrived at the

"Bridge of Kisses" at the other end of our street. It must have been the funeral of some personage of historical importance, but I have no recollection of his name. I was too young to be interested in his identity. My mind was completely absorbed by the procession that slowly proceeded past our windows.

I used to experience the same feeling of mixed awe and terror when I watched religious processions. They were not frequent but for that very reason the more impressive. The beautiful Cathedral of St. Nicolas the Miraculous (popularly called "St. Nicolas of the Navy") stood right opposite us. Only the width of the Ekaterinhofsky Prospect, and the garden which surrounded the Cathedral, lay between it and our house. The mass of the church rose high above the old birch trees in the garden, the cupolas shining and glittering in the sunshine. On moonlit nights the five cupolas of St. Nicolas, and especially the large central one, became transformed in my imagination into a group of giants with helmets on their heads, and in spite of my respect for the House of God, and in spite of the fact that I considered our church to be "the most beautiful church in the world," this nightly transformation filled me with fear. A little distance away from the church stood the golden-spired belfry from which rang out the joyous or sad tolling of bells. The sound of them used to fill all the rooms of our apartment, particularly in the summer months when the windows were thrown open.

Sometimes, during a church festival, the central doors of the Cathedral would be opened and a procession of the clergy and the congregation would pass slowly round the square occupied by the church and garden. The bells would ring out from the belfry and, thanks to their ceaseless pealing, the voices of the choir would sound dull and mournful. Above all, I was impressed by the numerous banners carried in front of the miracle-working ikon, which was borne in the centre of the procession. These crimson and golden banners, adorned with pictures of the saints, bent and trembled in the air, swaying from side to side, so that they seemed to be alive and threatening—as if they would approach and strangle me. It is possible that I had experienced something like this in my nightmares. My childhood's sleep was full of nightmares, and they too were, in a way, spectacular experiences, so terrifying at times that I used to wake in cold perspiration.

The reader may be surprised that I should link my youthful impressions of church ceremonies with the memories of my nightmares, but the fact that our family was Roman Catholic provides, perhaps, a partial explanation. Although my father's example taught us to treat all creeds with the greatest reverence, I found the ritual of the Orthodox Church strange and incomprehensible. I also thought Russian priests rather alien when they came to visit us with some of the choir-people on Feast days and celebrated a short *Te Deum* in our apartment, or when we were present at a christening in an Orthodox family. I could not restrain a certain feeling of aversion as I watched the long-haired and long-bearded men—especially when I had to approach them to receive the blessing and kiss their outstretched hand. I used to feel perplexed at their way of speaking, as it reminded me of the speech of the common people. But it was the deacons who terrified me most with their huge manes and fat stomachs and their thunderous chanting that made the windows rattle and set all the crystal drops of the chandeliers tinkling!

I used to compare the Orthodox clergy unfavourably with our own Catholic priests, who were polished and polite, who gesticulated little and spoke in subdued tones; whose robes, stately in appearance and made of soft white cloth, were pleasant to behold

and even to touch.[1] Catholic priests in St. Petersburg
were of various nationalities—Polish, French and
German.   The fact that they were all "foreigners"
(associated therefore in my imagination with far-
away, attractive countries—the birth-places of my best
toys and books) enhanced, for me, their natural
sanctity.

I felt infinitely more at home in a Catholic than
in an Orthodox Church—and was equally happy in
the big church of St. Catherine, where the members
of our family were christened, married and buried, or
in the small Polish Church of St. Stanislas, where
my father attended early mass on Sundays, it being
the nearest to our home. The mere fact that one
could be seated during the service in the Catholic
Church instead of standing was a great advantage
to my mind. I loved too the noble harmony of the
architecture of our Catholic churches; the serenity,
the poise of the angels on the cornices, balancing
their youthful bodies and unfolding their tremendous
wings; the beautiful pictures which, instead of ikons
dressed in gold and silver, adorned the altar and
the walls.   How interesting it was, during the service,
to contemplate the mural decorations of St. Stanislas!

Our Catholic churches were my first museums.
Here I made my first acquaintance—in copies it is
true—with St. Anthony by Murillo, the Descent from
the Cross by Rubens, a work by a very good master
of the Bolognese school, and other admirable paintings.
I also loved the whole ritual of the Catholic Service
from the mysterious murmuring of the priest to the
thunder of the organ; the genuflections, the gentle
ascending and descending from the altar. I loved
to see the priests stretch out their arms as if beholding

[1] There were several Catholic Churches in St. Petersburg, but the
chief parish church, which numbered our family amongst its congregation, was St. Catherine's on the Nevsky Prospect. It belonged
to the Dominican Monks—according to the wish of Catherine the
Great.

a celestial vision. When, at the end of mass, the priest slowly made the sign of the cross over all the rising assembly, I never doubted that a real beneficent power would guard and keep me safe from all evil. Even to-day I still await that moment with the same thrill, and when the liturgy is over I enjoy, as I did in my childhood, watching the clergy process with solemn modesty and downcast eyes towards the Sacristy, preceded by boys bearing the lighted candles and the loftily raised Cross.

Chapter III

THE BALAGANI

THERE is no doubt that the various visual impressions absorbed by me, before I had ever attended a theatrical performance, laid the foundation of a rich store from which I have been able to draw all my life and on which—to be quite frank—I still depend. I feel I owe a debt of gratitude to God for having endowed me with an exceptional gift of perception and an unusually tenacious memory. To me there seems nothing out of the ordinary about my memory until I come to compare it with that of my contemporaries. It is when we indulge in recollection of the past and discuss experiences we have had in common that I find they remember incomparably less than I do. It becomes clear that they were less capable of genuine appreciation than I was, even at a very early age.

But to continue the tale of my "sources"—I will now draw another picture from my store of memories, gathered in my pre-theatre period, to prove that the St. Petersburg of my childhood actually bore a traditional national character.

Twice in the year this generally "European" city was transformed into one frankly barbarian. I refer to the two Fairs which characterised the Russian Easter and Carnival, or Butter Week as it was called. These two Fairs occurred at varying dates because they depended on the date of Easter Sunday, as did of course the seven weeks of Lent. Sometimes it happened that Butter Week occurred during severe winter weather; in other years at the first breath of spring. Easter Week always had a definite feeling of spring about it, though the weather could sometimes be wintry, the Neva full of ice, and the tiny buds that had recently appeared on the trees all shrivelled up from the cold.

Of course the elements of which the Russian Carnival consisted have much in common with those to be found in the rest of Europe. Still, the Russian Fair did not resemble those one saw in Paris, Vienna or Rome. The "elements in common" consisted of covered stages on which all kinds of plays were produced, enormous swings and merry-go-rounds, and innumerable stalls selling sweet-meats. Yet even these "general European" elements were transformed into something peculiarly our own. The whole atmosphere was different; the gaiety more intense, the revelry more spontaneous and whole-hearted.

One of the outstanding national features of the Carnival Fair were the ice-switchbacks, which for some unknown reason were called "American Mountains." Beyond the borders of Russia these switch-backs never hide their Russian origin, but answer to the name of *Montagnes Russes.* They were constructed of timber and were of considerable height; their sliding surface was actually made of ice and had a long level run-out. The switchbacks usually stood in pairs, facing each other, so that, having come down the first, one could immediately climb up the other and slide down again. They had a defect, however; they would only work efficiently when there was a good frost to give the necessary hardness to the ice; as soon as the thaw set in, the ice-hills went on strike. It sometimes happened that even at Carnival the ice-hills would suffer from the premature warm weather, and at Easter they had always ceased to function. These "ice-hills" were really the prominent feature of

B*

the Fair amusements; indeed, the Fair itself was often referred to as "the Hills." It was quite usual, when hailing an *izvozchik* to drive to the Fair, to tell him to go "to the Hills" or "to the *Balagani*."

The *Balagani* were, strictly speaking, the covered stages I have already mentioned. For me they provided the chief attraction of the Fair. They satisfied the insatiable passion I had in my childhood and youth for every form of spectacle. But the whole Fair also went under the name of *Balagani*—that is to say, the whole agglomeration of temporarily erected wooden sheds put up anew every year.

There was much that I loved at the *Balagani* in my childhood, but there were many things of which I was afraid. I was frightened, for instance, by the noise—menacing, almost, rather than gay—that hung over the grounds and vibrated through the thin winter air for miles around. We would hear this noise distinctly from our carriage as we drove into the far end of the Millionaya Street—the noise of innumerable brass bands playing simultaneously, the dull rhythmical beating of the Turkish drums, the squeaking of the swings, the chatter and cries of the thousands of people assembled round the "ice-hills," or in the decorated lanes between the various pavilions and merry-go-rounds. I was frightened, too, by the enormous swing-boats, as they flew high up in the air, their brightly-coloured wagonettes filled with laughing and shrieking girls. There seemed to be a foreboding of evil in the strong smell of cooking pancakes and "Berlin" doughnuts, as it mixed with the rising vapours of vodka. But most of all I was afraid of the huge wooden buildings, decorated with gaily-coloured pictures, which served as enclosures for the various entertainments. A special feature of these coloured boxes was the showmen on the galleries outside. These men, called Grandads, dressed in light-coloured sheep-skin coats, and rather ridiculously disguised in long, flowing false beards, entertained the crowd which surged round the booths with their jokes and antics.

The noisy merriment of these make-believe Grandads, their reckless balancing on the parapets, from which, at any moment, they could tumble headlong into the street, the whistling, shouting and fun-making of the passers-by, gave me a feeling of something demoniacal. My uneasy forebodings reached their climax when two nightmare figures, dressed in white and wearing huge masks on their long, giraffe-like necks, would suddenly emerge from behind the crimson curtains. They were meant to represent the traditional figures of every national Russian Fun-Fair—the Goat and the Crane. These monsters, after their sudden appearance, would perform a short, grotesque dance and swiftly disappear again behind the curtains—in all probability to re-inforce themselves with another drink. An easy possibility of obtaining quantities of "spiritual" warming-up was provided by the badly-lit interiors of the merry-go-rounds, where the huge two-storied machine, with its noisy passengers, revolved to the deafening music of an orchestrion.

Amusements and distractions of this kind at the *Balagani* were indulged in by the common people, and were greatly enjoyed by our servants, for instance —this was their conception of the Carnival. But for us well-brought-up children, the whole scene ot revelry and rude gaiety formed a background for pleasures more suitable to our upbringing; by this I mean the enormous, gaily-painted pavilions in which were staged varied and highly attractive per-formances. These were the *Balagani* in the narrower sense of the word.

Military-patriotic plays used to be given in some of these "theatres." Even from the outside one could distinctly hear gun-fire and the noises which accompanied the battles of Geoktepe and Plevna. In others it would be fairy-tales of Princes and Princesses; and finally, in the two chief *Balagani*, kept by Berg and Yegarev, Harlequinades were presented to the public. When I look back at my life, I consider it a remarkable stroke of luck that I had the opportunity of seeing those traditional pantomimes before they disappeared, for, thanks to them, Pantaloon, Pierrot, Harlequin and Columbine are, for me, not characters constructed by learned research into the *Commedia dell' Arte*, but real figures that I have seen with my own eyes.

I fell completely in love with one of those figures from the first moment I saw it, from the moment that its multi-coloured costume and face half covered by a black mask began to flit in front of my eyes. Throughout my childhood and youth this figure never ceased to charm and lure me. It was not the ancient Harlequin, the artful dodger—robber almost—black-faced and curiously ugly. When, later on, I first saw the ancient Harlequin in the pictures of Watteau, Gillot and Lancret, I did not want to believe that *this* was Harlequin, the real, historical Harlequin. *My* Harlequin was youthful, ideally built, with a charming face that one imagined behind the mysterious mask. One was the Harlequin who had been adopted and transformed by the French of the eighteenth century; the other the darling of the fairies, who dressed in clothes sparkling with spangles and performed the most wonderful miracles. Such was the unfading youthfulness of Harlequin and such he remained for me until I was found worthy to see him. I must add that this was the way Harlequin was depicted in a beautifully illustrated book called *Les Aventures d'Arlequin* which I inherited from my brothers, and that the *fantocci* which my grandmother Cavos brought me from Venice were just as charmingly attractive. I had no reason for doubting the genuineness of this Harlequin, for at that age doubt never entered my mind. The charming Harlequin whom I first saw in 1874 (when I was four years old) in Yegarev's *balagan*, I accepted wholeheartedly as a kind of deity—having completely lost to him both my curly head and beating little heart. That visit to Yegarev's *balagan* was my *first* experience of the theatre and to this day I consider it to have been a most wonderful beginning to my artistic life, a beginning which had the greatest significance for the whole of my existence.

The charm of my first visit to the *Balagani* was enhanced by the presence of my brother Isha (Jules), whom we were, alas, to lose in the autumn of the same year. He was ten years older than I and was already a schoolboy of the fourth form at the time when I was only just learning to conform to the demands of culture—that is to say, to shake hands with my elders when greeting them, to avoid picking my nose and generally to behave decently. But the friendship between us was great—in fact, it was far deeper than that which existed between me and my brother Michael, who was nearest to me in age. Had Isha lived, I am sure he would have become an artist, and perhaps a very vital and original artist. In any case, he had a wonderful imagination and was tireless in his inventions. His favourite occupation was drawing, and, as he was also a great reader, his drawings were full of unusual interest. They were mostly improvisations depicting all sorts of adventures, both comical and tragic. Devils often figured in his pictures, but his principal subjects were heroes of ancient history and the Pharaohs of Egypt. A certain vein of cruelty gave spice to these drawings of Isha's and I must confess that it was I, the four-year-old brat, who insisted that there should be more cruelty, and was delighted to see the great block of stone falling off the pyramid in construction and crushing the crowds of slaves to death. . . . Such is the nature of mankind. The "innocent" infant is just as "sadistic" unconsciously as is the two-month-old kitten when it playfully tortures a mouse before finally killing it. Sitting on Isha's knee and watching new and interesting episodes growing from under his pencil, I experienced the same delight as when Albert "related" his stories on the piano, and I think that Isha, feeling the intense interest and deep enjoyment which he awakened in me, must himself have experienced a feeling of elation—the elation that fills the poet when he reads his work to a highly-strung and thrilled audience.

I was especially lucky to have had Isha as my companion and neighbour during that first visit of mine to the "theatre" at the *Balagani*, because his comments, suited to my age, explained the action that was unfolding on the stage; and it was Isha who insisted on our entering Yegarev's *balagan* because he himself was a passionate admirer of the Harlequinade. I can well imagine his delight to discover in me an ally who could immediately share all his own joys. My delight was truly unbounded and I was entirely engrossed in the performance. I ceased to feel even the biting frost—the *Balagani* were not heated—and when the time came to leave began to cry, so unwilling was I to part from what seemed to me to be the height of bliss.

The impression of what I had seen at that performance was so strong and so deep that I have remembered throughout my whole life every detail of what I saw there. I must add that my memory was reinforced by seeing the same performance in the following two or three years. The Harlequinades were repeated from year to year with but slight variations in detail. Towards the end of the 'seventies the producer Yegarev either ceased to interest himself in the people's theatre or else went bankrupt, for he no longer figured among the *Balagani* managers. His

THE BALAGANI 33

rival, Berg, continued to produce the Harlequinades, but they were not the same thing, for in Berg's production the pantomime gave place to dialogue, which of course lessened the poetry of the whole performance and did away with its characteristic mystery. In any case, if I continued to frequent Berg's Harlequinade, it was because I never ceased to be enchanted with Harlequin. I am very constant in my likes and dislikes, and this constancy developed in me before I became conscious of it.

That memorable performance, seen on a cold grey February afternoon in 1874 at Yegarev's, was a pantomime, and this I consider to have been an extraordinarily fortunate chance for me. The fact that I was enchanted with a performance in dumb-show, where everything depended on movement and acting, may be regarded as an omen that I was one day to become a promoter of the ballet.

I must add here that I had a predecessor (of whom at that time I knew nothing) who has also played an important part in the history of Russian Ballet and who was also inspired in his youth by the Harlequinade. This was Ivan Alexandrovitch Vsevolojsky, who became the Director of the Imperial Theatres at the beginning of the 'eighties. When a very old man, he used to tell me about the shattering impression that had been made on him by the Harlequinades he had seen in some Paris Theatre. It was with the desire to revive this impression that he created the charming ballet, *Les Millions d'Arlequin* in the theatre he directed, taking the subject from a French *féerie*. In this ballet Harlequin was given exactly the part that he played in our old *Balagani*. The pleasant music by Drigo was a welcome addition to this fancy of Vsevolojsky's and one of the chief items, the famous *Serenade*, became extremely popular and was played by the orchestras of all the world and can often be heard to this day.

My goodness! How long ago that was! How
fantastically enchanting and delightful are memories
of those happy days! They have the flavour of an
"historical romance," enchanting in its truth and in
its fiction. How improbable and impossible much of
this past seems to-day. . . . Can it really be true
that the square that has now been named *Uritzky
Place* in honour of some revolutionary policeman is
the same as what formerly bore the appropriate name
of *Square of the Winter Palace*? Is it possible that it
was here, on this very same place, under the walls
of the residence of the Tsar, that the famous Fair
took place—the Fair with the whirling swings and
merry-go-rounds, the Grandads shouting their vul-
garities, the drunken crowds revelling in the deafening
din of the barrel-organs? And can it be I myself,
that small boy of about forty inches high, wrapped
up like a parcel, a *bashlik* covering my fur cap to
protect my nose and ears from the sharp frost, who
stamped his tiny feet disguised in snow boots as he
waited in the entrance of the *Balagani*, the scent of
the freshly-sawn planks tickling his nose? How delightful was the tense excitement of anticipation, in
spite of the cold and the frost biting one's toes! How
thrilling were the sounds that reached us from behind
the wooden partition! Now and again the music
would be interrupted by bursts of laughter from
the audience—this meant that Harlequin had played
one of his tricks or that Pierrot, the miller, had been
fooled again; shrill whistles signified a change of
set, and the terrifying boom of the gong announced
the appearance of the inevitable devils. . . .

At last, when our time came, all that we had
imagined while listening outside would take place
before our enchanted eyes. Harlequin would be cut
into pieces—but they would join up again immediately
and he would appear as if nothing had happened.
The only difference was that before he had been

dressed in a dirty and dull-looking costume whereas now, at the touch of the magic wand, he was resplendent with beautiful, shining spangles. A moment ago Harlequin was only a servant, like the silly white Pierrot; now he was under the protection of the Fairy Fortuna herself—who appeared on a turning, shining wheel. A moment ago he had been trying to please and wait upon his tiresome master Pantaloon—now, there he was eloping with his master's daughter and impudently making fun of Pantaloon and all his friends.

How was it possible not to fall in love with this graceful, sparkling twirler, whose dark eyes shone from behind a mysterious black half-mask, whose vivid red lips showed the dazzle of his smile? Harlequin conquered not only the heart of Columbine, but that of the Fairy herself—a deity descended from an Olympus unknown to mythology. And how natural all this amazing nonsense seemed to be! It was natural that Harlequin should remain unhurt when he rolled off a stone balcony to the street level, while his pursuers disappeared into an abyss; natural that after falling through the floor into the kitchen he should jump unharmed out of the steaming cauldron and leap into the clock, only to emerge unexpectedly from the sideboard. . . . What joy it was when the fugitives, Harlequin and Columbine, chased to the very entrails of hell by Pantaloon's party, were saved by the same Fairy just as they were on the point of falling into the claws of the gigantic devils that lined the stage! And then the Fairy would lead them into a paradise lit up with pink Bengal lights. . . .

All this was certainly not a ballet in the proper sense, but it was impressed on my unspoilt child's imagination as a spectacle so wonderful and enchanting that the innumerable ballet performances I have since seen on the stages of St. Petersburg,

Paris and London, are nothing in comparison. Yet the Harlequinade certainly resembled a ballet. Harlequin and Columbine were both dancers; the other characters danced at every opportunity, and even the black, long-tailed and horned devils gambolled in a very sprightly manner. But the outstanding fact was that *nobody spoke*. The magic spell woven by the music, which, though faulty, was still "the celestial language of the gods," was unbroken by any foolish words. In those days my inexperienced and untrained ear was delighted by any tune, while some pieces—the *Réveil du Lion*, fragments from *Faust*, Schubert's *Forelle* or the march from *Russlan*—sent me into ecstasy. Therefore blessed be that day of February, 1874, when I was so happily led into the "Ballet World." I shall be eternally grateful to the Fairy whose protection I was under, though she did not appear to me in person. . . . For who but she herself could have brought me to that performance at the *right* moment? Who but she introduced me to her *protégé*, Harlequin? Who but she can have set me on the path I was later to follow—a path that led to happiness throughout the world for people who know how to be spectators, who possess the gift of theatrical enjoyment?

Chapter IV

THE REAL THEATRE

THE first real theatre I attended was the French
Opéra Bouffe. Is it not strange that my parents
should have chosen to take me for my first performance to the place where they gave *La Belle
Hélène* and *La Duchesse de Gerolstein* and where Judic
herself had the most frenzied success?

The Opéra Bouffe took place in a wooden theatre
which has long ceased to exist. It stood near the
Alexandryinsky Theatre and all I can remember of
it is that the house was elaborately decorated and
gilded and that the curtain was shaped like an
opened fan, on each side of which beautiful ladies
were painted. But I hasten to make a correction. I
was not taken to the Opéra Bouffe to see either *Les
Mousquetaires au Couvent* or *L'Ile Verte*, but to see a
special performance for children—a kind of fantasy
in fifteen scenes adapted from the story of Jules
Verne's *Voyage Round the World in Eighty Days*. This
was my second performance, given in a real theatre
this time, and I remember all the details just as
vividly as those of the first.

I greatly appreciated the story itself, the exciting
plot and the happy ending when Phineas Fogg arrives
in the nick of time at the club where the bet had
been proposed, accepted and now fulfilled at so great
a risk, in two and a half months. Certain episodes I
found particularly exciting—the rescue of the Rajah's
widow, for instance, at the foot of the funeral pyre,

by Fogg and his faithful servant Passepartout. Later
the beautiful creature narrowly escapes destruction
from snakes that emerge, in vast numbers, from every
corner of the cave in which she is sleeping. Equally
exciting were the Red Indians' attack on the train
as it crossed the snow-covered regions of North
America and the explosion of the steamer carrying
passengers at full speed from New York to Liverpool.
The steamer, tossed spasmodically on the green-blue
waves, suddenly breaks into two and, vomiting fountains of sparks, sinks slowly into the deep! The
passengers did not perish, however, for they appeared
at once, hale and hearty, to acknowledge the applause
of the audience.

In the following year, 1876, it was the Opera's
turn, and I went to a performance of *Faust*. It took
place not a hundred yards from my parents' house,
at the Bolshoy Theatre, where the Ballet and Italian
Opera were given.

I was deeply impressed, during this second visit
to the theatre, both by the varied and effective décors
and by the music, the melodies of which I knew
intimately, thanks to my brother Albert's infatuation
with *Faust*. The acting of the artist-singers impressed me no less strongly and I was especially
thrilled to see the famous Nielson, whose face I knew
well from the innumerable photographs belonging to
my brother Loulou, who adored her. I have, however, completely forgotten what singers took the
parts of Faust and Mephistopheles; in all probability
their names were unknown to me. Besides, their
identity did not interest me in the least; to me Faust
and his tempter were real and alive—was not Mephistopheles one of the devils with whom I was well
acquainted? I even secretly loved him—for how
could a child fail to be attracted by this cavalier clad
from head to foot in scarlet, with a feather to match
in his cap? The most amazing thing was that where-

THE REAL THEATRE 39

ever Mephistopheles moved he was accompanied by
a red light and that he emerged through a trap in the
first act. In the last act he disappeared once again
through the floor, only to appear immediately writh-
ing in agony under the winged archangel's spear,
while behind him, above the roofs of the town, clouds
of tulle represented the flight of Marguerite's soul to
Heaven. This was the naïve way in which the Faust
apotheosis was represented in those days, but it was
just this simplicity which enchanted me. I was delighted that poor Marguerite, who had met with so
many misfortunes, should fly up to God. The fact
that Faust grieved so deeply after her death and that
the devil was punished for his wickedness gave me
intense "moral satisfaction." I remember that Mama
was somewhat preoccupied when I asked her why
poor Marguerite had been put in prison. It appeared
that she had "accidentally" smothered her child,
like one of the two women judged by Solomon. I
was left to guess where the child had come from—
which was not difficult. It was obvious that Faust
and Marguerite were married and probably an angel
or a stork had brought them a baby. . . .

We all know that the second act of Gounod's
Faust contains delightful dances to the sounds of the
famous waltz. This dancing, however, did not move
me half so much as did the entrance of the "old
men" (a very popular item in those days and one
which was invariably encored) or the march of the
returning troops. It was one of the marches I heard
almost daily in our street and soon became part of
a new fairy-tale. I was therefore extremely surprised
when an obliging grown-up destroyer of childish
illusions there and then announced to me that the
Landsknechts who filed through the ancient German
city with feathered berets and banners flying were
none other than sailors of the 8th Naval Division
from the nearby barracks. My illusion was not

destroyed, however; on the contrary, my respect for our sailors grew even deeper. It was wonderful that they should be able to "pretend" so well, to look so handsome and to march in such perfect time to the music, performing all sorts of complicated antics—which served principally to dissimulate their somewhat scanty number.

At last, about ten months after seeing *Faust*, I was taken to my first ballet. But before I give an account of what I saw then and how I was affected by it, I must dwell a little on the theatre itself, for this was the place of my initiation. From that day, for eight consecutive years, till its last season of 1885-1886, the Bolshoy Theatre became the object of my cravings, my aspirations and my temple indeed. I must say that the outward appearance of the building—especially its colonnaded entrance, thronged with a constant stream of carriages—corresponded exactly to one's idea of a temple.

Opposite stood the Maryinsky Theatre, which was then the home of Russian Opera and Russian Drama. But in spite of its noble architecture (then still unspoilt by later decorations) it did not in the least resemble a temple, and this fact only emphasised the majesty and severity of its *vis-à-vis*.

The interior of the Bolshoy Theatre also gave the impression of a temple. The hall with its six tiers, the gilding and the crimson brocade draperies, was strongly reminiscent of the Scala in Milan. The curtain was highly original, for it was an enormous painting by Roller which was supposed to transport the audience into the serene world of ancient Greece. It was only later in life that I discovered how naïve and conventional this painting was, conceived in the spirit of the "classical" landscapes fashionable in the beginning of the nineteenth century. As a child I greatly admired the picture and would literally "enter into it," especially during the languishing

THE MARYINSKY THEATRE IN 1890

Facing page 40

A BOX AT THE CIRQUE IMPERIALE
Replaced after the fire of 1858 by the Maryinsky Theatre
From a water-colour by Nicolas Benois, c. 1850

Facing page 41

minutes before the performance started and during the intervals when one is so excited to know "what is going to happen." It was in those moments that I studied the curtain in its minutest details. How well I knew the two dark portals that served as *repoussoir* in the foreground, the cypresses and pines standing out against the cloudless sky and the ancient city with its rotundas, colonnades and pyramids against a background of blue mountains in the distance! What I loved most of all was the simple little scene painted in the foreground of the gigantic picture: a pretty, half-naked boy was burning flowers on an altar while another mischievous imp, disguised in a tragic mask, was teasing a little girl who had dropped her basket of fruit from sheer fright. Dear painted friends of my childhood! I wonder what has become of you? What happened to you when the temple where you had played the honoured role of serving at the altar was destroyed? Did you perish together with the canvas on which you were painted? Or do you exist to this day together with the decaying picture, rolled up in a tube, in some dusty storehouse? How sad is the fate of theatrical décors! How can I help recording here my regret that all the wonders created by Bibiena, Servandoni, Piranesi, Gonzago and Roller should have entirely disappeared, leaving at the most but a preliminary sketch . . . that nothing at all has remained from the décors which made people shout with delight or weep with emotion.

I do not remember the date of that remarkable event of my life—my first visit to the ballet. I only know that it was a matinée and that the invitation to my Uncle Caesar's box was quite unexpected, as it arrived just before the performance. I remember the terrific haste with which I was washed, combed, dressed and tidied up—the light grey suit with blue stripes, the blue prunella shoes of which I was so proud, the bright-coloured tie and even the eau-de-

Cologne with which I was sprayed. Tears rolled down my face while I was being dressed—I was so afraid of being late; but I meekly submitted to all the ministrations, feeling this was not the time for any obstruction as it might only make me still later. At last, looking more like a shapeless parcel than a human being, I was led by my German nurse to the same theatre where I had seen *Faust*, and which seemed to me the most wonderful and most mysterious place in the world. Even the smell of gas one felt on entering the great, over-heated building only added to its mysteriousness.

In spite of the hurry we were late. The first scene of the second act was about to close and several minutes were spent in "unpacking" me in the *avant-loge*. But at last I am ready and pushed into the semi-darkened box; somebody's lips kiss me, I am passed from one pair of tender hands to another as I brush past scented muslin dresses to find myself at the edge of the box, seated next to my favourite cousin Ina. The box was on the ground floor, next to the one occupied by the Director, on the same level as the stage and very close to it. This was not a suitable place to form any illusion from the sets, but, on the other hand, I found myself in unexpected contact with what was taking place on the stage. Oh, how exciting, how alluring that contact seemed to me! I was even enchanted by the fact that from my place I could watch the artists still in the wings preparing to make their entrance on the stage. This did not spoil the impression for me; on the contrary, it seemed to enhance it, and to add an extra spice of interest and amusement. I must really have been predestined by fate for the stage and all its temptations!

The ballet was *La Bayadère*. The stage was occupied by a pyre whose long tongues of flame leapt high into the air while wild-looking, bearded people, dressed in brown tights and red slips and wearing high turbans, fearlessly jumped over it. I hardly had time to glue my eyes to this wonderful scene when the curtain came down amidst a burst of applause. Several artists appeared to acknowledge it; the famous Troitsky (my cousin pointed him out to me) was the central figure, for it happened to be the benefit performance of this extremely popular dancer. The curtain soon rose again and I found myself in a magnificent tropical park with palm trees and baobabs growing in profusion. In the distance one could see a procession approaching; it consisted at first of tiny cardboard figures, but soon the real ones filed across the stage to disappear in the opposite wing and then form a group in the background. The appearance of the bejewelled elephant caused me to clap my hands with delight, but the innumerable heads and arms of the gilt idols made me feel distinctly uncomfortable, and I could hardly keep my seat at the sight of the "royal tiger" nodding his head from side to side. He was so convincing. But what enchanted me more than anything—more than the warriors in their golden armour, more than the beautiful veiled maidens whose arms and ankles jingled with bracelets—was the group of blackamoors who approached dancing, twirling and tinkling their bells. The winding lines of little blackamoors so amazed and delighted me—principally because they were of my own size—that during the following days I shamelessly lied and boasted to my little friends in the Kindergarten that I had actually taken part in that negro dance. I got so used to this lie that I actually began to believe it myself.

The ballerina who danced the part of *la bayadère* (I do not remember whether it was Ekaterina Vazem or Evgenia Sokolova) seemed to me of incomparable beauty, and I was indignant when I overheard the grown-ups behind me criticise her looks and her dancing. I was particularly thrilled when the ballerina

rose on her points—as if some invisible force lifted her
from the floor. It reminded me of the charm of my
favourite dreams when I felt myself walking not on
the earth but soaring just above the surface, a few
inches from the ground. As I watched the leading
dancer and her delightful companions, I could not
help thinking that they must experience an inde-
scribable joy in this gift of being able to soar and flit
about like birds; and for many months after having
seen *La Bayadère* I used to try to learn their difficult
art and even made some progress in it, in spite of the
painfulness of the process.

A dark fate hung over the ballerina: the charming
girl fell down dead, struck by a snake emerging from
a basket of flowers, to the skirling sound of a pipe.
From now on she was a shadow. Her silhouette
would suddenly flit upon the background of a wall or
she would appear to her lover looking like her old
self and lure him to the sad, dimly-lighted world
beyond the grave, which I identified as "our heaven"
—where all the good people went after their death.
What a hardened heart the lover must have had, for
in spite of such proof of Nikia's love, he gave in to the
persuasion of his relatives and married the princess
that had been chosen for him. His punishment
followed immediately. A vast number of princes and
priests assembled in the sumptuous temple decorated
by huge statues with heads of elephants and horses;
the ceremony was about to begin when suddenly,
at the last moment, terrific flashes of lightning sent by
the avenging gods destroyed the temple; the enormous
falling blocks crushed the crowds assembled there for
the marriage. For the last time, through a shower
of golden rain, we see *la bayadère* who has now become
a celestial being. The trick of the golden rain was
much admired and even commented on in the newspapers.

It is possible that my rendering of the story is not

quite correct and does not correspond with the fabula of the ballet, which I have seen innumerable times and whose naïve and melodious music I know by heart. But what I have related about my first ballet is just that blend of truth and fiction which was created by my first impression, and which, curiously enough, has remained in my memory, always obliterating the later corrections and verifications. The lesson of "romantic morality" which lies in the subject of *La Bayadère* also sank deep into my soul and I whole-heartedly believed in the righteousness of the heroine, and fell in love not so much with her as with her part, or rather with the idea she personifies. With all my love for things magnificent and brilliant, I would not have had a moment's doubt, had I been Solor, in choosing between the feelings of my heart and practical considerations.

These early impressions from *La Bayadère* and many other analogous works of art (Andersen's fairy-tales, for instance) gradually helped to determine the structure of my soul. Or perhaps it would be more true to say that all of it was to my liking and had found in my soul the kind of response from which there is no appeal. Small boy that I was (I was not more than seven years old) I began to understand what my "ideal in life" was, an ideal to which I have remained faithful in spite of compromises, digressions and sins.

Chapter V

BALLET IN MY CHILDHOOD

AFTER the age of eight I was taken more often to the theatre; not to the ballet but to the Italian Opera, to which my parents subscribed and where they had a box reserved for them every Monday. Thus it happened that at an early age I became acquainted with the classical repertoire of opera—*Il Trovatore, I Puritani, Rigoletto, Martha, Il Barbiere di Seviglia, Aïda,* etc.

Usually things happened this way. As soon as the weekly programme came out on the placards on Saturdays and I had discovered what was going to be given in our series, I would immediately announce my intention of going and begin to beg and wheedle to be taken. Sometimes my parents would succeed in putting me off by saying that the opera given that night was dull and interesting only to grown-ups. But when such tempting titles as *Robert le Diable, L'Africana* or *Les Huguenots* caught my eye, no arguments could succeed in dispelling my determination, and I would wangle a promise from my parents that if I were a good boy and worked at my lessons, I should be allowed to go to the theatre. Unendurable days of waiting would slowly follow, and on the day of the performance itself I usually found myself without appetite and quite incapable of even looking at my lesson-books. On the following morning I would be unable to get up early and would announce that I had a headache, whereupon my kind Mama would allow me to stay at home and so miss school. The result of my passion for the theatre was that I was becoming a regular slacker and my father was perfectly right when he protested against these treats, which had a bad effect on my studies. But, although my father was exceedingly kind, the kindness of my mother was greater still, and I lost no time in taking advantage of this fact, so that when the next occasion presented itself, I found no difficulty in getting my own way once again.

My visits to the ballet were far less frequent; there were no season tickets, for one thing, and also the ballet did not enjoy the same popularity as did the opera. Society in those days was still full of moral prejudices and ballet was considered just a shade questionable. We must remember that this was the epoch of dresses to the ground and even long trains, whereas in the ballet very scantily-dressed young ladies appeared in skirts not reaching to their knees. It is true *balletomanes* existed even then, and I remember a popular song of the time which ridiculed them. It began with the words: "*J'aime le ballet, ce n'est pas un secret.*" But the *balletomanes* formed a special clan of their own and had the reputation of being hopelessly incorrigible cranks; they were looked upon as somewhat eccentric and slightly depraved. Besides, in this epoch there prevailed in Russian society ideas of an utilitarian and materialist kind, born of the social movement which marked the beginning of Alexander II's reign. These ideas found expression in the aphorism of the time: "Boots come before Pushkin." It was only natural that from such a puritanically materialist point of view the ballet (which did not preach anything "useful," where nothing for the improvement of society was advocated, and people were only busy with such nonsense as dancing, and in very scanty costumes at that) was considered unworthy of the attention of serious people.

One of the chief reproaches made against the Tsar's Government was that it patronised and encouraged the ballet. We must not forget that up to the assassination of Alexander II a majority of the intelligentzia and even members of the highest circles, though not really at one with the extremists or nihilists, were, nevertheless, in warm sympathy with liberal ideals, and therefore considered it their duty to take an attitude of opposition to the government wherever and whenever they could. I was too young to take in all this, but I felt that ballet was appreciated in a lesser degree than opera or drama, and that grown-ups talked about it in the same vein as when they spoke of the circus or the operette.

Nevertheless, it was the custom to take children to the ballet, especially to the Christmas, Carnival and Easter *matinées*, in the idea that children, anyway, would not understand anything scandalous and that the performance would give them pleasure and entertainment. I too used to be taken to the ballet about twice a year, and these occasions had the character of picnics. We usually had a box in the first tier, opposite the stage, so that we should have a good view. Our little relatives of my own age—my cousins Cavos or Khrabro-Vassilevsky and later on, as they grew older, my little nephews and nieces—were invited. Sometimes we had to have two neighbouring boxes. In the intervals tea and cakes used to be served which made our party more than ever like a *folle-journée*. One of the boxes in the Bolshoy Theatre (the one near the Royal Box) had belonged to my grandfather, Albert Cavos, as the builder of the theatre, and this box was especially beloved by me because the furniture in the *avant-loge* belonged to my grandfather and had been placed there by him. The mirror in the carved black frame that hung on the wall formed the pair to the one we had inherited after grandfather's death; the little table under it was of extravagant Venetian Rococo, exactly like the one I had seen at my Uncle Caesar's. All this created the impression that we were "at home" and gave a particular charm to our theatrical picnic.

Between 1878-1883 I saw all the principal ballets of the period in the surroundings I have just described. The ballets I remember best are: *Roxana, Le Papillon, La Fille des Neiges,* a performance which consisted of three comic little ballets, *Don Quichotte,* and lastly *Koniok Gorbunok (The Hump-Backed Horse),* which I saw at least four times in those years. This would correspond, I should say, to seeing something forty times as a grown-up. *Roxana* was another ballet which I saw several times and therefore remember the details better than those of the other ballets. Only fragments remain in my memory of most of them, as, for instance, the amusing dance of the enormous vegetables in the first act of *Le Papillon,* the ice-grotto with the white bears in the polar ballet *La Fille des Neiges,* the battle with the windmills and the scene in the marionette theatre in *Don Quichotte.*

Roxana, the Belle of Montenegro, was produced in 1878 for patriotic reasons, in order to raise enthusiasm for the war against Turkey for the "freedom of the Slavs." The war was popular enough without the propaganda. In spite of the fact that it was taking place at an enormous distance from the capital, people followed the campaign with intense interest and sympathy. This attitude was entirely different from that which reigned thirty years later during the extremely unpopular Russo-Japanese War. The enthusiasm in the Turkish war was shown by young and old; even children (and I among them) took a lively interest in "our victories" and were full of deep pity for our "little brothers," the Slavs, who were so cruelly persecuted by the Turks. In spite of the fact that shredding old linen for field hospitals was a very tedious job, it was done in those days by everybody. Even children were expected to join in, and, as I plucked the white threads, I used often to be on the verge of tears, imagining how they would dress the wounds of "our heroes."

In the ballet *Roxana* "our little brothers the Slavs" actually appeared in person, looking clean and elegant and graceful in comparison with their odious oppressors, the *Bashibazouks*. Oh, how jubilant the audience became when one of those *Bashibazouks*, after attempting to make love to the beautiful Roxana, was thrown by her *fiancé* into the moon-lit waterfall! The conviction that everything in the world is bound to end happily and that vice is finally punished was the predominant feature of this ballet. How happy one felt when, in the last act, the Montenegrin peasants celebrated their liberation from their oppressors and enthusiastically danced their different folk-dances, supposed to have been studied by the ballet-master at the source.

The actual subject of *Roxana* was far more complicated and confused than what has remained in my memory. It rather resembled the story of *Giselle*, in a Balkan setting; the dark forces—represented by a Slav variation of the Wilis—played a prominent part. All this, however, has disappeared from my memory. Only the scene in which the *Bashibazouk* is hurled off the bridge still lives in my memory with astonishing vividness. The act used to end with the stimulating sounds of a march which became extremely popular and was played in parks and gardens for the following twenty years. To this very day I can still play it by heart from beginning to end. The entire "younger generation of Montenegro" stepped forward on to the stage to the brave sounds of the march. This jubilant crowd consisted of the entire junior classes of the Imperial Theatre School. What a brilliant sight it was! How glittering

and alluring were the white silk shirts worn by the
little girls, how gaily-coloured the cavalry uniforms
of their partners and red high-boots! These little
dancers, who were of the same age as I, seemed to
me to be privileged, unattainable beings. They performed the most wonderful figures in their dancing
as they advanced and retreated, forming a circle or
spreading out like a fan. All this was performed with
an extraordinary gaiety and vivacity that made the
public almost hysterical with delight. The applause
was so great that the children had to encore their
dance two or three times and even then the public was
not satisfied and continued to shout and cheer.

The principal part in this ballet was danced by
Evgenia Sokolova, one of our most celebrated dancers.
Her name became firmly rooted in my memory, but
I can say little about the way she performed her part.
I only know that, with the whole of the house
separating us, she seemed to me to be by far the
most beautiful and charming of all the dancers.
This, however, was not the opinion of the adult
occupiers of our box, who definitely preferred the
beautiful daughter of the ballet master Petipa, just
then at the beginning of her career.

About five years later, when my childish heart had
transformed itself into the heart of a youth, it too
was conquered by the exceptional charm of Marie
Mariusovna Petipa. As to Evgenia Sokolova—I had
later many occasions of watching her and I must
confess that I failed to see anything attractive in her.
She made the great mistake of appearing at her fare-
well performance together with the Italian *diva*
Zucchi, who was then at the height of her career,
and after that fatal occasion she lost much in my
estimation. Her masterly technique seemed quite
pitiable to me that evening, but I was then no
authority on the matter, being entirely infatuated
with Zucchi and raving about her alone. After

c

retiring from the stage, as it was then customary, as quite a young woman, Evgenia Sokolova devoted herself to teaching and continued to do so even after the Bolshevik Revolution. The ballerina Vazem followed in her footsteps and they both reaped great fame in their career, being considered remarkable teachers and outstanding exponents of the old traditions. Many of our great ballet stars, who afterwards became world-famous, continued to take private lessons from Vazem and Sokolova after they had finished the Imperial Ballet School, and were unanimous in admiration and praise of their profound knowledge and experience.

The ballerina whose name I first heard during the performance of *Roxana* and whom I hardly noticed then (she had a quite secondary part) became later, as I have already mentioned, my first ballet infatuation. I fell head over heels in love with this beautiful dancer, and it is perhaps from that moment, when my interest in the performances became more personal and I began to feel the special joy of *her* presence, that I gradually turned into a real *balletomane*. I was only thirteen at that time, and having read all the works of Fenimore Cooper, Mayne Reid and Jules Verne, I had turned to the novels of Alexandre Dumas *père*, whole hosts of whose small volumes I had found hidden behind the more serious books of my father's library—behind Rollin's *History of the Romans* and Anquetil's *History of France*. The reading of Dumas completely turned my head, or rather my heart, by arousing my senses. Under Dumas' influence I started my own little romances—falling in love with some picture in a book, with each of my cousins and nieces in succession, and lastly with so unattainable a person as Marie Mariusovna.

The *coup de foudre* which brought on this platonic infatuation (platonic *de facto*, but far from platonic in feeling) occurred at a performance of *The Hump-*

Backed Horse. I knew the ballet well, but wanted to show it to my little nephews and nieces, the Edwardes'. Once again two boxes in the first tier were taken for the occasion. And I, to be sure to be in good time for the performance on the next day, went to spend the night with my sister, who was married to the charming and unforgettable M. J. Edwardes, brother of the George Edwardes who played so prominent a part in London theatrical life.

They lived on the outskirts of St. Petersburg in a park formerly belonging to Count Bezborodko, situated near a factory belonging to my brother-in-law. Before going to my sister's, I had worked out a whole programme as to the way I was going to prepare my young friends for the forthcoming performance and was looking forward to how we would all enjoy it together. One is altruistic at that age and one enjoys pleasures far more if they can be shared with others. One derives even greater pleasure in helping others to discover and appreciate beauty. This pedagogic trend in æsthetic matters was already one of my chief characteristics. Later I always played the part of "leading spirit" or instructor among my friends.

On this memorable occasion, which took place during Carnival Week in 1883, the first part of the programme, namely the "preparation of the novices before the performance," had been carried out to perfection, and the curiosity of my young companions, which I had done my best to arouse, had reached the highest pitch. The second part, however, which consisted of "enjoying the performance all together," was quite unsuccessful. The thirteen-year-old instructor had suddenly awakened to a new and purely personal interest in the performance and everything else on the stage was dimmed for him except for one figure, who, as the favourite wife of the Tartar Khan, did more running about than dancing. She finally conquered my heart when, at the end of the Ukrainian dance, which she performed with magnificent brio, shaking seductively her incomparable shoulders, she received from her partner Lukyanov a resounding kiss on the lips.

I must add that there was another reason for my watching with a new interest what was going on on the stage. In the box next to us sat two gentlemen who, during the whole performance, did nothing but criticise and discuss the dancers, alluding to them as "girls" and calling them by their christian names— Lida, Masha, Nastia, Tania. I knew these gentlemen very well by sight, for they had attended every ballet performance I had ever been to; one of them looked very good natured and was remarkable for his girth, and the shrill accents of the other were audible over the whole of the house during the intervals. They usually sat in the stalls, but on this occasion—I don't know why—they occupied the box next to ours. Possibly it was just a wish to watch a ballet which had long become stale for them from a different point of vantage. But to me their neighbourhood proved fatal.

They were, as I found out later, the two chief *balletomanes* of our time. The shrill-voiced one was C. Skalkovsky. He occupied a high administrative post but was at the same time a theatrical critic, concerned particularly with the ballet. His inseparable companion was N. M. Bezobrazov—with whom, later on in life, when this rather stout young man had become a portly general, I formed a sort of friendship, based on our mutual infatuation for the ballet, of which there is more to come.

Their rather loose talk seemed to open my eyes to the personal attractions of Marussia Petipa, already familiar to me but somehow in a different way. After this performance I began to frequent the ballet more and more, not only for the pure enjoyment that it gave me but to watch, through opera-glasses, every movement of the enchanting Marussia, whose beauty was really outstanding. This new interest of mine in the ballet soon became obvious in our family and I was teased a good deal. All the gossip about Marie Petipa—and there was plenty of it about town—used to be poured into my ears. I have always remembered a fleeting remark made about her by a dear old friend of our family, the hunch-back S. I. Gadon, the renowned wit. This observation was in no way modest and I might have become indignant about it, had my inclinations towards M. M. Petipa been of a purely idealistic nature. It was, however, quite definitely of a sinful order and when our old friend uttered the phrase, "Elle a beaucoup de cochon," I was definitely pleased. These words seemed, somehow, to make her more accessible, and I began longing to make the acquaintance of this Venus who had nothing of Diana in her. I remember on one occasion how cunningly I managed to hide an empty cigarette box left behind by my tutor, V. A. Soloviev, because it had Marie Petipa's picture on the lid. It was a photograph of her taken in a very tantalising costume in which she really had *l'air très cochon*. That picture laid the foundation of my collection of ballet photographs. It grew rapidly and contained numerous genuine photographs of the same Petipa.

I must mention here that I did at last make the acquaintance of my goddess, but it happened at a time when she had long lost her divinity for me, and her charms were usually spoken of as *des beaux restes*. At that period Marie Mariusovna hardly resembled her former charming self; the childish inexpressive face that looked out from under a heap of dyed hair wore obvious signs of fading. There could be no talk of anything tempting or tantalising any more. Her tall, erect figure had become heavy and rather massive and her girlish affectations, little suited to her years, were distinctly in bad taste. However, this "retired beauty" was literally covered with diamonds and pearls. In character she had retained her easy-going good nature. This, by the way, was proved by the willingness with which she accepted Fokine's and my joint proposal that she should take part in an improvised performance—of which I shall speak later on.

I have somewhat digressed from my subject—from the very ballet which led me to these reminiscences, though they have actually nothing to do with the ballet itself. *The Hump-Backed Horse* was at that period our only national ballet. Produced for the first time in 1864, it won the public's sympathies straight away and is popular to this day, whereas other ballets of a national character, such as *Baba Yaga*, *The Goldfish* and *L'Oiseau de Feu*, never had any real success. It is not very easy to explain its great popularity. It may be partly due to Pugni's music, with its effective waltz *At the Fountain* and the gay march of *The Peoples of Russia*; partly to the successful scenery and general production. Adults appreciated the enormous variety of both classical and character dancing and the excellent cast, but it was the younger generation that particularly favoured and, probably, still favours *Koniok Gorbunok*, because it offers, during the three whole hours it takes to perform, an endless variety of entertaining incidents.

The hero in *Koniok Gorbunok*, instead of being the usual prince, is just a peasant, a simpleton—or village fool—at that. Nevertheless, he has extraordinary good luck. Having caught the magic mare, he agrees to release her when she bribes him with the little hump-backed foal. As it was impossible to give a ballet part to an animal, the author, Saint-Léon, decided to resort to a compromise. In the first act Ivanushka the Simpleton is given a property foal; in the second picture we see him flying up to the clouds seated on it, back to front; but after that we see only a funny, crooked little man dressed in a strange costume, with a horse's head, who hops incessantly. This strange creature, according to the programme, is the "genie of the hump-backed horse." Children readily believed that the colt they had seen in the last picture could take this shape, that this funny little man was *actually* the same hump-backed horse, which, when so disguised, possessed peculiar magic force. The unlimited power of the hump-backed horse is entirely devoted to the services of Ivanushka. He has but to crack his whip to make the genie appear, hopping round his lord and master and awaiting his will. It is thanks to the hump-backed horse that Ivanushka penetrates into the palace of the Tartar Khan, that he reaches a fantastic kingdom (where a huge playing fountain occupies the whole of the stage) and kidnaps a young girl of astonishing beauty. It is thanks once more to the hump-backed horse that he is able to descend to the bottom of the sea to search for a wedding ring for the Tsar-Maiden, and that, lastly, Ivan is able to dupe the Khan when he emerges from the boiling cauldron as a handsome Tsarevitch instead of a village fool. The nasty old Khan—this part was taken by old Kshesinsky—wishes to marry the princess himself and, hoping that he will be given back his youth and turn into a handsome young prince, follows Ivanushka's example. He jumps into the boiling cauldron and . . . disappears for ever.

The ballet used to end with an apotheosis of Russia. For some unknown reason the background consisted of a reproduction of the Thousand Year Jubilee Monument at Nijni-Novgorod. An enormous procession of all the different nations inhabiting the Russian Empire filed past to make obeisance to the fool who had become their ruler. In sign of their loyalty the warriors raise the fool and his bride on their shields and carry them round the stage—just as is done in almost all Lifar's ballets nowadays. It is surprising how such flagrant free-thinking was passed by the theatrical censors, and actually on the stage of the Imperial Theatre! Probably the keepers of orthodox views never imagines that one could find anything seditious in the triumph of a simpleton. Children, of course, were delighted to see the wicked Khan boiling in the cauldron, and their favourite Ivanushka (usually acted by the famous mime Stukolkin) receiving his reward—namely, the throne and the hand of his beloved.[1]

[1] *Koniok Gorbunok* contained several other incidents of historical interest. At one village fair in the first scene there appeared a long-haired pedlar named in the programme as the Jew. To the great delight of the young audience—in those days predominantly "Aryan" —all sorts of pranks were played on him, which ended with his traditional long black overcoat being torn to shreds.

Chapter VI

COPPÉLIA AND GISELLE

BEFORE the memorable performance of *The Hump-Backed Horse* which I have just described, I was interested in ballet to the same extent as I was in any *féerie*. I preferred what I saw in the Bolshoy Theatre because it was of a far higher quality than the shows at the *Balagani* or in the Zoological Gardens. I must mention here that the Zoo was one of the favourite places of recreation and amusement for the St. Petersburg public, especially during the summer months. There was an open stage where fairy-ballets were performed, and well-known foreign ballerinas of considerable attainments used to take part in them.

Though there can be no doubt that the performance of *The Hump-Backed Horse,* during which I was overwhelmed by Marussia Petipa, represented a very important landmark in my infatuation for the ballet, if only from the sentimental point of view, nevertheless my understanding of ballet was deepened still more after two other performances, one of which revealed to me the importance of music as a factor in ballet, while the other proved to me what deep feelings ballet-drama can awaken.

These two revelations occurred in 1884-85—when I was fourteen. I had already gained some personal sentimental experience. During the summer of 1885 the image of my unattainable Dulcinea Marussia Petipa had been overshadowed by a more realistic

c*

love. I had become an insatiable reader of Dumas, Turgeniev and Daudet, and also a lover of museums, where I was beginning to appreciate the distinction between old and modern paintings. In other words, I was gradually turning from a youth into a young man. My upper lip and cheeks were actually showing fluff and my voice was breaking. At the same time my school studies were growing steadily worse. I frankly hated school and was becoming more and more engrossed in my home life. My chief occupation was to arrange marionette performances, for which I was not content to buy ready-made puppets and sets, but made them myself. My audience consisted of the same cousins, nephews and nieces, and the repertory of a kind of harlequinade and greatly simplified versions of classical plays, such as *The Maid of Orleans, Macbeth* and *Hamlet*.

Tommaso Salvini was in St. Petersburg at that time and I saw him act in *Macbeth* and *Hamlet*, and although I did not understand a word of Italian, his acting made a profound impression on me. If I were not entirely engrossed by my story of the ballet, I should have liked to pause here and give a more detailed account of these performances of Salvini.

From the autumn of 1884 I began to frequent the theatre independently, usually accompanied by my brother-in-law, who was only two years my senior. We had our own pocket money, which sufficed, as a seat in the stalls cost only two roubles (four shillings) in those days. Thus I gradually left off asking my mother's permission "to go to the theatre." My father, deeply grieved by what he considered my gradual decline, had almost given me up, and our relations, thanks to my passion for the theatre, were distinctly estranged. My father was almost pedantic in his conscientiousness, and his sense of duty and respect for the principle of education could not be reconciled to the fact that, instead of preparing my lessons, I should spend all my evenings talking with my friends or "hanging about at the ballet." Every visit of mine to the theatre was accompanied by endless conversations and arguments with my friends, mostly in the street after the performance, and as I never got to bed before three o'clock in the morning, getting up at eight in time for school was naturally extremely difficult. I had to feign illness; my mother would then allow me to stay at home. My continued shirking from school led to stormy explanations with Papa, which might have led to still more violent scenes had it not been for my mother's interference.

I must now tell of an occurrence in our family which happened some years before the period I am describing, but which fits in here as it had a great influence on my whole life, affecting both the personal and the creative sides of my character. This event was my brother Albert's marriage to the beautiful Marie Carlovna Kind, an excellent pianist. Music had always occupied an important place in our house —thanks to Albert's brilliant piano and violin improvisations—but from the autumn of 1876 it gained as strong a hold as our interest in architecture and painting.

In 1882 Albert and his family, consisting by then of his wife Masha, two little girls and two boys, moved into the parental house to occupy the apartment just above ours. From then onwards, I began to spend a great deal of my time "upstairs," playing with Albert's children, arranging dances and pantomimes for the two little girls to the sound of their father's improvisations. I was equally fond of talking to my beautiful and very witty sister-in-law, while her brothers and sisters became my nearest friends. The eldest of her brothers, Volodia was my constant companion and Atia, the youngest sister, when we were both sixteen, became my *fiancée*—later my wife and "life-companion." I must, however, confess that, although Marie Carlovna was a brilliant pupil of the famous Leschitizky, I was not very fond of her playing. She was apt to practise endless scales, arpeggios and difficult passages which I could not help hearing even in my own study.

The sounds used to penetrate downstairs into our apartment and I was often, I confess, bored by this endless practising. There was more in my critical attitude towards her execution; it struck me as being rather showy and I felt her interpretation as too angular, hard and devoid of imaginative phrasing. What a contrast to Albert's playing—always rich in life and colour, though he was far from being a virtuoso. It was different when Marie Benois appeared at concerts. The volume and precision which seemed to cut one's ears in a room became, in the concert hall, indispensable to the necessary "perspective of sound."

The result of my listening constantly to the work of such composers as Bach, Beethoven, Chopin or Liszt, was to develop, unconsciously, my taste and knowledge of music. Even the endless irritating repetition of difficult passages helped to make the language of the great composers more comprehensible to me. I was learning, quite unconsciously, to *know* them and therefore also to love them. I would be moved—almost to tears—by Schubert's Waltzes in Liszt's transcription,[1] by some of Chopin's Mazurkas and by the beautiful *Tannhäuser Overture*.

I used to spend several months of the summer with Albert and Masha at their country house in Peterhof, and oh, the joy of listening, on a hot summer day, to the magic sounds of Chopin or Schubert floating through the open window into the garden, where

---

[1] It was in memory of my youthful love of Schubert's Waltzes that I arranged my ballet *La Bienaimée*, which I offered to Ida Rubinstein. The music of this ballet consists principally of Liszt's transcription of Schubert's waltzes and two pieces by Liszt himself.

they mingled with the sweet scent of the flowers! In those days the barbaric cult of sacrificing every-thing to size was unknown and flowers were still fulfilling their chief duty—that of gladdening both the eye and the nose.

Near our house was the sea. On the other side was the beautiful, somewhat overgrown, wooded park of "His Majesty's Own Datcha," where the birds sang and twittered happily to the mysterious rustling of the leaves, and where it was lovely to play hide-and-seek. After a good romp with my little friends, I used to lie down in the shade of the birch-trees and dreamily contemplate the blades of grass and tiny insects beside me or gaze at the clouds sailing over the tree-tops, as I listened to the sounds of Masha's playing, softened by the distance. During those moments of ecstasy I was not fourteen but already twenty-five. I was beginning to feel the charm and the tragedy of life . . . An hour passed and I would be playing croquet with the same Masha, who was a great master of the game. Then, instead of Schubert's melodies, loud laughter and silly disputes would fill the air, interrupted by the sharp blow of the mallets on the balls. . . . What happy times those were!

But I must return to my subject. It seems to me, that in the years that followed Albert and Masha's move into our house, my friendship with Marie Carlovna and the continual listening to her classical repertoire caused some new strings to vibrate in me— taught me a new appreciation of music. My passion for Italian Opera began to weaken and I gained a taste for things more subtle, more refined, but also, perhaps, in a sense more insidious. This change in my attitude towards music was reflected in my attitude towards ballet.

To conceive so supreme an absurdity as a ballet without music could, in our senseless time, be achieved only by such an *enfant gâté des snobs* as Lifar. Music, of course, is the chief stimulus and guiding principle of the ballet. I already sensed this fully when, as a child, I used to dance in front of the mirror in unconscious obedience to the music I heard—whether it was the loud chords of the *Réveil du Lion* or Albert's improvisations. When I frequented the opera or ballet, I memorised the music to which the action or dancing took place. Much of it I liked, parts I found dull, and others I could myself reproduce on the piano. I did not ascribe much importance to this; I was not carried away by it. If I became fascinated by some little tune from *La Bayadère*, *Roxana* or *The Hump-Backed Horse*, it was only because, when I hummed or played it, the images that had charmed me on the stage arose before me.

Something quite different happened after I first heard *Coppélia*—and I say "heard" deliberately, because I rather heard than saw it. Suddenly the music came to the forefront; other qualities seemed to have value only in relation to the music.

Some people may find it strange that after talking of Beethoven, Schubert and Chopin and the beneficial influence they had on me, I should give such significance to the work of the "graceful but light-minded Frenchman," Delibes. As a matter of fact, Delibes is not only a "graceful Frenchman," but one of the most *genuine* creators of music—even if some people consider that the scope of his creative work cannot be compared to that of the giants I have just mentioned. It is conceivable, surely, that Boccaccio and Ariosto should meet Dante and Tasso on Parnassus, that Watteau should speak as an equal to Raphael and Titian. Why, then, not admit that in the shade of Apollo's laurels—where earthly ideas of rank and place have no significance—the warmest of welcomes is waiting for Strauss, Lecocq, Offenbach and, above all, Delibes, who spoke the celestial language of music with an expressive beauty that might rouse the greatest genius to envy? Yes, Delibes is indeed a genius—a member of the same family as Scarlatti, Schubert, Schumann and Tchaikovsky. Delibes' works are not numerous and unfortunately one of his masterpieces—the opera *Lakmé*—has become vulgarised. *Coppélia*, with the exception of individual pieces, has escaped the fate of *Lakmé* and the music is still delightfully fresh, expressive and genuine. How perfectly wonderful this masterpiece must have seemed when it was first given. The ballet world of St. Petersburg received the new ballet with patronising approval; *Coppélia* was usually alluded to as "a very nice little ballet with very nice music," and the artists all agreed that "the music was easy to dance to." But there were some who immediately recognised *Coppélia* as something out of the ordinary, something as striking in its own way as *Carmen*, recently produced at the St. Petersburg opera. Among these enthusiasts were several musicians—headed by Tchaikovsky. Both my elder brothers, Albert and Louis, had appreciated *Coppélia*, which was all the more surprising as one of them was more or less indifferent to the theatre, while the other liked only Italian Opera.

I went to see *Coppélia* for the first time after having played through the music on the piano—following the advice of my brother Louis. But when I first heard the ballet in the theatre, it seemed somehow to move and delight me to the very depths of my soul. It is true that there was much that was delightful in the ballet besides the music. The part of Swanilda was charmingly danced by the pretty and graceful Varvara Nikitina, who was in those days one of the chief adornments of the Imperial stage. The famous Stukolkin was amusing and mysterious as the old Coppelius, while Gerdt made a delightful Franz. Marussia Petipa danced her *czardas* and *mazurka* most brilliantly, flashing her beautiful eyes in all directions. The mimed scenes in the first and second act were performed with both humour and taste, and lastly, every individual number in the final act was a real *chef-d'œuvre* of the ballet-master's inexhaustible imagination. But such merits are common to nearly all the famous ballets. In *Coppélia* there seemed to be something new, something that raised it on to another plane. The whole performance seemed to be dominated by some higher inspiration, to be penetrated with the essence of poetry; the artists themselves to have achieved unconsciously a greater vitality and an unusually noble demeanour in their gestures and dancing. This metamorphosis was *entirely due to the music.*

I saw *Coppélia* for the first time in December of 1884 and after that Volodia Kind and I never missed a single performance, taking care to reserve good seats in advance. In those days tickets were not so difficult to get, and both the stalls and the boxes had many empty gaps. Ballet in that period had not yet gained a great popularity with the general public, and the *balletomanes* only filled the first three rows of the stalls. My friend and I were bent on getting places in those privileged rows and to obtain them a little diplomacy had to be practised and friendly relations maintained with the box-office cashier.

I must say that our enjoyment of *Coppélia* was purely artistic. After Marussia Petipa's dances in the first act, the excitement they had aroused would change into pure artistic delight at Zhukova's wonderful gracefulness and the "old" Kshesinsky's brilliant, characteristically Polish way of dancing the *mazurka*. Another extremely vivacious dancer was the Hungarian Bekeffy, who, though known to be very gloomy in everyday life, became on the stage one of the most thrilling dancers to watch, firing both his partner and the public with his own enthusiasm.

My "passion" for Marussia Petipa now began to wane, for when I compared her dancing to that of these first-class artists the verdict was not in her favour.

The delight I experienced from the very first act of *Coppélia* continued to grow as the drama developed, and this again was due to the expressiveness of the music. It was impossible not to believe that Swanilda and her companions had really penetrated into Coppelius's gloomy panopticon, that the silent, immobile figures were not really made of wood or of wax, that one of the girls had not accidentally touched the springs and thus started the automatons on their absurd repetitive gestures: the Chinaman nodding his head and making rhythmic, jerky movements, the astrologer moving his telescope from one side to the other, the knight in armour sheathing and unsheathing his sword. How charming were Coppelia's girl-companions in their fright and how quickly they became reassured that the figures were nothing but dolls! How infectious was their laughter and how gracefully they danced, stepping daintily on their points, in and out between the figures, to the sounds of the snuff-box tune! This contrast of automatic, senseless movement with the playfulness of living people is one of the most charming *trouvailles* in the whole of ballet literature.

But there were other musical joys still in store for us. The scene where old Coppelius catches Franz as he climbs in through the window is really brilliant, particularly when the old man is struck by the great idea of extracting the vital force from the young lout in order to transfer it to his doll. Every theme in this part of the music is a gem and they follow each other naturally and logically; the music describing the angered Coppelius is succeeded by another melody which expresses the mask of benevolence he puts on in order to coax Franz into drinking the magic draught. As Franz listens to the gay sounds of the *Brindisi*, he gradually becomes completely drunk and in the end unconscious. Even to this day, though I know it is *nicht ernst gemeint*, whenever I hear this part of *Coppélia* I get "the creeps." The scene used to be acted by Stukolkin in the real Hoffmann manner, and inspired in me a love for "Hoffmannism," though I had not then read a line written by the author of *Kater Murr* and *Der goldene Topf*.

The spirit of Hoffmann lives in *Coppélia* in spite of the fact that the libretto is only a humorous parody of his gloomy fairy tale *Der Sandmann*. I am not certain whether Stukolkin himself was acquainted with Hoffmann's works, but I have no doubt that he did not merely act his part, but was actually transformed, body and soul, into the ridiculous and weird magician. It was ten years later, while acting this part, that Stukolkin collapsed and died from a fatal heart attack. The old man must surely have been in a trance; he always *lived* his part and was profoundly affected by everything the music made him feel.

I have dwelt somewhat longer on this scene not only because it is the climax of the whole ballet but because it made so deep an impression on me, that later on in life, when I created my ballets *Le Pavillon d'Armide* and *Petrouchka*, I seemed to be fulfilling ideas that had been born in me in the days of *Coppélia*. Nor was it by chance that in 1901 our circle, when choosing its first ballet production, should have turned (at my insistence) to Delibes, this time to his ballet *Sylvia*. I will return to this later. Although neither *Sylvia* nor *Coppélia* was ever produced by Diaghilev, it was not because we had ceased to dream about them. On the contrary, every year when we discussed our programme, choosing ballets that "should be shown in a revised form" and which were really worthy of being transfigured, the question of *Coppélia* would arise, and Diaghilev's only reason for not producing Delibes' ballets was that both of them were too hackneyed in Paris. One of the great disappointments of my life is that I have not been destined to produce my favourite ballet in the way I should have wished it to be produced, in the manner so clearly and eloquently indicated by Delibes' music.

It was during the season before Zucchi made her début in Russia that I first saw *Giselle*, and the impression this ballet left on me was profound, though of a different order from that made by *Coppélia*.

The sets on that occasion were old and shabby and so were the costumes; the part of Giselle was taken by the unattractive, long-limbed and bony Gorshenkova, who was not favoured by the management because she did not draw a public. Her movements were angular and clumsy and she lacked the charming *naïveté* the part demands. But in spite of all this, the performance moved me so deeply that the memory of it has remained fresh to this day. This, my first impression of *Giselle*, was not wiped out even after I had seen it perfectly performed by Pavlova, Karsavina and Spessiva. When, in 1910, I insisted that *Giselle* should be included in the programme of the second season of our ballets, it was chiefly my youthful memories of the matinée in 1885 that prompted me to do so.

What is the secret charm of this ballet? It is mainly due, one must confess, to its simplicity and clearness of plot, to the amazingly impetuous spontaneity with which the drama is developed. There is barely time to collect one's thoughts before the heroine, who but a moment ago charmed everybody with her vitality, is lying stiff and cold and dead at the feet of the lover who has deceived her.

The second act is devoted to Giselle's life beyond the grave and serves to make us feel her loss still more poignantly, just as we feel Euridice's second death even more keenly after Orpheus has succeeded in bringing her back to the earth. Something similar happens in *La Bayadère*, but the subject of that ballet is almost over-shadowed by the extravagant display of eastern luxury so alien to us Europeans. The "middle-aged Europeanism" of *Giselle* is extremely problematic and one wonders whether Théophile Gautier didn't invent the "Wilis" himself . . . Nevertheless the poetry is European, and it arouses a far deeper response in our hearts than the inventions born of inflamed Eastern imagination.

One thing is certain—*Giselle* is deeply moving, and the magic of a true poet such as Gautier consists in making us accept without question any absurdities he may choose to offer us. It is strange, for instance, that a perfectly healthy young girl should become insane and die for the sole reason that she discovered her lover's betrayal. The Wilis themselves, who are supposed to be maidens punished after death for having danced too much on the earth, sound most unplausible. It seems extraordinary there should be so many of these sinful young girls—as if there had ever been an epidemic of dancing in that quiet little corner of Germany. But no one is inclined to criticise while under the spell of this strange idyll, especially in the second act, when the charming phantoms assemble in the graveyard . . .

I must repeat that the outstanding place which *Giselle* occupies in the repertory of ballet is really due to its subject. It is in some respects an ideal ballet, for it is short (not heavy and long like *La Bayadère*), but comprehends nevertheless the whole gamut of human feelings. The subject is, within limits, both reasonable and unreasonable. A measure of fancy has been found and is so presented that it compels our belief. It is the same measure we find in our favourite fairy-tales; they are beloved by us because they fulfil the same demands. Further, the choreo-

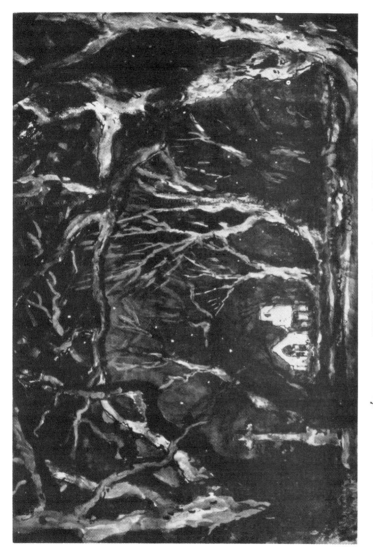

DÉCOR FOR THE SECOND ACT OF *GISELLE*
By Alexandre Benois

Facing page 70

NIJINSKY IN THE SECOND ACT OF *GISELLE*, 1910

Facing page 71

graphic story of *Giselle* has this advantage over many other ballet stories, that one of its chief elements is *the dance*. Thanks to this, *Giselle* remains something incomparable and inimitable. The number of similar subjects is very limited and they do not bear repetition. I am again tempted to compare it with *La Bayadère*, where the heroine is also a dancer and a professional dancer at that. The chief charm of Giselle's personality lies in the fact that she is a disinterested lover of the dance who indulges in it when inspired and cannot therefore fight against temptation. Her very love for Loys is aroused by his graceful dancing, whereas the amorous forester Hilarion has no chance of winning her heart because he dances like a bear, and the Wilis in the second act have no difficulty in exhausting the clumsy boor and then drowning him in the marshes.

The reader may find it strange that I am relating so much about the heroine and saying nothing about the hero, whose role was greatly improved later on by Nijinsky. But the part of the *premier danseur* in this ballet is only auxiliary. It was Nijinsky's genius which was needed to bring it to the fore and thus interest the audience not only in Giselle herself, but also in her unfaithful lover, who is cruelly punished in the second part of the ballet. It was here that Nijinsky rivalled the ballerina. He made the grief of the repentant seducer profoundly pathetic; the scene where the Wilis, exalted by Hilarion's doom, try to dance him too to his death became genuinely terrifying. But Nijinsky had not yet been born when I first saw *Giselle*, in the Spring of 1884 and the part of Loys-Albrecht was played not by a genius but by one of our excellent artists; I remember nothing of him, but Gisellè, though acted by the rather unsuitable Gorshenkova, still lives in my memory.

I have already said that *Coppélia* played a decisive part in my musical development and led me to demand from the ballet a high standard of music. *Giselle* played the same part in developing my ideas and standards for the dramatic side of choreographic art. The subject of *Giselle* is ideal material for a ballet, and it was towards that ideal that I afterwards aspired in *Pavillon d'Armide, Petrouchka, Schéhérazade* and *La Bienaimée*. How many other ballet themes I have dreamed of but, alas, have never been realised! It is due to the influence of *Giselle* that most of my ballets have a sad ending. *Giselle* has, as its poetical foundation, an elegiac quality that inspires the whole ballet with intoxicating sweetness and gives it a nobility which makes other, quite worthy, inventions seem trivial and flat. If only the music for *Giselle* had been written by Chopin or Tchaikovsky instead of by Adam! But let us not be unjust to him; some items in the ballet, especially the charming *Allegro louré* to which Giselle and Loys dance together, are full of moving poetry—inspired surely by the subject.

Chapter VII

THE DIVINE ZUCCHI

IN a current number of a weekly, family journal called *Niva*, an ultra-conservative publication, full of inferior illustrations for bits of Russian poetry, I found the portrait of an uncommonly vivacious and delightful young woman. Under this woodcut—which was of quite adequate workmanship—were the words: "Types of feminine beauty: Mlle. Zucchi, *première danseuse* of the Eden Theatre in Paris. In the part of Sieba." Being rather sophisticated in matters of art, I usually looked at a fresh number for the fun of laughing at the pictures, reproduced from the German *Gartenlaube* and *Ueber Land und See*. Quite unexpectedly there emerged among the pages of this journal a face not at all beautiful, but strangely piquant and attractive. I immediately longed to see the *diva* about whom, it was said, all Paris was raving. There was but little hope of my ever seeing her—foreign ballet stars seldom visited Russia at that time, and if they did, it was only for a short season on the stage of some summer-theatre, and their appearance was not even advertised. The times of Taglioni, Elssler, Cerito and Grantsova were over and we were expected to be entertained by our own national talent.

It is possible that it was not by chance that Zucchi's portrait was published in the *Niva*—it may have been part of her manager's plan to show this brilliant Parisian "Star of stars" to the St. Petersburg public. If this was the case, his idea could hardly have been

expected to succeed, because the majority of sub-
scribers to the *Niva* were far from being interested in
the ballet, and the writer of these lines was probably
the only one fully to appreciate the picture, which he
immediately cut out and added to the collection of
similar portraits stored in his writing-table drawer.
But what was the importance of this fourteen-year-
old schoolboy Shura Benois? I tried to find out
something about this new star from our family
"oracle," my uncle Misha Cavos, who was a great
æsthete and theatre-lover, but he had never heard of
Zucchi. Thus I had to resign myself to my dreams
and to admiring her portrait.

A year later, quite unexpectedly, my dream came
true: Zucchi was actually in St. Petersburg! She
could be seen any day in the suburban amusement
park Livadia, but so little notice did her appearance
attract that I only heard of her arrival after she had
been taking part in the performances for a whole
week. Her part consisted of dancing an entirely in-
appropriate solo in the operette *Voyage dans la Lune*.
The real attraction for the Russian public was the
pretty, vivacious Marussia Poiré, sister of the well-
known Paris caricaturist, "Caran d'Ache." But neither
she nor the gay, luxuriously produced operette, nor
the presence of the dancer who was soon to be called
"the Divine" seemed to attract the public. Livadia
was empty and business definitely bad.

The theatre presented rather a sad and desolate picture when I visited it about ten days after Zucchi's arrival. With me went a young Englishman—Reginald
L., a relation of the Edwardeses, with whom he had
come to stay. He was a delightful fellow but a bit
of a crank. I was fascinated by him because he was
of such a definite type: his long, thin figure—considered characteristic of an Englishman—his sense of
humour, the funny little pipe eternally sticking in
his mouth, his extraordinary coats which looked like

shooting jackets. He was also a great lover and collector of antiques, and this finally conquered me, for we spent days in the antique shops of the Alexandrovsky and Schukin markets buying up silver, china and old pictures. He loved the Russian manner of bargaining and indulged in lengthy conversations with the cunning, bearded shopmen in order to draw them out. His nickname for them was "those old *Zdrastis*"—derived from *zdravstvuite*, how-do-you-do, a greeting with which every Russian starts a conversation. I acted as his voluntary interpreter and expert at the same time. On one occasion we bought a picture for a hundred roubles—about ten pounds—which he re-sold in England for several hundred pounds. This raised us in each other's estimation. Though he was some ten years my senior, he was much more of a child than I was and, though endowed with a good brain, retained this childishness to the end of his days . . .

ꜟ The day on which I first saw Zucchi is fixed in my memory with exceptional vividness. It was certainly an important event in my life and Reginald's presence seemed to add a certain picturesqueness to it. It was a warm summer evening at the end of June, and though already eight o'clock, it was so light that when we reached the Summer Gardens landing-stage and stepped on board the tiny steamer which was to take us to "the Islands," the sun was still high in the heavens. Livadia was situated on one of the islands and this was the quickest way of getting there. When we stepped off the steamer and entered the amusement park the daylight seemed to emphasise the depression caused by the emptiness of the place. There were masses of empty seats in the theatre and one felt sorry for the artistes who had to perform to so poor an audience. However, my companion was soon tired of the performance and I found him in the interval at a shooting booth, surrounded by a gaping crowd watching the "English lord," attired, in spite of the warm summer weather, in a long, fox-fur coat —his way of expressing his sympathy with everything Russian—spending rouble after rouble in futile attempts to hit an egg bobbing on a jet of water. I must add that the rifles were being loaded and handed to him by two pretty, heavily made-up young women, and it was probably for their sake that my friend was "losing his fortune."

Two whole acts and two intervals passed before Zucchi's appearance on the stage, which itself lasted not more than ten minutes; but those ten minutes were a revelation to me. The ecstasy of delight that I experienced caused an utter revolution in my outlook on dancing and brought it into line with the ideal which was taking shape in my subconscious mind.

Zucchi was dancing accompanied by a small *corps de ballet* and a very indifferent partner; she represented some fantastic creature who could as well be imagined at the bottom of a moonlit sea as in the garden of the Hesperides. The ballet had nothing in common with the rest of the operette. It was just a choreographic number, devoid of subject or drama. I am laying special stress on this point as later on Virginia Zucchi aroused the wildest enthusiasm of the Russian public by the dramatic intensity of her miming. On this early occasion, even the small audience seated here and there in the stalls and boxes seemed instantly to appreciate Zucchi's appearance on the stage and showed this by the breathless intentness with which they watched her. Towards the end of her dance she rose on her points and, taking tiny steps, began gliding backwards to the music of a very popular song, *Nur für Natur*—it seemed as though she were being wafted by a gentle breeze. At first there were individual bursts of applause, but soon the whole audience broke out into a stormy ovation. Zucchi was forced to give two encores. Even then the public was not satisfied and remained in the empty, barn-like theatre applauding and shouting the name that was shortly to be on everybody's lips.

From then onwards, similar scenes took place in Livadia at every performance. Those who had seen her once became enthusiastic and spread the glad news throughout St. Petersburg that a marvellous dancer was appearing "on the Islands," thus, slowly but surely, the audience was augmented every night. Without the least help from advertisement (in those times still very primitive), the renown of the Italian dancer spread more and more widely among the Russian people. This was a source of great satisfaction to Skalkovsky, who had appreciated the genius of Zucchi when he was abroad a year before, and had insisted on her being engaged by the theatrical manager Lentovsky.

The rest of the performance lost all interest for me because Zucchi did not appear again. Having torn my companion, the "English lord," from his shooting exercises, I insisted on our returning home at once to my sister's house at Kushelevka. The good-natured Redge agreed to this, and, puffing at his pipe, listened patiently all the way to my excited descriptions of what I had seen. These continued at home in our room until the break of day, when, smiling slyly over the bowl of his interminable pipe, Redge proposed that we should drink to my new infatuation. After about five drinks of vodka, to which he was very partial, Redge proceeded to show me how he imagined Zucchi's manner of dancing, and I don't think I ever laughed so much as when I watched my fair-haired friend, in a night-shirt that hardly reached his knees, prancing with his thin legs about the parquet floor in a wild mixture of jig and *trepak*.

On all the following nights I went to Livadia,

more often by myself, but occasionally taking Volodia or his cousins. The theatre seemed fuller every time I went and the papers began to publish favourable accounts. My pilgrimages were, however, cut short because I had to accompany my parents to the government of Kharkov on a visit to my sister, Mme. Lanceray. Oh, how impatient I was to get back to St. Petersburg, as soon as I learned from the papers that the programme at Livadia had been altered, and that she was now creating a real sensation in the ballet *Brahma*.

On the evening of our return, I flew to the theatre with Volodia in the hope of seeing this wonderful ballet, and great was our disappointment when we found that all the tickets were sold out. We managed to get seats, however, by paying a tout three times the price, but this we didn't mind, for we found ourselves in the stalls actually watching *Brahma*.

The performance did not consist of the whole of Monplaisir's ballet but of several fragments. Only one of these has remained in my memory—the one that attracted the public and brought forth the wildest enthusiasm. This fragment showed the flight of the Bayadère (again a Bayadère!) and her lover Brahma from their enemies and the halt of the fugitives in a tropical forest. The scenery demanded a great deal of imagination from the audience, as the stage was ill-lit and what was visible was much more like a stunted St. Petersburg public square than a luxuriant tropical jungle. The lovers were discovered, faint and tired and hardly able to drag their feet along, peering with horror into the surrounding gloom and approaching a cardboard rock, on which Brahma sank down exhausted. Suddenly a band of bearded, white-clad men emerged from the darkness and crept towards the sleepers. But Zucchi the Bayadère was wide awake. From that moment onwards, thanks to the spotlight—electric sun, as it was then called—

every change of expression on her mobile face could be seen. She kissed lovingly the forehead of her prince. Lying by his side she first only senses and then, still feigning sleep, actually watches the approach of danger. Zucchi's change of expression was so marvellously beautiful that these few seconds alone were worth the whole ballet. The conspirators surround their victims and, pulling out their daggers, raise them, and are just about to plunge them into the sleeping prince when an extraordinary thing happens. The feeble, unarmed girl who, but a few moments ago, could hardly walk, rises suddenly to her feet and begins to advance towards the would-be murderers, holding them with her eyes. It is impossible to describe this moment. The scene when related is apt to appear as ridiculous as any melodramatic nonsense. But those who saw Zucchi could not have laughed. There was such pathos, such supreme self-sacrifice, such feminine fury in the woman fighting for the life of her beloved, and finally, such tremendous magnetic force! The play demanded that the plotters should withdraw, forced by the magic force of Padmana's eyes, and indeed it was obvious that they were not simply following the producer's directions, but were actually compelled to do so by Zucchi's piercing gaze.

My brother Louis corroborated this impression when, several months later, he told me about the following incident. At a dinner party given by the *balletomane* I. I. Rostovtsev in honour of Zucchi, it was decided to perform that scene to my brother Albert's improvisation on the piano. Dinner napkins were quickly transformed into turbans on the heads of the amateur actors, the prince turned his frock-coat inside out, and Zucchi ruffled the mass of her raven black hair and only slightly tucked up her evening dress. A couch served as the rock and two or three tropical plants in pots became the forest.

In spite of these surroundings, the scene was performed so convincingly that, after it was over, my brother felt as though his eyes had been blinded by some brilliant light . . .

How perfectly adorable Zucchi became after her victory, when, radiant with joy, she awakened her sleeping lover and insisted on continuing their journey! There was such genuine love in her eyes, such joy in every movement, such simplicity and unaffected charm in her whole personality. How worthy of love she seemed and how one hoped and wished that this happiness would not forsake her! The whole audience, which had just been trembling for her, now heaved a sigh of relief and relaxed, believing that she would be saved.

All this took place to the sounds of the most ordinary, uninspiring and even vulgar music, played by a miserable little orchestra, with the poorest setting, without the aid of any producer's artifice. The ballet itself had been hastily arranged and it was said that it had cost the management less than ten pounds. This nightly performance on the St. Petersburg islands was nothing short of a miracle. Not only the Brahmins but the entire audience was bewitched by Zucchi. A success so extraordinary and unprecedented began to penetrate into higher spheres and the Emperor expressed the wish to see the dancer who was the talk of the town. A performance was given in Krasnoye Selo—the summer camp of the Guards Brigade. Zucchi was favourably received by the Emperor and after this Vsevelojsky, the Director of the Imperial Theatres, decided to sign a contract with her, though he had refused to do so earlier, in spite of Skalkovsky's urging.

The divine Virginia was to appear on the Imperial stage in the ballet that had so pleased Alexander III and the Empress Marie Feodorovna. But things turned out differently. Evgenia Sokolova's benefit night was at hand, for which the long ballet *La Fille du Pharaon* was being revived. She was to have danced the part in which Rosati and Vazem had starred in former days, but because of her sudden serious indisposition the role of the princess Aspicia was given to Zucchi. She had just returned to St. Petersburg from a visit to Milan and was met at the station with the news that, instead of having the part of a simple little shepherdess, she was to appear as a King's daughter. Zucchi got frightened, tried to refuse, but when the subject of the ballet—taken from Théophile Gautier's *Le Roman de la Momie*—was explained to her in detail, she immediately realised the possibilities the part offered, and drove straight from the station to rehearsal at the Imperial School of Ballet, having gained confidence and giving herself entirely into the hands of Marius Petipa.

Many rumours circulated about the rehearsals and preparations for this ballet. According to some, the great Marius had frequent fits of despair about Zucchi, for she did not coincide with his conception of an ideal dancer. He greatly appreciated a certain severity and reserve—classicism in the full meaning of the word—and demanded, above all, absolute subordination to his own ideas. With Zucchi this was difficult; her temperament generally got the upper hand in spite of her goodwill, and she always put too much fire, too much passion into everything she did. The other rumour was that Petipa was raving about her, even more so her partner, the outstanding *jeune premier* of the company, P. A. Gerdt, so that the rehearsals took place in an atmosphere of mutual delight. It is probable that both these rumours had some truth in them, but it seems that only at the beginning things did not run quite smoothly, as they did later on when the artists had learned to know each other, and Petipa had realised what a guarantee of success lay in the exceptional temperament of the

artiste; while she, for her part, had understood what
was wanted of her. It was then that the rehearsals
began to improve; in a week and a half everything
was ready and Saint-Georges' ballet *La Fille du
Pharaon* was presented to the public.

Zucchi's name was now famous in St. Petersburg
and there was a tremendous audience at the first
night. I was then but a fifteen-year-old schoolboy,
yet I managed to get a seat in the stalls. I felt I *had*
to be at this performance not only because I was
one of the first people to "discover" Zucchi, but also
because there were rumours that her enemies were
likely to arrange a hostile demonstration that evening.
Volodia and I were firmly resolved to defend "our
goddess," even if it came to fighting for her. But
this proved unnecessary. From her first entrance the
whole theatre was overwhelmed by a feeling of
exaltation—from that first moment of her appearance,
when the resurrected Aspicia leaves her sarcophagus
and steps out on to the proscenium, her whole being
radiant with happiness at having awakened from the
sleep of death, at being alive and just as beautiful
as she was four thousand years ago.

This was not a usual, simple, well-rehearsed
performance, but something well-nigh supernatural.
The stage of the Bolshoy Theatre had never seen
anything like it. Nobody commented upon the fact
that Aspicia's gestures were not quite like those that
were taught to the pupils in the Theatre School,
that there was too much sensuality in the curves and
movements of this ancient Egyptian. Everyone was
conquered by the extraordinary sincerity, the absolute
conviction which she inspired. The whole performance,
in spite of faults and shortcomings, was of the same
quality. The public laughed heartily during the first
scene when a hideous monkey jumps about the stage;[1]

[1] The monkey was played by the pupil Nicolas Legat, who later
on became the pride of the Imperial Ballet.

the laughter became Homeric when Aspicia first chases the monkey but then flees in terror as a lion, suspended on wires, but more reminiscent of a hearth-rug, appears above the rocks. But one had only to transfer one's eyes from these curios to Zucchi to forget all about the comic part. When she was chasing the monkey, Aspicia's face expressed such excitement and intentness that one thought she was Artemis herself; when she was escaping from the lion, her terror was such that the audience became infected with her panic. Here again, as in *Brahma*, the reaction of joy which overcame Zucchi when she was saved at the last minute—Ta-Hor's arrow pierces the lion just in time—was communicated to the entire audience.

I must add a few words about Zucchi's outward appearance. She could in no case be called beautiful, but she was *mieux que belle et mieux que jolie*. Her eyes had a somewhat Chinese slant, but could widen and sparkle at the proper occasions; her mouth was large, with perfect teeth; her jet black hair was unruly and could not be coaxed into any style of *coiffure*. At supremely dramatic moments Zucchi made clever use of this artistic untidiness of her hair, for she would push it up with a perfectly natural gesture, and the effect was wonderful. She had an unusually thin natural waist—Zucchi never wore a corset—and a very flexible body with a small chest, round hips and not very slim but perfectly shaped legs. All this created an image which does not correspond to the modern idea of "beautiful line," but was extremely attractive nevertheless. Zucchi's back and shoulders were her chief beauty—they were truly perfect. Skalkovsky used to assure us that Zucchi's back contained a whole world of poetry. But her charm had really nothing to do with any one of her features. It lay in her wonderful, radiant femininity.

This radiance was expressed most vividly in her

D

face. Zucchi's capacity for expressing shades of emotion was really remarkable. At the same time her face was extraordinarily suitable for the stage. Nowadays it is essential for cinema artists that their outward appearance should be *photogénique*. The theatre has its own laws about looks and these too are of immense importance. Some beautiful faces are entirely lost on the stage, for one has to depend on strong opera glasses to discover their admirable qualities. No opera glasses were needed to see Zucchi's face, and to admire every fleeting expression on it.

La Fille du Pharaon was not the perfect role for Zucchi. The parts of "king's daughters," "fairies" or "goddesses" did not suit her character—she was too much nature's child, too alive, too spontaneous. This purely Italian vivacity would sometimes become trivial, but it never ceased to be charming. The parts she was most suited for were the roles of simple, naïve, and impulsive young girls. In spite of this, her interpretation of so unsuitable a part as Aspicia, for which she had to prepare at extremely short notice, was perfect. This was more obviously apparent when the same ballet was performed again with Evgenia Sokolova after she had recovered from her illness. She danced with the usual classical restraint and dignity that suited the part, but at the same time seemed to *kill* the ballet, which had, but a few weeks before, been resurrected by the "divine Virginia." With Sokolova in the chief part the seven acts, prologue and epilogue seemed endless, tiring and dull. One could hardly believe that, only a few days ago, this same ballet had been breathlessly watched by an enthusiastic audience which left the theatre with regret, wishing they could see the whole performance over again.

The story of the ballet is indeed very moving. The outlines were taken from Théophile Gautier, but actually the only point in common was the resurrection of the mummy. In the ballet the scene where the young Lord Wilson falls asleep in the pyramid was totally different from Gautier's version. The young lord dreamed that he had taken the form of the noble Egyptian Ta-Hor. He saved Aspicia from the lion and was graciously rewarded by Pharaoh, her father. In the second act the Nubian King (this part was magnificently played by Kshesinsky) appeared to beg for Aspicia's hand in marriage. Pharaoh agreed and therefore the young lovers, Aspicia and Ta-Hor, decided to escape. They plotted and made all their arrangements during the famous *grand pas d'action*. This *grand pas d'action* remains a perfect example of Petipa's art and is still one of the high-lights of dramatic choregraphy—where dance is imperatively united to the development of the plot.

Zucchi was not, perhaps, entirely convincing as a princess of royal blood at the moment when she was presented to the black monarch, but she certainly triumphed in the *grand pas d'action* when using her divine gift of "speaking with her face and her whole body." Here she had an opportunity of displaying a whole gamut of feelings. She tried to resist Ta-Hor, shuddered at the thought that their flight would arouse her father's anger, and then, little by little, gave way to the persuasion of her fiery lover and of her followers. All this has to be clearly interpreted so that the side-play is obvious to the audience, while remaining hidden from the two feasting rulers. The lovers escape and, as soon as this is discovered, they are pursued.

In the next scene the fugitives seek refuge in a humble fisherman's hut. Here Zucchi's natural gifts of acting were given full scope. Pretending she was a simple fisherwoman, she described to the guests assembled there for a wedding how she and her lover had been overtaken by a storm on the Nile, in which they nearly lost their lives. Having finished her story, she gaily takes part in the general dancing and merriment. This act closes with a dramatic scene between Aspicia and the Nubian King, who has overtaken the fugitives and tries to take possession of Aspicia. After several attempts to escape from the embraces of the impassioned black monarch, Pharaoh's daughter jumps on to the window-sill, threatening to drown herself in the Nile, and when even this fails to bring the barbarian to his senses, full of despair, she flings herself into the water.

Thenceforward the young lord's dream becomes still more improbable. Aspicia appears at the bottom of the Nile. The dignified, long-bearded ruler of the watery kingdom is touched by the beauty of his earthly colleague's daughter, and when she implores him to allow her to return to earth he grants her request. Before she leaves his kingdom, a ball is given in her honour. One by one all the great rivers of the world appear in national costume and perform the dances of their countries. The Tiber dances a tarantella, the Guadalquivir a bolero; then comes a jig by the Thames and a Russian dance by the Neva.

At the end of this water *divertissement* the Nile gave his blessing to Aspicia for her safe return home and sent two "streams" to accompany her. All three of them were lifted high above the stage by a real spout of water. The effect was great, but on one occasion it cost the life of the dancer who was doubling the prima-ballerina. The platform, which rose behind the water spout, had almost reached the top when it suddenly collapsed, and the three unfortunate girls fell with it. Two of them survived, but Zucchi's double died after several months of struggle between life and death. I hasten to assure the reader that similar accidents were extremely rare on the Imperial stage; this was the one and only case during all the years I frequented the theatres.

The *dénouement* of the drama was successfully reached in the last scene but one. Having left the Nile, Aspicia arrives home just in time to save her lover and his faithful servant from execution. This servant refuses to leave his master even in the dream and becomes transformed from the valet John Bull into the Egyptian Passifont. Here Aspicia had to act a most complicated and effective scene. She describes the infamous behaviour of the Nubian king and decides to awaken her father's pity by throwing herself on to the basket of flowers that contains the snake destined to poison Ta-Hor and Passifont. Papa Pharaoh is deeply touched by this proof of his daughter's love and immediately gives his consent to the marriage. The scene is brought to an end by a brilliantly gay *pas de crotales*, after which the stage is shrouded in mist. When it disperses, one sees the interior of the pyramid and the sleeping travellers. The final chord of the performance was the inevitable apotheosis: the stage opened up and the whole scene was transformed into a brilliantly illuminated conglomeration of the monuments of ancient Egypt.

I have dwelt so long on *La Fille du Pharaon* partly because it was the ballet that determined Zucchi's success in St. Petersburg, but also because it played a decisive part in my personal life.

I saw *La Fille du Pharaon* innumerable times and could play the entire score from beginning to end by heart on the piano. My enthusiasm was due not only to the "divine Virginia," but to the performance as a whole. At that period I preferred *Aïda* to all other operas; apart from its magnificent music, *Aïda* transferred me to a world that seemed strangely familiar. *La Fille du Pharaon* awoke in me again my fascination for ancient Egypt, chiefly, I think, on account of Pugni's music. It is true that it is inferior to Verdi's, being much coarser—probably because Pugni composed in such haste. Still, the music is full of colour and life and, thanks to this, certainly stimulates the imagination.

My friends and I were so enthusiastic about *La Fille du Pharaon* that we decided to produce this ballet in my doll's theatre. A portal in Egyptian style reaching to the very ceiling was built in our ballroom; the performance itself took place on a rather high platform. The décors for my ballet were painted by me, and the dolls' costumes were made by my sisters and my future *fiancée* according to my designs. No details were forgotten—even the Pharaoh's chariot on which he appears at the end of the hunting scene was there and so were the luxurious accessories for the royal banquet. The only scene we omitted was the watery kingdom at the bottom of the Nile. A piano and harmonium taking the place of the orchestra, played the most colourful parts of Pugni's score, while I handled the dolls with the help of my future brother-in-law, Volodia Kind, his sister, with whom I was already desperately in love, and my friends, Kolia Cheremisinov and the two brothers Fenoult. The elder Fenoult composed the libretto of our play in verse, as it was a dramatic performance and not a pantomime.

After many rehearsals our play was ready; the oil-lamps, which stood at our feet in the wings, failed, by some miracle, to cause a fire, and the performance proved a great success. There was one drop of bitterness in my triumph, namely in the attitude of my Uncle Misha Cavos, who always made fun of everything. He was, however, punished for this by his nephew, for I refused to speak to him during a whole year! The result of this estrangement proved beneficial; the uncle developed a certain respect for his young nephew and later on in life, in spite of the forty years' difference between us, we became real friends. I owe much to this friendship, as Michel Cavos was one of the most cultured men of his time, the friend of famous writers, musicians and artists.

Zucchi's second triumph on the Imperial Stage was her appearance in *La Fille Mal Gardée*. This was the ballet that had delighted the Imperial family in Krasnoye Selo and it was now chosen by the management for Zucchi's début in her new engagement. Her success in *La Fille Mal Gardée* was perhaps even greater than in *La Fille du Pharaon*. To begin with, the part of the village maiden Lise suited her far better than that of the Princess Aspicia. Though she had managed to perform the part of the Pharaoh's daughter so brilliantly, it had really been a kind of *tour de force*. There were no such difficulties to surmount in the new ballet. Zucchi had only to be herself. Her spontaneity gave the performance an exceptional freshness.

La Fille Mal Gardée is a naïve story in the style of a *bergerie* of the eighteenth century, but, thanks to Zucchi and in spite of the faded décors—the management had not wished to have any expenses and had merely restored the old scenery which dated from Nicolas I—and the very modest music of Hertel, the performance seemed actually to exude the fresh fragrance of fields and meadows and to create a full illusion of the charm of country life.

In the third act, which shows Lise slowly succumbing to the temptation of her lover's importunity, Zucchi gave a strikingly sincere and realistic performance. Here was a genuinely inexperienced girl who first felt the danger of temptation and then, moved by her passion for Colas, gave in to his tender entreaties without losing her charming shyness. Some people might say that this was a subject for "nasty old men" because the very youthfulness of the heroine—the forty-year-old Zucchi gave the full illusion of being fifteen—gave a kind of lewd piquancy to what was going on on the stage and also to what was hidden from the spectators' eyes—at a certain moment Lise's mother locks her up in a loft where Colas has concealed himself. There were many years between me and old age then, yet this ballet caused both me and all the younger part of the audience to *live through* the performance, for we watched it with the purest feelings and all the exaltation of youth. Each of us seemed to recognise in the play the happy moments that we had ourselves experienced at some time or other and which had remained in our hearts as the "blessed moments that made life worth living."

Zucchi's dancing in *La Fille Mal Gardée* was so enchanting that no other artist before or after could ever be compared with her. Her technique was perfect and included many difficult novelties hitherto unseen in St. Petersburg; but, more than this, she put genuine feeling and significance into every dance. How full of childish grace, without the least sign of affectation, was the *pas de deux* in the second act! It consisted of three different parts which were connected between themselves: first the happy, playful work of churning the butter, then the *valse à trois temps* and finally the lovers, who were still children at heart, playing hobby-horses. Even more moving was Zucchi's performance in the classic "choreographic duet" of the second act, where every step seemed to be a declaration of the feelings of an innocent young girl to her beloved. This was performed with such sincerity that many people in the theatre wept as they watched her, and an old friend of our family, the famous sculptor Aubert, was so moved that he had to retire to the *avant-loge* to have a good cry—his tears were coming down in streams and choking him.

Those who never saw Zucchi can hardly imagine how wonderful it was, but some of our great ballerinas who were afterwards to create the world-wide celebrity of the Russian ballet did actually witness the miracles I have been describing and have preserved an ineffaceable memory of it all. M. F. Kshesinskaya and O. O. Preobrazhenskaya speak of Zucchi, whom they saw in *La Fille Mal Gardée*, with a profound reverence. There can be no doubt that our great ballerinas were influenced by this example at the beginning of their career; that it played an important part in forming their artistic personality and was transferred through them to the entire Academy of St. Petersburg.

Zucchi's success overwhelmed St. Petersburg. The whole town demanded seats in the Bolshoy Theatre, then in its last season. Society talked only of the "divine Virginia" and only to praise her. Still more important was the fact that since Zucchi's success in the autumn of 1885, there was a definite revival of interest among the Russian public for the ballet—an interest that has never waned since then and never died. It has outlived even the Bolshevist Revolution. There was, of course, unfavourable criticism. Part of it was due to the jealous attacks of those who disliked Zucchi for undermining the success of their own *protegées* in the ballet; part of it, however, was based on genuine questions of principle. Zucchi was blamed for going against the chief tradition of the old Russian ballet, the aspiration towards pure and noble classicism. She was accused of introducing "vulgarity" into the Imperial Ballet, the "vulgarity" that was supposed to have ruined the once-famous ballet schools of Milan and Paris. But what could such solitary voices do against the *vox populi*, which grew louder and louder every day? The Court, headed by the Emperor himself, were firm supporters of Zucchi. Alexander III, who hated all falsehood and pretence as did the entire Imperial family, was delighted with Zucchi's simplicity and genuineness.

The artist's simplicity and sincerity impregnated all those with whom she came into contact on the stage. Her usual partner, P. A. Gerdt, had always

D*

been a first-class artist, but even he loved to say that, although he had been on the stage for twenty years,[1] "working with Zucchi had opened his eyes to many things." Indeed, it would be difficult to imagine anything more harmonious than the co-operation between these two first-class artists.

But nothing lasts for ever and even the light of Zucchi's fantastic success began to fade. The first premonitions of twilight were apparent at her own benefit performance, which was given in the second half of the season of 1885–1886, just before its close. After this Zucchi continued to charm the St. Petersburg public for another whole season, but at the performance I have just mentioned something happened which showed that the Divine One did not possess everything. Even her genius could not overcome bad music or absurd plot. When she first came to St. Petersburg to perform in *Le Voyage dans la Lune*, nobody knew her and those who saw her were amazed to watch her create a masterpiece out of the trivial, small part that had been given to her. It was quite different when the management forced her to perform a new ballet, *L'Ordre du Roi*, a heavy, muddled, incomprehensible choreographic story set to music by M. Vizentini, the former producer of the Italian Opera. Zucchi did everything in her power to save this nonsense, but the failure of the performance as a whole was so obvious that the public, used to seeing the artiste who triumphed in everything, was

---

[1] The ballet *La Fille Mal Gardée* was chosen to celebrate Gerdt's twenty-fifth anniversary on the Imperial stage. When he appeared as Colas, everybody who was present—even those who knew him well—could hardly believe that "the young lad playing horses with Lise" was actually forty years old. It must be said that Gerdt's artistic adaptability was such that when the part demanded it he could assume the type of perfect manliness and virility. Such was his performance as Lord Wilson, as the Roman proconsul in *La Vestale*, etc. Five years after his benefit night in *La Fille Mal Gardée*, he created his best part—that of the Prince in *La Belle au Bois Dormant*—and two years later he became an ideal Blue-Beard.

puzzled to see her struggling hopelessly—for the performance remained stone dead.

That evening is impressed on my memory because I had waited for it with a kind of nervous terror; I had even secretly ordered my first dress-coat for the occasion—in honour of my goddess! Alas! I never got to know Virginia personally, though my brother Louis presented her with a first edition of one of Noverre's works from me. That evening was doubly memorable because of the fearful suspense I went through on account of the dress-coat. It was already time to go to the theatre where my mother had, at my insistence, taken an expensive box in the first tier —but the wretched tailor had not brought the coat. It only arrived at five minutes to eight and I hastily got into it and dashed off to the theatre, buttoning up my fur coat on the way, but alas! the first act was almost over. The fact that such a thing should have happened to me on the day of "her" benefit greatly upset me. But I became steadily more and more upset as the performance proceeded, for a fiasco was in the air—a fiasco, it is true, of the ballet, though not of Virginia. The theatre burst into applause every time Zucchi appeared, but one felt that the public was expressing its delight and admiration for Zucchi *in general* and not for her in this particular part.

The celebration of Zucchi as the holder of the benefit took place after the second act. The whole theatre shouted as it had never shouted before. The ballerina had to come out innumerable times in front of the curtain and keep on bowing, bowing, bowing. It was Zucchi who introduced the new manner of thanking the public. Before her appearance in St. Petersburg our ballerinas just made the classical curtsey—the curtsey they were taught at the Imperial School. This was very charming but too old-fashioned; it reminded one of a *pensionnat de jeunes filles*. When Zucchi acknowledged applause she expressed by her gestures, her eyes, and her whole figure how deeply moved she was by such appreciation, how she reciprocated the feelings, how she *loved* her audience. Every time Zucchi bowed, flowers were handed to her from the orchestra till at last the whole stage was covered with them and looked like a garden through which Virginia tripped gracefully. The climax of the celebration was when an open box was handed to Zucchi in which sparkled a necklace of enormous diamonds. It was a present from her chief admirer, who had decided to express his adoration in so public a manner. Comments spread throughout the theatre instantaneously— "Prince B. Vassiltchikov has presented his beloved with a necklace for which he paid thirty thousand roubles!" It even became known at once where he bought the necklace. Immediately there were rumours that the Tsar was extremely displeased at Vassiltchikov's extravagance and that he was henceforward to be placed under a guardian. Exaggeration is never to be recommended and this exhibition of feelings was tactless though quite comprehensible, and to a certain extent did the artiste more harm than good.

When Zucchi returned to the Imperial Stage after the summer vacation of 1886, she met with the same admiration, but it was *La Fille du Pharaon* and *La Fille Mal Gardée* that aroused the most fiery enthusiasm. Her success in *Esmeralda, Paquita,* Auber's opera *Fenella la Muette de Portici*—specially revived for her—had already a certain flavour of *un succès d'estime*.

In spite of this, some scenes have remained vividly in my memory. Zucchi was unforgettable in *Paquita* as the gypsy girl who turns out to be the daughter of a Spanish Grandee, and likewise as Esmeralda in her *pas de deux* with Gringoire. But the scene of Esmeralda proceeding to her execution did not impress me much, possibly because the very idea of showing a young girl weakened by torture was out of harmony with the usual atmosphere of the ballet. In general, *Esmeralda* is a long and rather absurd ballet with an ugly setting and extremely banal décors and costumes. The greatest success fell to Bekeffy, who created the part of a truly terrifying Quasimodo.

The enthusiasm aroused by Zucchi began to wear off rather obviously—even I, her ardent admirer, only saw her twice in *Esmeralda* and once in *Fenella*. This, or possibly some intrigue behind the scenes, may have been the reason for the management's not wishing to engage the divine Virginia for a third season. The news spread through the town and the public expressed their protest by giving Zucchi a hitherto unparalleled ovation. The ovation took place not when she was on the stage, but while she was watching one of the performances from a box. It was obviously a sort of conspiracy organised by Bezobrazov, both Skalkovskys and several other leading *balletomanes*. Zucchi's box seemed to be attracting general interest and when several claps gave the signal the whole theatre burst into frenzied applause. Those who had gone out into the foyer hastened back to the theatre. All eyes were turned towards the favourite ballerina's box, everybody clapped and innumerable voices shouted: "Do not go away! Do not leave us! Come back to us! We will not let you go!"[1] But plotting was not considered favourably in Russia and this demonstration not only failed to influence the management to renew the contract with Zucchi, but, on the

[1] I cannot resist the temptation of boasting that I know, from similar experience, how exciting it is when the whole theatre turns towards one to express their enthusiasm. It is quite a different feeling when one is applauded while on the stage. From behind the footlights the auditorium is a confused, turbid mass. I experienced the honour and happiness of a similar ovation when I remained in my box after the act showing the Novgorod Harbour in *Sadko*. This was at the première of *Sadko* in Paris in 1930.

contrary, caused it to persist in its decision. It is possible that the conspiracy made a bad impression in the higher spheres, because the Emperor, in spite of his approval of Zucchi, did not express any wish that the artiste should renew her contract. This was a heavy blow for Zucchi. During the two years she had spent in Russia, she had learned to love the Russian mode of life and nowhere did she feel herself at home as in St. Petersburg. Nowhere else in the world did she meet with such sympathy and understanding, and certainly nothing could compare with the artistic environment she found on the St. Petersburg stage, where many a *coryphée* was equal to a first-class ballerina in Western Europe, and the atmosphere entirely free from the usual petty theatrical intrigue. How delightful it was to dance with so confident and graceful a partner as Gerdt! How quick was everyone to grasp the finest point, the remotest allusion! How delightful were the youthful pupils of the Theatrical School—a school with the traditions and character of an aristocratic *pension*. The mere fact that there were as many men on the Russian stage as women gave work in the ballet the strength and vitality that springs from a harmony of contrasts—very different from the usual atmosphere of a "kingdom of women." Lastly, Zucchi found in the person of Marius Petipa a ballet-master unequalled in Western Europe. A persistent and at times a capricious tyrant, he was, nevertheless, a master unusually sensitive to every artistic manifestation. It was a joy to give oneself into the hands of this "painter and sculptor," to guess his unuttered intentions, to follow one's own instinct while carrying out his lightest hints. And having succeeded, what a joy it was to feel that the "ruler of the stage" was satisfied and pleased.

The St. Petersburg ballet in those days was dominated by a very remarkable spirit of friendly collaboration. It probably reigns there even now, in spite of everything, but at that period the artists were entirely united by an unlimited confidence in their leader. This created an atmosphere of wonderful harmony. One must add that Petipa had found his ideal in Zucchi, though he did grumble at her lack of elevation and at her temperament, which was apt to carry her away from the subject. Petipa believed that the dance could and should be full of meaning, but by this he did not imply anything "literary." Being a first-class mime himself, Petipa hated soulless dancing, however perfect the technique. In Zucchi he had a wonderful dancer and an actress of exceptional power and ability, both in tragedy and comedy. Zucchi was the ideal artist for any thoughtful and sensitive producer, but she would not have suited those who are apt to treat their subordinates as soldiers or marionettes.

In the following year Zucchi came to St. Petersburg at her own risk—she was confident that the former enthusiasm of the St. Petersburg public was still alive and would support her. But she was bitterly disappointed. It would not be just to accuse the Russian public of inconstancy. Zucchi appeared in very shabby surroundings, supported by a third-class company, in the very small, and ugly theatre Nemetti. She continued to thrill her audience in scenes from *Brahma* and *Paquita*, but the performance, as a whole, was second-rate and dull. The public applauded violently nevertheless, and when she left the theatre the pavement leading to Zucchi's carriage was strewn with coats, laid there by young enthusiasts in spite of the winter cold. My coat, too, once had the honour of being trodden upon by the feet of the divine Virginia, but I must confess quite frankly that, though I took part in this symbolic demonstration, my heart was cold. On the same evening I promised myself to keep sacred in my memory all the joys I owed to Zucchi, but never to go to another of her performances. I wished to preserve, untarnished, the ideal she had become for me in 1885. Alas, how many artists since then, no less distinguished than Zucchi, have provoked me to the same vows!

Chapter VIII

THE ACADEMY OF ARTS

THE period of my life between 1887–1890 must be considered "empty" from the point of view of ballet impressions. For two years I scarcely visited the theatre and one whole season passed without my having been inside one. At that time I was passing through a period of retirement and inner seclusion. I so completely lost the habit of going to any performance that when I did at last hear an opera again, I was overwhelmed by the imposing beauty of orchestral sound; it was almost as if I had never heard one before. A change was going on within me, for from a rather flighty and foppish young man I was turning into an unusually serious one. This seriousness, however, did not improve my studies or help to make me more diligent. On the contrary, I continued to be just as careless with my lessons in spite of the fact that I had left the Public High School, which I hated, and had entered the private school of Karl May where I was very happy.

I think that my laziness at lessons was partly excused and overlooked because I possessed an unusually good memory; also because the staff were favourably inclined towards me, being impressed, perhaps, by my "artistic" nature. The old headmaster May was adored by all the pupils, and when I presented him with an album of my water-colours as a birthday present I was regarded from that day as a sort of prodigy. In fact, the water-colours were nothing but the rather indifferent work of a beginner.

My lesson books and rough note-books were covered with drawings, the greater part of which were devoted to ballet impressions, and these, again, were not forbidden by my teachers but often aroused their sincere delight. I was far more serious about my education outside school. This was pursued without any programme and was extremely unpedantic. I was becoming more and more engrossed in my studies of literature and the history of art, and was trying at the same time to perfect myself in painting. Obviously, with my passion for the theatre still burning fiercely—though I abstained from indulging it—my dream was to become a painter for the stage. I have already told about my "home-made" theatrical enterprise which ended with the "grand" performance of *La Fille du Pharaon*. I now gave up such childish diversions altogether and imagined myself a future creator of something wonderful for the real stage, something that would rival the creations of past centuries.

My father had seen in his youth theatrical décors by the famous Pietro Gonzago and had often told me about them. He, too, had been a passionate theatre-goer in his young days, and at that time—1820–1830—the majority of performances on the Imperial Stage were given in the beautiful architectural settings created by the great Italian and his son. My father used to tell me that some of Gonzago's décors aroused such enthusiasm that the ovations in their honour actually held up the performance. Other masters of scenic painting and art in Russia were Corsini, Canoppi and Quaglio, who were hardly inferior to Gonzago. The famous writer, D. V. Grigorovitch, who was a great friend of my father's and whose fervent admirer I was, on being shown my childish efforts at creating some doll's performance, exclaimed : "This is a future Bibiena!" These friendly condescending words remained imprinted in my heart and

NICOLAS BENOIS.   FATHER OF THE AUTHOR
From an etching by V. V. Matthé

Facing page 100

DÉCOR FOR THE FIRST AND THIRD SCENES OF *LE PAVILLON D'ARMIDE,*
By Alexandre Benois, 1907

Facing page 101

certainly served later on as a stimulus in my choice of a profession. I should add that my father had in his collection three magnificent large theatrical sketches by the last Bibiena, which I greatly admired. They made me prize the art of the great Bolognese master very highly and gave weight to Grigorovitch's words.

Another occurrence in our family life encouraged me, to a certain extent, to prepare for the career of a painter for the stage. The flat on the top floor of our house was to let and the French artist Levogt, who had recently arrived in St. Petersburg at the invitation of the management of the Imperial Theatres, was greatly attracted by it. In those days I believed blindly that everything that came from Paris was faultless and therefore considered it would be a stroke of extraordinary luck that a Parisian stage painter should live in the same house. I used all my endeavours to persuade my parents to agree to the considerable reduction that he—a real Frenchman— insisted on. It is true that there was much that I did not care for in Levogt, but I forgave the stout, grey-haired, red-faced old man, who was almost always drunk, his typically French *blagues* and his vulgar familiarity, because I chose to see in him the successor of Gonzago and Bibiena, or rather of Cambon and Cicéri, who were nearer to him. My respect for Levogt became still greater when the five rooms of his flat were heaped with masses of books on art.

My confidence in his powers was soon to be cruelly shattered. It happened in the autumn of 1887 when I saw Levogt's first work for the Maryinsky Theatre— the *maquettes* he made for the ballet *La Tulipe de Haarlem*. The landscapes and interiors were worked out in minutest detail, the wings were drawn in pencil and cut out with a penknife and really looked like lace. But the general impression of these miniature theatres was a dull lack of talent. If my acquaintance with Levogt served any useful purpose, it was to provide me with an example of what should never be imitated.

During the summer of 1887, while I was still intending to embark on a theatrical career, I began composing my own ballet, for which I was not only to be the librettist, but also composer of the music and the artist who was to create the whole production. This new enterprise was not less childish than my grandiose *Fille du Pharaon* had been. In spite of my good intentions, my "work" was that of a pure dilettante, for I had no idea of the theory of music and could not even write down what I played on the piano. I do not in the least regret that not a line has remained of all that nonsense. But it gave me the joy of creation, and in my dreams I could see my four-act ballet *Die Kette der Nixe* produced on the stage. The fact that one person was responsible for the entire performance was supposed to give it a special *cachet*.

Sometimes when I played my different scenes and dances on the piano, my future father-in-law, the venerable Karl Ivanovitch Kind, would praise some passage, smiling benevolently. This approval, coming from the lips of so great a connoisseur of music, was extremely encouraging. At the same time Papa Kind would tactfully try to make me understand that I should take up music seriously, and this pleased me much less, for in my heart of hearts I felt sure that my invention was perfect. Moreover, I was enthusiastically confirmed in this opinion by my Atia and her two brothers. I had chosen as subject for my ballet a fairy-tale from one of my favourite German collections called *Elfenreigen* and was enchanted with the idea that my subject rather resembled the opera by E. T. A. Hoffmann—for whom I had just conceived almost fanatical adoration.

Moved by the same idea of becoming a painter for the theatre and thus "creating a new era in theatrical productions," I decided to start without delay along the road that was to lead me straight to the heights of Parnassus. This meant that I resolved to combine my school work with that of the Academy of Arts where I could take evening classes. I was coached in drawing from plaster casts by our dear Arthur Aubert, and presented myself at the Academy for the entrance examination, which consisted of making a drawing—within a given time of two hours—of an antique head cast in plaster. And so it came to pass that I now entered the same institution that had bestowed honours on my father and brothers!

I adored the beautiful building of the Academy— that masterpiece of the so-called Louis XV *classique,* which remains to this day one of the finest adornments of the Neva. I loved the porch, the cupola, the imposing windows, the landing-stage on the river with its two granite Sphinxes, brought from Thebes during the reign of Nicolas I.

Every time I entered the enormous building, I was struck by a feeling of almost religious awe at the sight of the vast, incomparable staircase, its sloping, rounded steps and many-columned peristyles. Even at the age of four I would be overcome with delight when I caught a glimpse in the Raphael Hall of the life-sized copies of the frescoes from the Vatican Stanze, while a gigantic cast of one of the Dioscuri which stood at the end of the Titian Hall appealed to the feeling of holy terror and adoration that everything colossal awakened in me. I must mention too the narrow, vaulted corridors, extraordinarily high and light, into which opened the doors of the class-rooms and the professors' apartments. The walls of the corridors were hung with bas-reliefs. All this I found highly interesting and attractive when I marched along them holding Papa's hand—for I loved accompanying him on his visits to the "competitors'" studies. And I cannot refrain from mentioning the round Conference Hall with its beautiful multi-coloured windows and Shebuev's fresco of Apollo in his chariot that occupied the entire ceiling. I would have a feeling of intoxication when I entered this hall, for it was here that all my nearest relations were fêted and received their honours. This was the hall where the yearly ceremony took place, attended by numerous patrons of art, professors and pupils; in their midst, under the marble statue of Catherine II, sat the august President of the Academy himself.

It was in circumstances no less solemn, in the very same hall, that my father's jubilee had been triumphantly celebrated a year before (1886). Trumpets sounded in his honour and there was a great gathering of dignitaries of high rank, whose chests were covered with orders of merit, medals, stars and ribbons.

The Academy of Arts belonged to the Imperial Court and its uniforms were remarkable for their magnificence. When my father attended the Academy celebrations he wore a uniform embroidered in gold, white trousers with a golden stripe, a sword and a three-cornered plumed hat. His chest was covered with masses of decorations and cut across by the red ribbon of St. Anne. All this greatly impressed my youthful imagination and helped to awaken dreams of ambition; it also helped me to regard the Academy as a real Alma Mater, into whose embrace I readily threw myself.

Unfortunately, in spite of my enthusiasm and readiness to fly into her arms with real filial love, the Alma Mater herself showed neither pleasure nor interest in me. I just managed to pass the entrance examination and what followed was unbearably dull and uninteresting. I now walked along my favourite corridors every evening, but they did not lead me into the studies of the painters, the Museum or the beautiful Conference Hall, but into the class-rooms which were crowded with twice as many people as they could contain. The big gas lamp that hung in the middle of the class-room, lighting up some head of Jupiter or Cicero, and the over-heated stoves made the room stiflingly hot. My fellow-students, most of whom were not too clean, did not help to purify the atmosphere. How I disliked my new comrades! Especially those who, like myself, were preparing to become painters! I made friends only with two future architects, one of whom is at present in charge of all the principal architectural works in U.S.S.R. I disliked the coarse manners of most of my companions and the conversations, which had nothing in common with art but concerned questions of everyday life and especially of daily bread, which I, being one of the lucky ones, never had to bother about!

The professors who went round from pupil to pupil were no more inspiring. There were four of them, three old and one young, but they were all equally helpless at teaching. They crossed silently from one pupil to another, mumbling something under their noses, and then made two or three lines across the drawing without explaining their corrections. And that was the sum total of their efforts. One of them was distinguished by a kind of nervous *tic*. He used to approach the pupil, a smelly cigar in his mouth, and if the drawing were a profile, invariably uttered the sentence: "Must add some back to the head." Whereupon he would proceed to spoil the sketch by drawing energetically—in greasy Italian pencil—a fresh line about an inch away from the old one.

At first I tried to bear up, assuring myself that such were the thorns on every road leading to art and that those who survived these ordeals could later consider themselves "worthy priests of Apollo." I would try and go through with it for the first three months, after which I would surely be transferred to the figure classes, where work would be much more interesting, and very soon I would find myself in the class where they drew from nature. I never doubted that it would take me at the most a year to pass through the first stages, at the end of which I would be given paint brushes and palette, taught the technique of painting and perspective, and so approach the special branch I had chosen.

In the decorative class I would be taught to use the special glue-paints for painting the enormous pictures which create the "place of action" in the theatre, and in this I would doubtless be able to show myself at my best. Samples of decorative art were hung on the walls of the cast-iron staircases leading to the classes on the top floor of the Academy. They were the work of our famous decorators Botcharov and Shishkov during their Academy years. They represented ruins and I never ceased to admire the infinite illusion that their details created—the layers of bricks, the leaves of the bushes and trees and even the grass in the foreground.

I was soon to experience a severe blow. Every month all the pupils of the Academy were given a problem for composition. In a special hall, whose walls were covered with the sketches of former pupils, amongst which were the works of Semiradsky, Surikov, Repin and Vrubel, a small note giving the subject and signed by one of the professors would be exposed on the board. Near it lay several books of reference, among them the inevitable volumes of Racinet and Hottenroth. The pupil was expected to read the subject and, as it was usually historical, could immediately study the costumes and properties suited to the given epoch. The one and only time I risked taking part in such a competition was several weeks after my entrance into the Academy.

The subject was a scene from Pushkin's drama

Mozart and Salieri and was to represent the moment when the untalented and perfidious Salieri pours poison into the wine of the great composer. I cannot say that I was much attracted by the subject, as it did not give me the opportunity of showing what I considered to be my strong points—decorative display in appropriate surroundings. Pushkin's scene is laid in the private room of a modest Viennese inn. I was very keen, nevertheless, to distinguish myself and set to work eagerly. I completed and handed in my work in time, not doubting for a moment that it would be appreciated according to its merits. What was my surprise and distress when, on entering the halls hung with drawings, I found that instead of being in the first category, as I had expected, my drawing was placed among the *very last!* It is true it did not bear the mark of final disgrace, an inscription which meant that the drawing was so weak that the author should go back to copying engravings (this shows what the system of our artistic education was like before it was reformed); still, my "Mozart" was disgraced by having been placed in the fourth category. This distressed me to such an extent that I never brought my drawing home, but left it in the Academy, where some caretaker probably used this masterpiece for lighting a stove.

It was during this episode that I began to suspect that the "crying injustice" I had suffered was due not to sheer chance or lack of interest, but to evil purpose. The administration of the Academy was in the hands of a certain Iseyev, a great favourite of the Grand Duke Vladimir, who was President of the Academy. This Iseyev, who was a typical *parvenu*, was on very bad terms with my father. They were both on the same committees and my father invariably brought to light the abuses which, later on, brought Iseyev to the Courts of Justice, where he eventually got a severe sentence. . . . In the days of his favour, however, Iseyev, a man of domineering disposition, was greatly feared by the entire staff of professors, amongst whom were many good friends of my father, including the Rector of the Academy, A. I. Resanov. I was well aware of all this and therefore, when I found myself disgraced at the composition examination, began to suspect that this was a "cabal" against me, or rather a caddish trick deliberately arranged to annoy my father. After this episode I did not feel any happier within the walls of Alma Mater and never ventured again to take part in the "free competitions." At the same time I began to realise how difficult it was to combine my school studies with those of the Academy.

One can well imagine how hopelessly dull and dreary work in the Academy seemed under these conditions, how sick I was of the professors' senseless roaming from table to table, how aimless it all seemed to me. I managed to drag on till January, when I left the Academy without ever having passed into the next class. I must confess that my feelings were very different from those with which I had entered.

The episode at the Academy had a definite influence on my whole life. To begin with, I began to hate the education that was given there in those days and to loathe the bureaucratic world of red tape that seemed to have attached itself to art. Further, any sort of "state service" seemed absolutely unbearable to me. This, undoubtedly, was the reason why I did not follow in the footsteps of all the other members of my family, but remained independent, valuing my freedom more and more. Admittedly, prompted by material considerations, I tried several times to enter service—that is, to become a salary earner; but I never got used to it, and my service was generally of an unusual kind. The post I occupied for the longest period was that of curator of the Hermitage.

The chief reason for my remaining in this post for eight years was the attitude towards me of the Director, S. N. Troinitsky, who carefully protected me from any trouble with the higher authorities and, together with the other members of the staff, did everything in his power to make me feel at home in the Hermitage. To feel oneself at home in so incomparable a place as the Hermitage was an experience that I treasure to this day.

My decision to leave the Academy dampened considerably my ambition to become a painter for the stage. Nor was I encouraged by the thought that I would have to serve in the theatrical management and so become a civil servant and join the hated tribe of bureaucrats. My visits to Levogt's studios produced the same effect. Two of Levogt's pupils—one of whom, O. C. Allegri, was later an excellent master of décors—did their best to discourage me from joining their profession, but this I disregarded, thinking it inspired by fear of my "competition." But chiefly I was disgusted by the atmosphere of Levogt's studio—a particular blend of mercenary craftsmanship. There was even less of art in Levogt's studio than there had been in the Academy classes and I only continued to go there because this studio was situated in a new wing of the Maryinsky Theatre, from where I could watch what was going on on the stage.

It is true that from my look-out, which was several yards above the stage, the figures that I saw seemed minute; but that only made some of the scenes and dances the more fantastic. There was something peculiarly enchanting in the muffled sounds of the music. I always tried to visit Levogt in the evenings and afternoons of ballet performances, but, unfortunately, before slipping up to the fire-bars—the little bridges over the stage—I had to stop and listen to the idiotic conversation of the owner of the studio.

The final blow would come when he chose to accompany me—then all my evening was spoilt, all the poetry gone. . . . But it was due to Levogt's studio that I saw the rehearsal of Drigo's new ballet *The Talisman*, which, later, when I began going to the theatre again, I watched from the stalls.

Chapter IX

THE FILOSOFOV FAMILY

MY period of abstinence from theatres and performances lasted for almost a whole year and was an unique experience in the lives of my *fiancée* and myself. Our self-imposed privation was, I think, due partly to our satiety with theatrical pleasure. As regards ballet, no performances now given could bear comparison with those in which Zucchi had once taken part, and we simply detested the Italian dance-virtuosi with whom the theatrical management endeavoured to recompense the St. Petersburg public, after having deprived it of the *diva* who had conquered every heart. We were undoubtedly prejudiced and unfair when we refused to see anything good in the pretty Algisi, the rather coarse but athletically strong Cornalba, or the excellent dancer Bessone.

During that season several ballets were revived, among them *La Vestale*, the cruel music for which had been composed by the ungifted but influential critic of the *Novoye Vremya*, M. Ivanov. Others were *La Tulipe de Haarlem, Catarina Fille du Bandit*, in which Salvator Rosa's studio was shown, and *Fiammetta* with M. M. Petipa looking charming in *travesti*. But none of these ballets had any attraction for us. There was, I must admit, another more profound reason for our abstaining from theatres. Partly from jealousy and partly owing to a religious crisis that we were both experiencing, my *fiancée* and I began to forbid each other to visit places where people met and enjoyed themselves, be it a theatre, a dance, or a family party. We were influenced too by the differences arising* between my brother Albert and his wife, who was my Atia's sister. These differences finally resulted in a break for both our couples, but it was only the elder couple's separation that was permanent, for Atia and I soon came together again. Our reunion was not achieved without a long and difficult struggle, for we had to contend with opposition from our relatives on both sides. My parents were particularly indignant that I, the younger brother, should wish again to become related to the family with whom my elder brother had just broken. We managed nevertheless to overcome the obstacles put in our way, and the romance that had begun in the days of our early youth was renewed and continued the whole of our lives. During the short period of our separation we grew to understand each other far better and to feel the necessity of being together. The foolishness of depriving each other of every enjoyment—with which we had so tormented ourselves—was done away with for ever. During our estrangement we had begun, individually, to visit the theatre again; when we were reunited we continued the practice together.

Among the greatest theatrical events of that period was the appearance in 1890 of the Duke of Meiningen's company, in which I was deeply interested, but I will refrain from describing it, as it would mean digressing too far from my subject. I cannot, however, remain silent about Neumann's enterprise of bringing *The Ring of the Nibelungs* to St. Petersburg in March of 1889, because these performances played a decisive part in developing and educating my taste in music. I was already acquainted with Wagner's text and, as soon as *The Ring* was announced, I became deeply interested in the dramatic side of the production. I had tremendous expectations at the thought of the event, i.e. the "exact reproduction of the performance at Bayreuth." But from the moment that the music started, my interest in the stage was relegated to second place. It seemed to me, under the spell of those magic sounds, that I had become regenerated and had gained an entirely new perspective and understanding of life.

I must confess that it was difficult to take Loge and Siegfried seriously as impersonated by Vogel. What could he have meant by wearing on his head a ridiculous red topee borrowed from some circus clown? Was it credible that this same venerable gentleman, whose voice had lost all trace of youthful freshness, was the demi-god, for love of whom the Valkyrie Brünnhilde throws herself on to the funeral pyre in the final scene of *Götterdämmerung*? It was just as difficult to be convinced by the plump little German girls who were supposed to represent enchanting mermaids, austere goddesses and fairy princesses. Nor did their fat-bellied companions, whose voices resounded like beer-barrels, look anything like the mythological giants they were meant to represent. Sublimely ludicrous and ridiculous was the dragon Fafner—a worthy brother of the famous Lion in our own *La Fille du Pharaon*! I was even more grieved by the décors, which, though said to have been approved by Wagner himself, were, alas, indescribably far from the ideal I had formed after reading the great composer's detailed scenarios. These sets differed from those current in our Russian productions only by being far harder in execution, more tasteless in colouring and by having an even greater wealth of unnecessary detail. Even then, there was no attempt to indicate what is suggested by the music —no rippling of the waters of the Rhine, no mystery of dark forests, no threatening grandeur of rocks and caves, no primitive solemnity in the castle of the Gibichungen . . . Where Wagner had meant to blend a genuine feeling of nature with the poetical vision that inspired his genius there reigned nothing but banal routine and trite convention.

The very first chords of *Rheingold* made me feel that here was a new elemental force, and this feeling persisted during all the four days the tetralogy lasted. For a considerable time afterwards I remained under the spell of the music; I was in a state of exaltation, not unlike what one experiences on mountain heights or on the shore of the ocean . . .

In 1889 my summer holidays started unusually early. Owing to my poor school-work throughout the winter, I had not been admitted to the examinations at the end of the term. Thus, after a break of many years, I was able once again to enjoy the spring whole-heartedly, free from the nauseating fear of examinations and the imminent necessity of "cramming."

I moved to the country, to stay with my brother Albert, at the very beginning of May, when the snow still lay in patches in the deep ravines and in the shade of the woods, when the birch trees, just beginning to show their delicate green, contrasted with the still lifeless branches of the mighty oaks. The air was full of the scent of life being renewed, the grass was awakening from its long winter sleep, the ditches, puddles, bogs were swarming with myriads of tiny beings performing the great work of reproduction. All these impressions of life in nature—a world that hitherto had escaped my attention—became intermingled with my "Wagner experiences," with the magic sounds of the tetralogy I had heard in March, and aroused in me a joy that sometimes called forth my tears. I roamed for days on end through the wild surroundings of Peterhof and Oranienbaum, making new discoveries everywhere; yet I never thought of taking a pencil or a paint-brush, of progressing from passive contemplation to an artistic representation of what I had seen. The fact that I was "not an artist" in those days had, nevertheless, its good side and proved very useful. I studied nature disinterestedly; I seemed to discover all sorts of feeling in nature, to understand her language. I was but nineteen years old, and there was still much childish nonsense in me, mingled with the first sensations of ripening manhood.

The fact that both I and my school-fellow and great friend, Valetchka Nouvel, had been left in the same seventh form, brought us together with another friend who had been set back owing to illness a couple of years previously. This was Dima Filosofov, who had caught up with us again. Thenceforward we formed an inseparable trio, of which I, as the eldest and also perhaps the most fully developed in artistic sensibility, occupied, to a certain extent, the position of leader and initiator. Nouvel was a passionate musician, a magnificent reader of music, deeply interested in its theory and history. Our friendship was really based on musical "reminiscences." Dima was a great lover of literature. He was the son of Anna Pavlovna Filosofov, the well-known social worker, whose house was a centre for all progressive intellectual workers and thinkers. From his cradle, so to speak, Dima had assimilated all sorts of ideas, though there were many with which he did not agree. His love of literature and the theatre was the link between us, but while it was the music that was the chief attraction in the theatre for Valetchka and me, Dima's interest lay almost entirely in the literary side.

Very soon I infected my friends with my own infatuation for painting and the plastic arts. I had formed, by that time, a very considerable library of books on art and subscribed to several foreign art

E

reviews. My father's excellent though somewhat austere library was also at our disposal. Consequently, during our friendly talks, much of the time was spent in looking at and discussing pictures. I must here confess that I was extremely despotic and inclined to consider my own opinion as absolutely infallible. It is a well-known fact that those who firmly believe that their taste is faultless and impeccable are the people most capable of convincing others and making them agree with their point of view.

Our small circle began gradually to grow and to resemble, in some respects, a sort of artistic club. We were joined by our old school-fellow from May's, Constantin Somov, and two others, Nicolas Skalon and Gregor Kalin. We usually assembled about three times a week, almost always in my "red study," the walls of which were hung with pictures belonging to my father and engravings bought by me. The furniture in this room was rather modest, on the whole, but a prominent place was occupied by a large sofa with a folding back, the other side of which served as a bed. My father had ordered this sofa for me from Birkenfeld, the cabinet-maker, at the time when German Renaissance was very fashionable, and I had been especially anxious that my sofa should be like the attractive furniture, adorned with shelves, that were depicted in the German editions of Hirth's *Das deutsche Zimmer* and *Der Formenschatz*. The shelf was built over the back of the sofa and I hastened to place on it some of the old bronzes which had hitherto stood in small cupboards in the hall or on my father's mantelpiece. This shelf was heartily hated by Dima Filosofov, who, though younger than we, was quite half a head taller, so that when he followed his usual habit of throwing himself down on the sofa, it invariably resulted in his knocking the back of his head against the edge of the shelf, after which, almost crying from pain, he would curse it unrestrainedly.

Often, so as not to interrupt our discussions, we preferred not to go to the dining-room for our evening tea. Our old maid Stepanida would bring tea, biscuits and fruit into my study. Every time this happened, Dima, who always liked making fun of everything, would begin to remonstrate, for my room was certainly the most unsuitable place for comfortable enjoyment of food and drink. All the tables, chairs and armchairs and even the wide window-sill were heaped with books and reviews—there was literally no place where one could put down a cup of tea or a fruit plate; we were obliged to balance these objects in our hands or on our knees, with the result that the contents were spilled over our clothes or on to the floor. My other friends were reconciled to this, but Dima prided himself on a greater knowledge of the manners and ways of society and pretended to be deeply shocked by the defects of this arrangement and by many other shortcomings in our old-fashioned, patriarchal household.

One must not imagine that gloomy conventions were enforced in the Filosofov household. On the contrary, it was the nicest, cosiest and most home-like place I have ever seen. In those years Dima's father, a very important official, renowned for great severity during the time he had occupied the post of Military Prosecutor, had withdrawn from active service. He had retired and been appointed member of the Council of State. Consequently the Filosofovs no longer lived in their former colossal government apartments, but had taken a very nice, though far from luxurious, flat which occupied the ground floor of an old house on the Galernaya Street. The father's large study, Anna Pavlovna's drawing-room and bedroom all faced the street, while the long, narrow dining-room and Dima's still narrower and half-dark bedroom looked out on the yard. The interior of their house was, on the whole, more modest, perhaps, than ours, but there hung on the walls good Dutch and Italian pictures, amongst which I appreciated particularly the charming little "Feast" by Dirk Hals. They were the remains of the "gallery" collected by Dima's grandfather, a rich landowner who had spent a substantial part of his fortune on all kinds of whims. The magnificent oval portrait of this grandfather holding a long-stemmed pipe in his hand, and the companion portrait of his wife, were the works of Kiprensky and Venetzianov—two of the most eminent Russian painters of the early nineteenth century.

I was still more attracted by a portrait of Vladimir Dmitrievitch himself when he was but two or three years old. He was painted in a red Russian shirt, sitting in his high baby-chair on the terrace, against the colonnade of the balcony of an old country-house. This quiet-looking child was surrounded by his toys, amongst which was a carriage made of multi-coloured cards. It was difficult to believe that the charming baby and the tall, bent, baggy-eyed old man were the same person. The portrait had a special interest for me because it was the work of a serf artist, as were also several other pictures representing the rooms in Bogdanovskoye—the Filosofovs' family estate. The painting was rather pedantic in a primitive way, but showed considerable mastery and talent. The fact that my friends the Filosofovs had so recently had a serf as their private painter not only struck me as anomalous, but seemed somehow to throw light on the whole mode of life of my friend's family. Although I had many acquaintances amongst the nobility, was very fond of good society and was accustomed to houses that displayed the wealth of their owners—in short, to the class which in their time had owned serfs, and to whom more than half of Russian classical literature is devoted—it was the first time that I had come into close touch with the atmosphere and spirit of the class for which Tolstoy has coined the name of "middle high." Now, thanks to the school friendship between Dima and myself, which resulted in my being so intimately received in the Filosofov family, I was discovering for myself an entirely new social outlook. When compared with my own home, their house seemed to be "the same and yet not the same"— "not the same" because, first of all, the Filosofov family was entirely Russian, and second, because it was a family typical of the nobility and landowners. The difference was keenly felt in the attitude towards art. In our family and in those of the majority of our relations, art was a kind of family professional prerogative. To the Filosofovs it was something apart, something that Dima's grandfather had *patronised*, that he had encouraged—yet, at the same time, it was something that could be created by his serfs. This was an important *nuance*, of which I was to become fully and intelligently aware only a great deal later. At the time of my first acquaintance with the new world, I merely felt the distinction subconsciously.

I am dwelling on my memories of Dima Filosofov and his family circle because one of the chief characters in these memoirs was nearly related to them and it was in the Filosofov family that I first met him. I speak of Diaghilev. Diaghilev was Dima's first cousin, being the son of Anna Pavlovna's brother. He had spent all his earliest years in the provinces and first came to St. Petersburg in 1890. He made friends with Dima, with whom he had only been in correspondence up to then, and thus entered the Filosofov circle owing not only to the fact that he was a relative, but also to his personal inclination. The fact that, for the first few months, Seriozha Diaghilev stayed in their house, sharing Dima's room, made the process still easier. Diaghilev's adoption by the Filosofov "clan" was a factor of great signifi-

cance and importance in his life.   He was very much
of a provincial when he first arrived in St. Petersburg
and Valetchka, Kostia Somov and I were even shocked
by his rather uncouth manners and primitive views,
though this was only natural to one who had lived
all his life in the depths of the Perm countryside.

Seriozha's new life in the metropolis, the pleasant
atmosphere of home and family life that prevailed
in his aunt's house, his friendship with so refined a
youth as Dima and the members of his circle, began
very soon to tell on him, and it was not long before
he was acquiring all that he had hitherto lacked.
What he gained was not only the outward polish
which he could have acquired by frequenting "polite
society," but a certain degree of breeding, a proof
of being *de bonne maison.* This manner of *bonne
maison* proved extremely useful to him in later years.

It is true that he did not always manage to preserve
the manners he then acquired.   They had not been
imbued in him from childhood and were in contradiction to much in his nature and character.   When
lapses occurred, we, who knew him so well, would
recognise the "primitive, provincial Seriozha of
Perm" and his *mauvais genre.*   These outbursts did
harm to Seriozha in St. Petersburg society, which
never really accepted him as one of themselves.
Abroad they were looked upon as "remnants of the
Tartar in the Russian Boyar" and were supposed to
give M. Serge de Diaghilev an attractive local colour.
Sergei himself did not mind this at all, and fully aware
of human folly and an expert in exploiting it, often
exaggerated and flaunted his "barbarism."

Chapter X

LA BELLE AU BOIS DORMANT

I HAVE jumped ahead by a few months and must now retrace my steps. Diaghilev appeared on our horizon in the summer of 1890, but this event was preceded by a still greater one which had occurred during the late winter. This was the production of *La Belle au Bois Dormant,* presented to the St. Petersburg public in the first days of January, 1890. I must add that, at the time, the appearance of *La Belle au Bois Dormant* was an outstanding event for us, while the arrival of Seriozha was just an episode of minor importance—it had more significance for Dima's family than for our small circle.

At that time I had been completely neglecting the ballet. I had become interested in the opera, the French Theatre, the Russian Drama, and especially in concerts, as a result of my new passion for Wagner. The ballet, except for a short infatuation with *Le Talisman,* had almost ceased to interest me. The action of *Le Talisman* took place in India and the whole ballet greatly resembled *La Bayadère,* with the difference that it was not a human girl who penetrates into Brahma's paradise but a goddess who finds herself among human beings. On the whole, it was not the ballet itself that I admired, for it was produced without enthusiasm, with indifferent décors and rather absurd costumes, and the chief part was danced by the unattractive Cornalba. It was Drigo's simple and charming music that had attracted both Valetchka and me. In fact, we had been so delighted with it during the *première* that our noisy approval had attracted the attention and seemed to shock the then rather popular governor of St. Petersburg, General Grösser. From the first row of the stalls, where he had his permanent seat, he turned round, affecting a severe expression, and shook his finger at us. My enthusiasm was so great, however, that I could not stop applauding and even felt compelled to exclaim: *Mais puisque, Excellence, c'est un chef d'œuvre*—upon which his Excellency deigned to bestow on me a fatherly smile.

Still, we only went about three times to see *Le Talisman*, and even then it was not entirely on account of the music, but rather because we greatly admired the charming young dancer Vinogradova—who, alas, very soon after that production was carried away by consumption.

A proof of my neglect of the ballet can be seen in the fact that I actually took no steps to obtain tickets for the *première* of *La Belle au Bois Dormant*. My brother Louis, who attended the dress rehearsal, had told me that the new ballet was heavy and unwieldy, that Tchaikovsky's music was muddled, and that many of the artists said it was impossible to dance to it. There were rumours that the Emperor and Grand Dukes, who had been present at the rehearsal and had actually sat in the first rows of the stalls instead of in the Imperial Box, were unfavourably impressed with the ballet. All this, it was said, had somewhat shaken the position of the Director of the Imperial Theatres, I. A. Vsevolojsky, whom it had become the fashion to criticise in society, although it was obvious to everyone that his management was distinguished by a period of great progress for the Imperial Theatres.

I must here confess that, although since 1889 I had become a firm Wagnerian, I still continued to ignore Russian music. It is true that when, occasionally, I heard some work of Tchaikovsky or Rimsky-Korsakov during a concert, I used to feel a certain premonition of delight—to which, however, I attached no importance, since the prejudice that Russian composers could not be compared to foreigners was firmly rooted in me.

This prejudice prevailed in my family and in our circle of friends, and was disputed only by two people: my mother's friend, E. I. Raevskaya—who even had a season ticket to the Russian Opera—and V. S. Rossolovsky, a great friend of the family. "Aunt Lisa's" opinion carried little weight with us, because this dear, kind lady, a typical old maid, worshipped anything and everything Russian from a rather narrow national prejudice, and was, on the whole, a slightly comic figure. As for "Uncle Zozo" Rossolovsky, his authority was lessened by the fact of his being collaborator in the *Novoye Vremya*, and he was accused of the same tendencies *ex officio*. As to the other members of our family: Uncle Misha Cavos preferred to deride everything both Russian and foreign and only made some exceptions for Wagner, whereas my father, who appreciated the Russian composers of his young days like Glinka and Verstovsky, was quite indifferent to anything that had been created during the last forty years. My Italian grandmother Cavos was also an enemy of Russian art, as was Uncle Kostia, the Voltairian, my brothers, and most of our relations and friends. They were unsparing in their criticism of Russian painting and Russian music and enjoyed reading Zoilus Burenin's articles, in which Stassov, that champion of nationalism in art, was cruelly mocked for his "exaggerated patriotism."

I went to the second performance of *La Belle au Bois Dormant* and left the theatre in a rather hazy state, only feeling that I had just heard and seen something that I was *going* to love. When I try to

E*

analyse the feeling that came over me then, it seems to me that I simply could not believe in my own joy; that, subconsciously, I was already completely in the power of something entirely new, but for which, nevertheless, my soul had been waiting, for a long, long while. As soon as possible I saw *La Belle au Bois Dormant* a second time, and then a third and a fourth. The more I listened to the music, the more I seemed to discover in it greater and greater beauty— a beauty that was not universally understood but that was absolutely in harmony with me, that aroused the sweetest languor and an almost celestial joy.

One of the great attractions of *La Belle au Bois Dormant* was the historical reminiscences that it evoked. No music had ever so successfully resuscitated the distant past as was done in the hunting scene and in the last divertissement of *La Belle au Bois Dormant*. Gradually my visits to the ballet became almost a sort of obsession. Not only did I know the entire score by heart, but I *had* to hear it played by the orchestra, again and again. The rapture it aroused in me was different from the thrill provoked by Wagner; still, there was no clash between them and my new infatuation was as great, or even greater than the first had been. It seemed to have penetrated my whole being.

Let me repeat again, Tchaikovsky's music was what I seemed to have been waiting for since my earliest childhood. It generally happens that each generation is influenced and most deeply stirred by the art and music created *within its time*. Their understanding and perception is aided by certain cultural conditions that both the creator and those who enjoy his creations have in common. Bach, Handel, Gluck, Mozart, Beethoven seem divine to us, but I do not doubt that those who heard their work when it had just been created experienced a joy and rapture that is beyond comparison with ours. It is true that Tchaikovsky did not belong strictly to my generation, for he was fifty at the time he composed *La Belle au Bois Dormant* whereas I was only twenty, but there was not a great difference in the cultural conditions which had helped to form his personality and mine. One word would have been enough to make our understanding of each other complete. This kind of understanding between human beings is the greatest happiness that can be attained by mankind; the joy which is born of spiritual union and relationship is so intense that any other fades into insignificance in comparison with it.

But here I must make one reservation on the subject of the *union of souls*. This must be understood in a special way. The union of my soul with Tchaikovsky's was felt by me alone. Peter Ilyitch himself never even suspected the existence of the youthful schoolboy who was raving about his music. I had many occasions and possibilities of having personal contact with the composer, who had so suddenly (within a few weeks actually) become my idol, but I purposely avoided making his acquaintance, believing "it to be better so." It seemed to me that I had so deeply understood Tchaikovsky and had received such intense happiness through him that there was nothing more to wish for, while to get to know him personally might prove to be a disappointment . . .

It would be superfluous to describe in detail all my musical reactions of that period. Those who love Tchaikovsky as I do, who love his way of thinking and feeling in music, the wonderful mastery with which he conveys the most varied sensations—whether they be of a purely psychological nature, or merely descriptive—will already have understood me. On the other hand, there is no use in arguing with those who profess to have "ideas that are more advanced," who consider Tchaikovsky's music as old-fashioned as some Victorian table or sofa, or that it is not sufficiently "national"—we Russians know that, although Tchaikovsky did not draw much from folk-lore, he is nevertheless the most national of our composers. Let those people hold their own opinion; they are sufficiently punished for it by being debarred from a region so vast and so enchanting.

I must add a few words about the ballet of *La Belle au Bois Dormant* in general and explain why it proved to be a novelty of such outstanding significance on our stage. *La Belle au Bois Dormant* actually belongs to the type of heavy ballets, whose traditions have become obsolete in Europe and are now regarded as belonging to *féeries* or musical revues. It is a ballet *à grand spectacle* similar to *La Fille du Pharaon, Koniok Gorbunok* or *Le Talisman*. Its author, Vsevolojsky, never intended to try any new experiments or present a new formula of ballet in the stage production which had been entrusted to him. He was by nature too great a conservative for this, and jealously guarded the old traditions. During the time of Vsevolojsky's management, *La Belle au Bois Dormant* was followed by other, similarly massive, productions with subjects based on fairy tales—*Barbe Blue, Cendrillon, Raymonda*.

The purely choreographic production of *La Belle au Bois Dormant* belonged to Marius Petipa, who, though venerable in years, was still young in spirit, and who did not consider it necessary in this case to alter his usual methods of production, methods to which he had remained faithful ever since the beginning of his brilliant career in the 1840's.

The production of *La Belle au Bois Dormant* had all the usual qualities and shortcomings of the Imperial Stage—great luxury and at the same time lack of taste in the choice of costumes—especially with regard to colours. The décors were technically perfect, but lacked any poetical quality. In a word, everything seemed to be as usual, and yet the production of *La Belle au Bois Dormant* was a most significant turning-

point in the history of the Theatre because it put an
end to the back-water slackness that had prevailed
on the stage of the Maryinsky Theatre since the
departure of Zucchi.

Interest in the ballet, which had been somehow
declining, was suddenly regenerated with fresh vigour
and has never lessened since. It can be said with
confidence that, had this production not proved to
be such an outstanding success, the whole history of
the ballet in general—not only that of the Russian
ballet—would have been totally different. The *Ballets
Russes* themselves would never have seen the light of
day had not the *Belle au Bois Dormant* awakened in a
group of Russian youths a fiery enthusiasm that
developed into a kind of frenzy. It is a curious fact
that Diaghilev had not at that time arrived in St.
Petersburg. When he came, he did not at first share
our enthusiasm, possibly because he was not as fully
prepared as we were for artistic appreciation; but
later on he also became infected. By contrast, Dima
Filosofov was, after me, the most enthusiastic admirer
of *La Belle au Bois Dormant*. He actually "went quite
mad over it." This was all the more wonderful as
Dima was, on the whole, of a very reserved nature,
inclined to analyse and be sceptical about most things
—often, in consequence, considered "hard" by those
who did not know him well. He raved about the
new ballet and when Seriozha arrived to spend the
summer with his cousin, he must doubtless have
heard endless descriptions of the winter season that
had been such an eventful one for Dima.

There can be no doubt that the chief reason for
the success of the ballet *La Belle au Bois Dormant* lies in
Tchaikovsky's music, which the composer considered
his *chef d'œuvre*. The music really possesses so strong
a power of suggestion that those who give themselves
up to it are completely transported from reality into
the magic world of fairy tale. Marius Petipa, himself

inspired by the music, achieved in the composition of the dances a height of perfection hitherto unsurpassed by him.   It is enough to recall the *variations* of the fairies in the prologue, the *grand pas de deux* in the third scene and, the greatest masterpiece of all, the dance of the Blue Bird and the enchanted Princess. But what innumerable other gems of choreographic art are scattered by Petipa throughout *La Belle au Bois Dormant!* The *grande valse* in the second act, all the fairy-tale dances, the *mazurka*, the *sarabande!* The ballet-master was no less inspired when he created the mimed scenes which abound in *La Belle au Bois Dormant*—all so expressive and in such perfect taste. What other scene of fairy-tale grotesque can stand comparison with the arrival of the wicked fairy Carabosse and her horrible attendants?   How enchanting is the reproduction of the most poetical pictures of Watteau and Lancret in the scene of the hunt in the forest!   How delightful is the arrival of Prince Charming at the enchanted castle, what perfect style and solemnity in the final act—later to become one of Diaghilev's greatest successes under the title of *Le Mariage d'Aurore!*

In the enumeration of all these successes I must not forget to add that never before had the St. Petersburg ballet stage possessed so perfect and harmonious a company of artistes as were at the disposal of Vsevolojsky and Petipa at the time of the creation of *La Belle au Bois Dormant.*   It is true that the prima ballerina of the ballet—Carlotta Brianza—could in no way be compared with Zucchi, but she was nevertheless attractive, very graceful, very accomplished technically, and had at the same time an extremely agreeable personality.   Her dancing was faultless and she succeeded in conveying all the waywardness with which Tchaikovsky has characterised the heroine. Gerdt, who was the Prince Charming, was ideal, for he gave the absolute illusion of a genuine prince—in fact, he seemed to be Louis XIV in person. Those who did not see this miracle for themselves can hardly imagine how perfectly suited this fine artist was to the role, how obvious were the traditions that he had inherited from Johannsen and Petipa, traditions which went back to the days when the youthful *Roi Soleil* himself would deign to appear on the stage as a ballet dancer.

In the last act Gerdt performed a short *variation*. Although perfectly simple and lasting less than a minute, it aroused such enthusiasm in the public that even people who knew nothing of the history of the *Grand Siècle* seemed, during the dance, to achieve a clear vision of the distant past.[1] An incomparable Master of Ceremonies was my favourite artist Stukolkin, the creator of the roles of Ivan the Simpleton and Coppélius. In this case Vsevolojsky's wide experience of court life was a great help and enabled the artist to parody it very subtly. In his Cantalbutte, Stukolkin impersonated the very type of the absurdly zealous, conceited and servile courtier. There was no exaggeration or malice, but good-natured humour, behind which one felt the typical smile of Ivan Alexandrovitch himself—a great but good-natured joker.

Among the best dancers in the ballet—from the point of view of dancing, in fact, the very best—was Enrico Cecchetti, the Italian who had recently been engaged by the Imperial Theatres. The Russian School had had no part in his education, but he had fortunately preserved enough of the excellent Italian traditions which had, in their time, so strongly influenced the elder Vestris of the French ballet, and, through the influence of French ballet-masters, had

[1] One of Diaghilev's "vandalisms" in *Le Mariage d'Aurore* was the arrangement of a Russian dance to this music under the pretext that there was a Russian theme in the melody of the variation. On the other hand, what artist since then could possibly have repeated Gerdt's performance—with the exception of Legat, Fokine or Nijinsky.

reached the Russian ballet too. Cecchetti's ardent southern temperament was perhaps a trifle out of tune with the severe *bon ton* of the Imperial stage—as had also been Zucchi's. Now and again there would burst forth from Enrico something of Truffaldino and Pulcinella. But in the present case, in the role of the terrifying yet comical witch Carabosse, those traits were only an asset, as they helped to make him all the more alive and convincing. And how wonderful it was when, in the last act, the same artist, who had just been so ingenuous a grotesque, suddenly appeared in the beautiful dance of the Blue Bird as partner to the charming Nikitina. Here he amazed and enchanted the Russian public with his extraordinary softness and grace, performing intricate *entrechats* and *pirouettes* as yet inaccessible to Russian artists, who had not even been taught to attempt them.

La Belle au Bois Dormant was first presented to the St. Petersburg public on the 3rd of January, 1890. It has never since then been taken off the repertoire and remains to this day the highest achievement of the Russian Ballet. Let who likes say that this ballet cannot be considered purely Russian because the subject is a fairy tale of Perrault, because the music is written by Tchaikovsky, whose work many Western judges refuse to pass as characteristically Russian, because it was produced by the *marseillais* Petipa, because the two principal roles were created by the Italians, Brianza and Cecchetti. In spite of all this, the ballet of *La Belle au Bois Dormant* is a typical production of Russian or rather St. Petersburg culture. Nowhere else in the world could this fairy-tale have been produced on the stage as it was in those days in the Maryinsky Theatre. To make this achievement possible, the coincidence of various factors in the mode of life of the country was essential: the aristocratic spirit, untouched by any democratic deviations, which reigned in Russia under the sceptre of Alexander III; the unique atmosphere of the St. Petersburg Theatre School and the traditions that had been formed in consequence; and finally a rejuvenation of these traditions so that, on this occasion, shaking off the dust of routine, they should appear in all the freshness of something newly-born.

Chief credit for this triumph of resuscitated traditions belongs to Vsevolojsky. Although the costumes invented by him could be criticised for their rather helpless amateurishness, he was the person responsible for *creating this masterpiece*, for he made the production of the ballet his own personal work. It was he who, by entering into all the details, became the link as well as the head of the whole production— a feature indispensable in the creation of a *Gesamtkunstwerk*. This resulted in a coherence and polish hitherto unseen. Vsevolojsky had exceptional tact and never forced his ideas on anyone, striving to convince by persuasion, and, as Ivan Alexandrovitch was a great charmer by nature, he found it very easy to convince. Thanks to his aristocratic politeness, he always managed to get what he wanted from people without using the authority to which he was entitled.

It was Vsevolojsky's idea to contrast two different epochs, divided by a hundred years. According to his version, Aurora falls asleep in the middle of the sixteenth century and wakes up in the days of the youthful Louis XIV. This "bridge," joining two centuries, gives the ballet a special poetical charm. The idea was executed by Vsevolojsky with remarkable tact in the style of the days of Perrault himself. The more distant epoch was presented in a somewhat fantastic transformation; the period contemporary to Perrault was realistically historical. Tchaikovsky was enchanted with the problem and followed the programme with all his heart, and this is why the music of the first part is lyrical and free in character, while that of the second half is more classical in style. But even the second part, though formally imitative of the style of Lully and Couperin, bears the stamp of Tchaikovsky's creative invention.

Twenty years later, when Teliakovsky was Director of the Imperial Theatres, *La Belle au Bois Dormant* was given in a new setting. One of the chief mistakes of that production lay in the fact that too little attention had been paid to the principal problem. In artistic quality Korovin's sets surpassed by far the conventional and rather timid work of Levogt, Botcharov, Shishkov and Ivanov—though one must acknowledge that Ivanov's *trompe l'œil* of "Aurora's bedroom" gave one a complete illusion. From an artistic point of view Korovin's costumes were better still and in colouring incomparably superior to Vsevolojsky's somewhat dilettante and tasteless inventions. But no artistic perfection of colouring in the new version could make up for the loss of the poetry—the poetry that was so apparent in Vsevolojsky's production.

Korovin moved the epoch of the first part of the ballet forward by eighty years, which made the court of Florestan XXIV resemble in character the court of Louis XIII. This proved that our excellent artist and the director who had allowed him to take this liberty had failed to appreciate the chief charm of the first production. Bakst tried to correct this mistake in Diaghilev's London production of the *Sleeping Princess* in 1922, but instead of frankly going back to the first version he introduced too much elaboration—as was his habit—and the principal idea was again weakened and obscured. The production certainly gained in grandeur, but, as before, it lost its poetic quality.

Chapter XI

TCHAIKOVSKY'S LAST BALLET

UNFORTUNATELY, Vsevolojsky, although he had at his disposal such composers as Tchaikovsky and, after Tchaikovsky's death, Glazunov, was not destined to produce another ballet as successful as *La Belle au Bois Dormant*. In opera a similar success was vouchsafed to him at the end of the year in which *La Belle au Bois Dormant* was produced. This was the opera *La Dame de Pique*, which must be considered as the crowning glory and chief masterpiece of Vsevolojsky's work in general.

The ballets that followed *La Belle au Bois Dormant* were Tchaikovsky's *Casse-Noisette* in 1892, Glazunov's *Raymonda* in 1898, *Les Saisons* and *Ruses d'Amour* in 1900. The two other novelties—*Barbe Bleu* and *Cendrillon*—did not remain in the repertoire of the Maryinsky Theatre, although they contained many charming and witty items. The reason for this lay chiefly in the music, for though it may not have been inferior to that of Pugni and Minkus, it seemed both banal and colourless to the public who had now learned to appreciate and love Tchaikovsky.

It was through my infatuation for *La Belle au Bois Dormant* that I began to develop into a conscious and convinced *balletomane*. But, in truth, I never actually became a complete *balletomane*. I was too devoted to the theatre in general, or rather to art in general, to limit myself to a special sphere—though I must say that during those years I certainly developed a conscious and well-based *culte* of the ballet. I willingly talked about ballet with my friends and when in later years I published my first efforts in print they were full of glowing enthusiasm about the ballet. My preference for the ballet has lasted to this day, though I must confess that the exaggerated passion for stage dancing, which has nowadays taken the form of an epidemic, irritates me intensely. I am revolted, too, by the snobbish absurdity and ugliness that are exhibited on many once famous stages; they only prove that we have come to a standstill and that the epoch of inspiration and genuine creativeness is over. . . . Let us hope not for ever.

I have just said that Tchaikovsky's ballet *Casse-Noisette*, which proved to be his last "gift to the stage," cannot be placed on the same level as *La Belle au Bois Dormant* or *La Dame de Pique*. If, however, we refrain from comparison and regard the two works separately, or, better still, if one could alter the dates of their appearance, making *Casse-Noisette* the first, in 1890, and *La Belle au Bois Dormant* the second, in 1892, the development of the great composer's creative genius in ballet would seem to be more logical and more harmonious. *La Belle au Bois Dormant* would then be the crowning apotheosis of Tchaikovsky's choreographic · music, while *Casse-Noisette* would be its wonderful forerunner. But, putting aside all these fancies, one must acknowledge that the music of *Casse-Noisette* is excellent on the whole and in parts even more mature than that of *La Belle au Bois Dormant*. In spite of this, *Casse-Noisette* never had the same success as *La Belle au Bois Dormant* and the reason lies principally in the fact that the subject is badly constructed. It is presented only in the first scene; the following two scenes are just "tacked on."

The purely choreographic action of *Casse-Noisette* has little in common with the subject and cannot be called successful. The unaccountable appearance of the unruly French Incroyables at the patriarchal Christmas-tree party spoils the atmosphere of "good old times," while the famous battle between the mice and the tin soldiers was so chaotically presented in the first version that it only aroused perplexity and boredom. It was impossible to imagine anything more cheerless than the décors of the first act: the ballroom in President Stahlbaum's house reminded one rather of a *Bierstube* decorated in German Renaissance style instead of being one of the cosy and poetical interiors of the eighteenth century that one so often meets in the old-fashioned provincial towns of Germany. The décor of the kingdom of sweets was more suitable for some *féerie* in the Châtelet than for the stage of the Imperial Ballet, where its gaudy brilliance was strangely incongruous. The only setting of artistic merit was Botcharov's moonlit and snow-covered forest which formed the background for the "white" or "snow-flake" ballet in the second scene, but this décor had no connection with either the first or third scenes and so emphasised the inconsequent construction of the whole act—which had in any case the air of an interlude.[1]

---

[1] In my production of *Casse-Noisette* in 1938 at the Scala in Milan, I tried to correct some of the absurdities of the first scenario and was greatly helped in this by the talented ballet-mistress, Mme. Froman, who now occupies the post of "ballet-master of the National Theatre" in Zagreb. I joined the intermediate "Snow-flake" ballet with the Christmas-tree party scene; when the President's ballroom was transformed into a snow-covered magic forest, the little girl Clara became a grown-up beauty and the little Casse-Noisette changed into a Prince. They danced a *pas de deux* to the beautiful music which used formerly to be played in the interval, after which the couple, wrapped up in their white fur coats, drove away in a sleigh drawn by white polar bears. They arrived at the Kingdom of Sweets, where they were received by Clara's godfather, Drosselmeyer, who turned out to be the king of the country of Sweets. This new incident was consistent with Hoffmann's tale and served as link between the first and third acts.

I would like to quote here an extract from my diary dated December 7th, 1892, where I describe two premières—both by Tchaikovsky—given on the same night—the one-act opera *Yolande* and the ballet *Casse-Noisette*. After the description of *Yolande*, which disappointed even Tchaikovsky's most ardent admirers, follows the account of the ballet.

". . . But alas! *Casse-Noisette* has not turned out a success! And it was just in this ballet that I had placed all my hopes, knowing Tchaikovsky's talent for creating a fairy-tale atmosphere. But perhaps the chief cause of my disappointment lies not in the music but in the *hideous* production. The overture (which I already knew on the piano) was hurried through at the tempo of a can-can gallop, and entirely lacked the salt that the orchestra should have given it. The décor of Scene I, though by Ivanov,[1] is both disgusting and profoundly shocking. It spoilt the whole impression from the start. Instead of having an elaborate chamber in Rococo or Louis XVI style, lit up by chandeliers and sconces, but conveying at the same time an atmosphere of good-natured bourgeoisie, we were obliged to contemplate during a whole hour the *salon* of some rich *parvenu* banker in the Friedrichstrasse style. It was stupid, coarse, heavy and dark. How absurd the kind of fresco portraits of Tchaikovsky, Petipa and the rest of them on the walls! Absolute lack of taste in all the ornaments, furniture, etc. The costumes, too, are *stupidly* chosen. The period of 1770–1780 would have best suited the fairy-tale, whereas here they have chosen the Directoire—in purely French manner! What is more—a company of Merveilleuses and Incroyables appear in the old-fashioned, conventional, prim Germany of those days! Valetchka

[1] Ivanov had exceptional success with his décors for *La Belle au Bois Dormant* and *La Dame de Pique.*

tries to explain all these mistakes by saying that it
is meant to be a masquerade, but even this goes
against good taste and the whole spirit and atmosphere of the fairy-tale. The ladies have long trains
which they pull up higher than their knees—and that
is quite indecent. I was indignant!

"Both Stukolkins—grandfather and grandson—
were magnificent. The elder (in the part of the godfather, Drosselmeyer) entered completely into the eerie
spirit of the part. The music that accompanies his
entrance is, I think, the best in the ballet. It is
really the work of a genius. Unfortunately, his
entrance is so stupidly staged that it passes unnoticed.
Drosselmeyer jumps out of a side-door and disappears
at once among the romping children. . . . The
music of the night scene is again enchanting; both
horror and mystery are expressed with a wonderful
feeling for *das Grausige*. But the battle of the mice and
the tin soldiers is disgracefully produced—one cannot
understand anything. Disorderly pushing about
from corner to corner and running backwards and
forwards—quite senseless and amateurish. The
moonlight (how effective it could be in creating an
atmosphere) is produced as usual by blazing spotlights
from the side instead of through the window. The
décor of the forest buried under the winter snow is
magnificent, but the whole scene is squeezed in to no
purpose, as Clara's and Casse-Noisette's flight through
it passes quite unnoticed.

"The second act is still worse. Levogt's décor is
effective in a showy way, while at times the music
reminds one of an open-air military band.[1] Tchaikovsky has never written anything more banal than
some of these numbers! Nevertheless *Thé*, *Chocolat*,
the *trepak* and part of the *pas de deux* are delightful.
The costumes are elaborate but lacking in taste;

[1] The serene unconcern of this judgment is due to my being twenty-
two years old at that time.

some of the dancers are in bright yellow, others in bright pink and the effect can only be called 'loud.'

"The performance dragged on from 8 o'clock to midnight. We were both tired out! When it was over one did not feel inclined to see the ballet all over again, and even to-day, which is the day after, I do not feel drawn to go, although I should like to *hear* the first act another time.

"We returned home to a festive family supper (in honour of Papa's nameday). Though I was feeling both ill and tired, I had to describe my impressions, argue with Valetchka, drink to the health of relations and listen to all sorts of stupid toasts."

I have quoted in full my own entry of so long ago because it seems to me to be of certain documentary interest with regard to my views on ballet at that period, views which were shared by all our circle. Another point of interest in this passage from my diary is that I do not even mention the starring prima ballerina Dell'Era who took the part of the Fée Dragée—the Sugar-Plum Fairy—in the third scene. The reason for this omission must be that I was not in the least impressed by her, but I hasten to add that the fault was not so much in the artiste herself as in the unsuccessful setting of her dances, which only consisted of one *grand pas de deux*, Dell'Era performed all that was demanded of her with precision and skill and pleasing grace, but she was not the only one to be perfect in *tours, cabrioles* and *arabesques*! Without mentioning Zucchi, we had seen, during the last years, a number of technically excellent Italian dancers and there were several of our own ballerinas whose skill could surpass that of any foreign visitor.

It is interesting to pause and consider here that the music written by Tchaikovsky for this *pas de deux* is not ordinary ballet music. It was composed by

him a year before he wrote the sixth Symphony—
the *Pathétique*—which is permeated with a sense of
approaching death, alternating with moments full
of a passionate thirst for life. The music of the *pas
de deux* in *Casse-Noisette* has many similar features.
Why did Tchaikovsky impart a tragic character to
the dances of the Fée Dragée? He has taken the
answer to that question with him to his grave—
but there is no doubt that this music does not express
the personality of the playful "sugar-plum" fairy.
Is not this *pas de deux* rather an attempt to restore a
"Hoffmann" atmosphere to the ballet? Beneath the
humour of Hoffmann's tale there is a feeling of tension,
a kind of delirious languor, as if the heroine, Clara,
were both overjoyed and tormented by all that happens
to her. The only light-hearted part in the *pas de deux*
is the dancer's *variation*—the tarantella—and even
that seems out-of-place here. The dances of the
ballerina herself, including the wonderful *variation*
to the accompaniment of the celesta, are in turn
solemn and pathetic or melancholy and restless.

Lev Ivanov, who, because of Petipa's illness, was
entrusted with the production of the ballet,
evidently did not understand what the music of this
part implied, that it was in direct contradiction to
the general atmosphere of the rest of the second scene.
The ballerina's dances, though no worse than usual,
have nothing remarkable about them, even when
performed by a first class virtuoso.

I am approaching the end of the first part of my
tale—the part which is devoted to my reminiscences
as a spectator. Several years were destined to pass
before I took an active part in the productions.
These last years as a member of the audience (1892–
1900) produced no new impressions that could alter
my views or re-orientate the dreams I had formed
of an ideal ballet. But I cannot refrain from men-

tioning my favourite Gerdt's interpretation of the
dramatic part of Bluebeard, which amazed both me
and my friends, and the highly ingenious mirror
dance in *Cendrillon*, in which the prima ballerina's
double was performed by that original and charming
dancer, Kulichevskaya.

Lastly, I must add that we derived some comfort
for our grief at Tchaikovsky's death from the belated
production of his earlier ballet *Le Lac des Cygnes* and
from the appearance of Glazunov's ballets: *Raymonda,
Les Saisons* and *Ruses d'Amour*. But this comfort was
only relative, for although the charming, melancholy
and poetical *Lac des Cygnes* contains much that is
dear to me, it fails to arouse real enthusiasm, having
been presented after works that are infinitely more
mature. As for Glazunov's ballets, in spite of their
musical qualities, it is impossible to be absorbed by
them. In *Raymonda* the fault lies in the absurdity of
the subject, of which nobody could ever make head
or tail—which is rather awkward as the performance
lasts for three whole hours. In *Ruses d'Amour* the
eighteenth century subject is graceful, but too light
to be moving. The ballet is just a *bagatelle* suitable
for a Court Gala in the Hermitage Theatre. The
subject of *Les Saisons*, inspired by the phenomena of
nature, gave occasion to both composer and ballet-
master to create a series of highly poetical dances.
But as it so happened that I failed to see it when it
was first produced in 1900, and only got to know it
considerably later, I cannot include it in my reminiscences of that period. I must add that, in spite of
my real admiration for Glazunov's music, I do not
consider him an ideal composer of ballets. Such
enchanting musical pieces as *La Romanesque* in
Raymonda, and *Hoar Frost, Snow, Autumn* and
The Awakening of Spring, in *Les Saisons*, are rare exceptions. When listening to them, one cannot help
wondering how so heavy and massive a man (he was

almost grotesque in figure) could achieve such delicate grace, such strength of temperament, so sensitive an understanding of nature. In general, the bulk of Glazunov's music is too materialistic. There seems to be no air in it; it oppresses and chokes the listener. That is the reason why Glazunov's music cannot be considered suitable for the ballet, where we are accustomed to airy, soaring music, that defies, as it were, the laws of gravity.

PART TWO

WORKER FOR THE BALLET

Chapter I

MY MARRIAGE

BEFORE I begin my reminiscences of the time when our group and I embarked on active theatrical work—of which ballet production was the predominant feature—I must relate the principal events that occurred both in my personal life and in that of our circle during the years 1890–1900.

Within these ten years I had left High School, made my first independent trip abroad, studied law for four years in the St. Petersburg University and lived three years in Paris.

In April, 1891, I had the great sorrow of losing my beloved mother. My father, who adored her as much as we did, outlived my mother by seven years and died in December, 1898, at the age of eighty-five. His death put an end to our old home. The last days spent there were unutterably sad, for we knew that the surroundings that were so dear to us were soon to disappear. A characteristic feature of our home was the way in which outstandingly beautiful things, worthy of any art collection, were kept side by side with quite ordinary objects, preserved solely out of family sentiment. Thus in the drawing-room, where stood the dark blue velvet-covered furniture of the '40's, two of my humble water-colours presented to my father on his birthday hung beside a magnificent portrait of my mother by Kapkov; in my father's study, furnished with curious old-fashioned Karelian birch, incomparable sepias of Guardi and excellent family portraits again hung side by side with the feebler and sometimes tasteless work of children and grandchildren. A similar medley could be found in every room of my parents' large apartment, but perhaps it was just this feature—then greatly despised by me, and certainly to be criticised from the point of view of taste—which imparted to our home that particular cosiness which was noticed by all who came to visit us, making them feel at once "quite at home" —which meant in most cases, "much better than in their own homes."

My parents' house had actually ceased to be my own home a few years before the final breaking up of 1899. In 1894, after a long engagement, my youthful romance came at last to a happy conclusion, for we were married on the 29th of June in the beautiful church of St. Catherine on the Nevsky Prospect. This was the church where, during a whole century, most of the members of our family had been married, christened and buried and where I had been confirmed in 1883. It was in this church that I had first seen my future *fiancée*, Atia, when we were both only six years old. It was on the occasion of my brother Albert's marriage to Marie Kind, Atia's sister. I vaguely remember the figure of the nice and very shy little girl standing in the group of the bride's relations. Years passed and the little girl became a maiden, a young woman. I myself had turned from a boy into a youth and a young man; our meetings became more and more frequent, through the relationship between our families, until one day we suddenly discovered that we "could not live without each other." From that moment began our romance, which was looked upon good-naturedly by our elders, for it was considered as *une chose sans conséquence*; nevertheless, after my brother Albert's divorce from Atia's sister, our friendship was forbidden. Three years passed and both the hostile parties decided that they could do nothing with us and ceased to oppose our union.

It was a clear, hot day in June, 1894, a month after I had passed my last university examination—and therefore had become a full member of society—that our marriage took place. We stood radiantly happy at the steps of the light-flooded altar, where we exchanged rings; then proceeded to the vestry to sign the register, surrounded by a crowd of relations and friends. Atia's signature of "Anne Benois" was hardly legible and this was due not only to excitement, but also to the fact that she had a temperature, for she had just got up to come to church for her wedding. Her illness—tonsilitis—had disappeared on the following day, but unfortunately she caught cold while we were staying with my brother Michael in Peterhof. To my horror, she now developed a very severe form of rheumatic fever and our honeymoon was spent in torturing physical pain for her and the most terrible anxiety for me, especially as her illness dragged on, owing to the unsuitable treatment prescribed by our family doctor, who, declining in years, had lost all faith in his own professional skill. It was Bakst, it must be said, who then saved Atia—he insisted on calling in L. M. Kliachko, a famous young doctor who was one of his friends. The very first thing Kliachko did was to transfer the patient from the gloomy "green" room, into which the sun hardly ever penetrated, into my old "red" room usually flooded with sunshine. This measure acted miraculously on my wife's condition and she began rapidly to recover. Two weeks later found us both in the compartment of a railway carriage at the Warsaw Station, for we were going abroad.

This was the beginning of our honeymoon which lasted four months. The first part of it was devoted to re-establishing Atia's health and was spent in Wiesbaden, where she underwent the full cure.

F

Only after this did she regain her full strength and feel as well as she had before her illness. We left Wiesbaden full of vigour, energy and gaiety accumulated during the months of our trials, and proceeded to places more tempting and wonderful than the famous German Spa, for which we retained, nevertheless, a grateful memory.

We returned to St. Petersburg in January 1895, and lived at first in my parents' apartment. In August, during our stay in Peterhof, we were gladdened by the birth of our first child, who was named Anna after her mother. In the autumn we moved into a small separate flat, but I still had such a need not to lose touch with the old house, where I had been born and where I had grown up, that we made our first home only a few steps away. It was on the first floor, the windows overlooking a large light yard, the whole atmosphere being pleasant and cosy. The walls were hung with pictures and prints which had already adorned my old room; Atia's wedding gift had been some charming old-fashioned mahogany furniture, and all our relations and friends brought us heaps of presents. The chief feature of my study was the famous old sofa and a huge *empire* bookcase filled with books on art. I had also inherited the old piano on which Albert used to play to me in the days of my childhood.

I liked to improvise on it myself in the twilight hours. My ballet, composed eight years ago, had by now been completely forgotten and, feeling disappointed in my musical capacities, I had entirely given up the idea of ever composing anything of importance. However, I dearly loved to let loose my imagination in music. I was caught improvising one day by Somov, who made a sketch of me, and now, when I see that sketch, I can hardly recognise myself in the curious creature depicted, for I look like an unkempt and bearded Bohemian.

ALEXANDRE BENOIS

From a sketch by Constantine Somov, 1896

Facing page 148

NICOLAS BENOIS AND HIS FAMILY IN HIS STUDY, 1895

Left to right: Michel Benois, Nicolas Benois, Mlle. Raevsky, Marie Lanceray, Sophie Lanceray, Anne Benois, Catherine Lanceray, Catherine Lanceray-fille, Zénaïde Lanceray, Nicolas Lanceray, Eugène Lanceray, Alexandre Benois. *From the sepia drawing by Nicolas Benois*

Facing page 149

Chapter II

PRODUCTS OF ST. PETERSBURG

DURING the years that preceded the birth of the *World of Art*, many changes took place in our little circle, from which sprang the *World of Art* and many other artistic creations. In writing about this, I shall try to resist the temptation of reviving in memory all the events that moved, grieved or gladdened me, and shall endeavour to limit myself to the theme of this book—that is to say, I shall write only of things concerning the ballet directly or indirectly.

We moved into our own apartment in 1895. At that period the original form and character of our circle had already undergone considerable changes. The four schoolfellows—Somov, Nouvel, Filosofov and myself—continued to be the nucleus, but in the spring of 1890 we had been joined by L. Bakst, a few months later by Diaghilev, and later still by the Frenchman Charles Birlé and the half-English Nourok; my nephew Genia Lanceray had also been accepted in our circle. On the other hand, several members had fallen away and we eventually quite lost sight of each other. These were the two Fenoult brothers, with whom I had been inseparable at one time, the witty G. Kalin and his friend N. Skalon, who incidentally was the only one of us who in his social outlook inclined towards advanced ideas. Looking back at our group, which was later on to become the head-quarters of the *World of Art*, one has to note that the chief link binding us was Art and that the members who broke away were those to whom Art was insuperably alien, although they were charming and pleasant friends. Another important bond was our Europeanism or Westernism. By nature we all belonged to Europe rather than to Russia. The majority of us—Nouvel, Lanceray, Bakst, Nourok, Birlé and myself—had no Russian blood in us. And if it is true that Somov and Filosofov belonged to the old Russian gentry, their upbringing and personal inclinations were impregnated through and through with western culture.

The most Russian of us all was perhaps Diaghilev, and it was just this "Russian side" of Diaghilev that aroused our antagonism—all the more because his characteristically Russian qualities were, from a universal point of view, the least acceptable. Moreover, his Russianism had for a long time a strong provincial flavour. It was not that he was uncouth, or "simple" in a provincial way; yet he was infinitely less educated than we and often shocked us by his manners and a very disagreeable *sans gêne*, that was at times most embarrassing. For a considerable period, too, he surprised and irritated us by his indifference to the plastic arts, to history and literature —to all the things, in fact, that chiefly interested us. Diaghilev set to work to catch us up by becoming more and more of a "Westerner," until there came a moment when the position seemed to be reversed; it was we who had to defend everything Russian, now thoroughly despised by him.

What I have just written needs an explanation. French, English or German people can easily misunderstand me and give the wrong interpretation to my words. They may find it extraordinary and strange that a group of young men should sweep aside all that was characteristic of their country. It seems almost like an act of treason. Such a conclusion would not be correct.   It is necessary to have an insight into Russian life and its development since the reforms of Peter the Great fully to understand how normal it was to yearn after the West, to endeavour to become a "Westerner."   This attitude was in no way treasonable.   It was prevalent all over Russia, and in St. Petersburg especially it was almost impossible *not* to become a "Westerner," because the very soil seemed to *infect* one with the yearning for the West.

The spirit of its founder seemed to dominate St. Petersburg right down to the days of Bolshevism, and it was this spirit which gave our city its original character and its unique charm.   Paris, London, Berlin, Vienna are all cities of a universal character and they all have features that resemble the typical features of St. Petersburg, yet each of these cities represents the heart of its country; they are deeply national and entirely self-sufficient.   They willingly receive guests, live with them and even periodically become infatuated with them, yet every one of these capitals in its heart of hearts is always deeply convinced of its own superiority to anything foreign.

The enemies of St. Petersburg, who were numerous in Russia, used to throw at our city the accusation that it owed its existence to a whim.   One cannot deny that St. Petersburg actually emerged from an empty waste, from the marshes, solely as an act of will of the Great Peter.   But this act cannot be called a fantastic whim, for it was founded on the conviction that only an entirely new mode of life and the foundation of a new society for Russian people was capable of supporting the reforms that had already been inaugurated and those that were planned for the future. The creation of St. Petersburg was an act of the greatest importance performed by a man of genius, who, with unceasing energy and persistence, followed one purpose.   This purpose was to lead his country out of the darkness and bring the people who had been entrusted to him by Providence in closer contact with their brothers by race, culture and Christianity. Had Muscovy remained cut off from the rest of the world as she had been during the reign of Peter's father, Tsar Alexei the Meek, she would probably have ceased to exist as a country of any importance. Her borders would have fallen under the sway of Sweden, Germany, Poland and Turkey, while the heart of the country, having no outlet to the sea, would have dragged out the pitiful existence of a third-rate, vast, poverty-stricken and half-savage country. She would have had no part in the concert of great European Powers and would have shared the fate of Moldavia, Wallachia or the Crimean Khanate.

It was not only that Peter nourished ambitious plans for Russia's future greatness and dignity; he was personally repelled by much that was characteristic—·"picturesque" and "amusing," it would be called nowadays—in his subjects. These characteristics consisted of many negative qualities, which could only be called national. Whether they were racial, organically inherent in the Russian people, or whether they had been assimilated during centuries when Russia was under the yoke of the Tartars, will be eternally disputed. But there can be no doubt that they were repulsive to Peter and that he tried to uproot them. His idea was to make St. Petersburg a *new brain* for his country, an organ of control and conscience. The success of Peter and those who followed him during the next two hundred years is proved by what is happening in Russia to-day. The present horrors and absurdities are clear proof that the rebellion of "characteristic" Russians against Peter's propagation of foreign influence has taken elemental proportions. It is the reaction of the dark elements against the harmonious tenor of life. It is not by chance that Moscow—the "geographical heart of Russia"—has once more regained its power.   These fundamental Russian attributes are discussed throughout Russian literature, and that is why our literature can only be understood by those who are acquainted with the typical psychology of Russians.   One can boldly affirm that without Peter, without all that contributed to the predominance of St. Petersburg and St. Petersburg culture, there would have been no Russian literature—created by the typical representatives of St. Petersburg, Pushkin, Gogol, Dostoievsky—no Russian painters, such as Levitsky, Ivanov, Surikov and Repin, no Russian architecture or sculpture, no Russian theatre, no Russian music.

The fact that many of the artists of genius that I have named were not born in St. Petersburg does not weaken my argument.   They could have been born and brought up and lived for many years in any part of Russia, but their artistry, their artistic conscience, their sense of value, their acuteness of perception and judgment were acquired in St. Petersburg, where they spent the most important years of their training.

Thus it happened that our circle could not be called typically Russian.   On the contrary, we undoubtedly disapproved of many typically Russian features.   We objected both to Russian coarseness and to the decorative complacency that many Russians love to parade.   We disliked and distrusted the superficial sincerity that so often slips into deceit and falsehood; we distrusted, too, irresponsible "confusion of feelings," though all of us, from personal experience, were familiar with its tempting charms.   Our circle must therefore be regarded as a typical product of St. Petersburg. From this description I cannot exclude the member of our circle who gained the widest fame outside the borders of Russia—namely, Diaghilev—even though he was born and spent his childhood and youth in Perm, and only joined us when he was nineteen.

It would be a mistake to consider our circle, which
had been formed during our school-days and developed during our student years, as a sort of society
which pursued definite moral aims. This was not
so. Questions of morality and philosophy interested
us deeply and at one time several of us—including
Nouvel and myself—came under the strong influence
of Tolstoy. But, on the whole, our circle had a purely
artistic and æsthetic character, which did not blend
easily with any kind of rigorous morality. One of its
characteristics was our love of a joke and appreciation
of the comic side of life. Each of us expressed it in
his own way. Some of us frankly played the fool,
others liked to assume the mask of mystery, others
were cynical, others again played the part of thorough
sentimentalists. These roles were not permanent
ones; we often exchanged parts—that is to say, the
cynic became sentimental or the fool mysterious. A
certain similarity in our upbringing helped to establish
the harmony that reigned among us, but besides this
we were really united by a passionate interest in art.
We all burned with the same passion, with the result
that, in spite of only very slight differences of opinion,
our arguments were extremely violent. But there
was nothing fanatical in our disputes and we all
agreed in a certain eclecticism. Each one had his
own sympathies, but all of us were far from any kind
of doctrine.

Chapter III

LEADERS OF OUR CIRCLE

TOWARDS the end of our High School days we suddenly decided to re-organise the life of our circle and transform it into a sort of society or club with regular meetings, reports and debates. Regulations of this "Society for Self-Improvement" were drawn up, which we all duly signed, vowing to follow the rules scrupulously. The Society began to function in the autumn of 1889 and continued for over two years.

I was the one who treated the matter most seriously, for I delivered to my friends a long series of lectures on the great artists of the German School and prepared a cycle devoted to French painting of the nineteenth century for the third year. I often wonder to-day how I had the patience to compose these "popular compilations" and wonder even more how my friends had the patience to listen to them! I must add that my lectures were embellished by numerous graphic illustrations, so that when the talking became tedious the pictures made up for it.

Nouvel, after me, concerned himself most about our "mutual education"; he gave a course of lectures on the origins of opera, which he accompanied with musical illustrations on the piano, whereas Kalin, with his usual wit, gave an outline of Turgeniev's life and works. Bakst's efforts to establish his favourites— Makovsky and Semiradsky—were not without charm, while our youngest member Filosofov chose the difficult subject of the "Reign of Alexander I," a task

F*

with which he could not quite cope. E. Fenoult decided that we ought to know something about positive science and started a course about the then sensational discoveries of micro-organisms. His first lecture, however, was in no way better than any article that could be found in a popular review and had no success. Having understood this, he did not continue his enlightening activities.

All this was really very touching and amusing, but gradually the interest in our lectures began to flag, the discipline to slacken (our "Speaker" Bakst once broke the bell while ringing frantically to call for order) and at the beginning of the third year even the founders themselves had no illusions about its being worth while to continue. . . . Everybody was delighted at the announcement that our Society was to be liquidated, though this did not in the least imply that our circle would cease to exist or that we should all be dispersed. Kalin, Skalon and Fenoult did depart from us, but the reason was not one of principle; their departure was due, rather, to incompatibility of character. Their falling away had no effect on the core of our circle, for we seemed now to be tied with still stronger bonds—in fact, for several years we found it impossible to exist without each other.

Our meetings generally took place at my house, because I had a large room to myself and we were allowed to use the drawing-room for our musical activities. I had collected during those years a vast library of books on art and had also acquired a certain amount of knowledge which, though far from being scientific, I imparted to my friends with excessive enthusiasm. I felt in those years a thirst to teach and to influence people—also, perhaps, a love of power. I liked to play the part of leader, chairman, guide. My comrades both loved and respected me, and sometimes even feared me a little, for though I was the first

to play practical jokes—having always retained my
harlequin spirit—I never allowed any jesting about
the sanctity of my ideals and could not bear them
to be treated lightly or indifferently. I was continually attacking my friends and reproaching them
for their denseness and their lack of attention and
understanding, but as there was nothing personal or
unkind in these outbursts, my friends bore them
meekly and perhaps respected me all the more.

Nouvel, Bakst and Diaghilev were the chief offenders
and therefore used to "catch it" the most, each in
their several ways. Nouvel used to irritate me by his
self-possession and pretence of knowing everything.
I would accuse him, too, of being hard and unfeeling,
sometimes, I must say, not without reason; but
Nouvel always was—and has remained till this day—
an absolutely indispensable element in our circle, not
because he had much practical knowledge and
common sense, but because all his faults were balanced
by contrasting good qualities. Thus, in spite of a
certain hardness, which prevented him perhaps from
developing his marked musical talent, he was at the
same time sincere and warm-hearted, and though
inclined to be snobbish, could easily drop any prejudiced ideas and even confess to them publicly. He
was a gossip and loved egging on his friends against
each other, but could also be extremely discreet and
keep a secret faithfully.

Nouvel's value in our circle was indisputable
because of his passionate interest in art, not only
in music but in all other branches. In his young
days it had been partly the wish "to keep up with
the others" that was responsible for his interest; but
this was not the only motive that stimulated Nouvel,
for he was endowed with a genuine and insatiable
curiosity. Different surroundings would have probably made of Valetchka Nouvel an excellent man of
science or critic, especially as he was inclined, thanks

to his German origin, to pedantic systematisation. It was perhaps our fault that Nouvel never became a man of science, for he was corrupted by our dilettantism. But this dilettantism was an indispensable element in our versality, our encyclopædism, so to speak, and was instrumental in helping us to fulfil our part in cultural life. Each of us had, more or less, his own special subject; but if he had sacrificed everything to his special subject and locked himself up within the narrow region of his own interests, we would never have become united. There would never have been a *World of Art* nor any of the things that sprang from it, which include the *Ballets Russes*, the most remarkable development resulting from our union.

Levushka Bakst was another object of my criticism during the years when I played the part of mentor. He did not belong to our original first group of school-fellows, for, as I have already mentioned, I only got to know him in the spring of 1890 at my brother Albert's house. We made friends during that summer and I introduced him to our circle in the autumn. Levushka very quickly became a "competent Pickwickian" (as we jokingly called ourselves) and a feeling of real friendship developed and survived unchanged until his death. Everyone who saw Bakst will agree with me that he was a man of great charm, but the Bakst of *those* days was quite exceptionally delightful. Later, when he was at the height of his fame, it was difficult to imagine how modest and shy he had been as a young fellow. His near-sighted eyes and very fair lashes, his sibilant voice and slight lisp, imparted something half-comical and touching to his personality.

Levushka used to tell us about his childhood, which had been happy and prosperous until his father's death. After that life had become very difficult, for he had to earn what he could to keep his mother,

V. F. NOUVEL
From a pastel by C. Somov, 1914

Facing page 158

LÉON BAKST
From a sketch by M. Dobuzhinsky, 1908

grandmother, one brother and two sisters while he studied in the Academy of Arts. His artistic judgment was often incoherent, but the fire and vehemence with which he defended his absurdities was so genuine that one felt genuinely touched when listening to or even arguing with him. In those days we were all "encyclopædic-eclectics"—and extremely immature ones at that. We drew our knowledge of art from visits to exhibitions and museums and from reading and looking at books and magazines. But alas, exhibitions in St. Petersburg were very poor in comparison to those in Western Europe; the museums contained no examples of contemporary Western Art and even the best foreign books and journals that I received could not take the place of direct visual experience.

Levushka's immaturity differed from ours because he still admired things we had ceased to admire and now disdained. For instance, he admired, and considered excellent, Russian painters whom we hated for their triviality, whereas among German, French and English artists (with whom we were acquainted through our books and journals) he considered favourites of ours like Böcklin, Menzel, Bastien Lepage, Dagnan-Bouveret, Holman Hunt, Millais, Burne-Jones to be on the same level as such "unacceptable" painters as Zichel, Kiesel, Benjamin Constant, Alma Tadema, etc.

It was on account of these infatuations that Bakst was usually called to task, but he was also criticised for his own pictures, which vividly expressed the incoherence of his ideas. We were in fact justified in doing this, for it was difficult not to feel indignant when one so gifted as he, wasted his talent in creating comical anecdotes like *The Drunken Torch-bearer* or *The Mésalliance*. I used to get still more worried when he attempted to create something "profound." During the first months of our acquaintance he was full of

the idea of picturing *Despair*—a woman just about to
throw herself under a train. It was to be a life-sized
figure standing near the rails, with the smoke of the
approaching engine in the distance. A little later on
he started a picture of *Judas conversing with Christ*, in
which he endeavoured to express his special understanding of the traitor disciple. In Bakst's opinion
Judas was not a traitor; on the contrary, he considered
him as the wisest and most faithful of Christ's
disciples. . . . Judas' doubts were the result of his
wisdom and he confided his doubts to his Teacher. It
was obvious that Bakst was erring while he persisted
in following this road and running the risk of ruining
his talent. From the purely "picturesque" angle his
experiments were equally pitiful.

These paintings showed that Levushka, who was so
modest in ordinary life, was nursing a secret ambition
to become "a great and remarkable artist." On the
other hand, the "scraps" that sprang from his pencil
or brush—he had started working in water-colour,
following Somov's, Albert's and my example—disclosed even then the technique of a virtuoso and
an incomparable intensity of colour. Whenever we
were assembled together Bakst never ceased drawing
or painting small pictures, sometimes in the style
of Isabey and at others in the style of Fortuny.
I had such a collection of these trifles that I used
to give them away right and left or present them
to lotteries. It was remarkable that, although
Bakst did not seem to value these productions in the
least, he nevertheless signed every one of the hastily
sketched water-colours with his full name—which
proves that, in spite of his modesty, there was alive
in him even at that time a feeling of strong ambition,
the feeling that helped him later on in life, when he
occupied a prominent position in both the Old World
and the New. Possibly this characteristic was simply
typical of his race. Bakst was the only Jew among

us. That is perhaps why his manner of life differed in some respects from ours. Although he appeared to be extremely unpractical, he could be more tenacious and persistent than any of us; equally, he had a talent for extracting the greatest advantage out of every possibility. I am not blaming him for this, but mention it in order to make his personality more comprehensible. There was so much sincerity and simplicity in his nature that his ambition only irritated us sometimes without altering our feeling of friendship towards him. Everybody was fond of Bakst and he had the gift of creating, by his mere presence, an atmosphere of friendliness and ease.

Chapter IV

EDUCATION OF DIAGHILEV

I GOT to know Diaghilev a few months after Bakst,
but while our friendship with Levushka had a
purely artistic basis, the *rapprochement* with Seriozha was
due solely to his being the cousin of Dima Filosofov.
He had arrived in St. Petersburg from Perm in order
to enter the University with us and we had welcomed
him amiably as one usually welcomes a relation who
lands on one from the blue. Seriozha remained a
newcomer with us for quite a long time; when I say
"long," I am speaking from the point of view of
childhood and youth, that is, counting weeks as
months and months as years. At first we found his
presence only just tolerable and nobody took any
notice of his opinions. Moreover, he did not frequent
our group meetings regularly. He showed himself
incapable of following our lectures closely or taking
part in any æsthetic, philosophical or religious discussions, and showed it so obviously, yawning un-
restrainedly to make clear how remote and boring it
all was, that at times we became very angry. I used
to shout and stamp at him, accusing him of being a
thick-skinned Philistine and God knows what else.
Seriozha took all this abuse very meekly, without any
protest, and would even try to reform himself, being
influenced by heart-to-heart talks with his cousin at
home. But it was all useless, for the very next time
we had our meeting Seriozha would again go to
sleep, overcome by irresistible boredom.

Diaghilev used further to annoy us by his "society manners," thinking it his duty to perform the thousand and one social conventions which we all despised and hated—to our parents' great disappointment. Seriozha made innumerable social calls, leaving cards and putting down his name wherever he could. He was infinitely more refined and careful in his way of dressing than were any of his comrades and even managed to look elegant in our clumsy student's uniform. In short, he tried to represent a real man about town and member of high society. None of us were in the least democratic. We all felt, quite consciously, an absolute indifference to politics and every shade of it; yet, at the same time, we had a certain reverence for whatever appeared to us to be a "living emblem of history," and to that category belonged Monarchy and the Sovereign himself, his court and the nobility represented in it. But we did not therefore try to penetrate into high society or to "bow" before anybody. It was loathsome to see Seriozha's ingratiating manner when he approached personalities of high standing in the first rows of the stalls, or when he went his rounds through the boxes in the first tiers. He seemed to assume a special insolence when performing these social "functions" and this manner of his was attacked and criticised by us so mercilessly that it was surprising how he tolerated it. His behaviour angered and annoyed not only his own friends, but our whole circle of acquaintances. My brothers and sister-in-law and all the Filosofov relations used to be furious with him. As a student, Diaghilev was never alluded to otherwise than as a "terrible fop," and this reputation continued to stick to him among his relations and intimate friends even in later years, after his merits had become obvious to all. It prevented Seriozha Diaghilev from being taken seriously for a considerable time. I ought perhaps to add here that none of us was taken

seriously outside our own circle and that our group
was quite unjustly nicknamed "the decadents."
The years when Seriozha was so meek and modest
in the company of his friends and so ridiculously
foppish in St. Petersburg society were years of growth.
Without any visible signs, concealing his inner life
from all of us except Dima Filosofov, Diaghilev was
rapidly filling up the blanks that were the result of
his provincial life. He also possessed "his own
baggage," but as it was not very brilliant it did not
impress anybody very much. By "his own baggage"
I mean music. The Diaghilevs' house in Perm had
once been a centre of culture not only for the town
itself, but for the whole district. In later years it
somewhat lost its significance owing to the change in
their financial circumstances, but music continued to
be cultivated far more seriously than it was wont to
be in the provinces. Seriozha's stepmother, who
loved him as if he were her own son, was especially
devoted to music. She was Elena Valerianovna,
née Panaev, the sister of the well-known singer and
daughter of the queer, extravagant old gentleman
who ruined himself in building an extremely ugly
theatre for private opera in St. Petersburg. Seriozha's
father was also said to be a fine singer and used to
sing in the circle of his friends and relations; the
musical taste of this retired guardsman was even
rather advanced for the time. Seriozha evidently
grew up in an atmosphere of music and was himself
extremely musical by nature.

Seriozha was slow and rather reluctant to acquaint
us with his musical "baggage." Having entered
our circle of "young men of the capital," who were,
on the whole, far more developed than he was and
expressed their opinions and taste in a very authoritative manner, he felt extreme embarrassment that
took some time to work off. But it was only natural
that Seriozha's opinions and convictions should be

rather muddled and inconsistent. We were all of us far from being mature. At that moment we had just discovered Wagner; next followed our infatuation for Russian music when we were ready to kill anyone who dared to disagree with us that Tchaikovsky's symphonies and some of Rimsky-Korsakov's orchestral compositions were the works of genius. We *swore* by them, and now despised what we had admired but a short time ago. I still vividly remember my indignation when I revisited the Italian Opera after a long interval and heard Donizetti's *Lucrezia Borgia*. I remember how enraged and insulted I was by anything typically Italian, including the extremely popular *Cavalleria Rusticana*, which had just then aroused such delight throughout the whole world, a delight that was also shared by Bakst. The main reason why we could not admit Seriozha at his full value even in his own sphere of music was that he not only loved *bel canto*, and admired above all, broad and expressive melody, but even went so far as to take singing lessons from the famous Italian baritone Cotogni, then living retired in St. Petersburg, and was prepared to sing in drawing-rooms that "despicable Italian stuff." Who could go further in vulgarity!

Nor were we in full agreement with Seriozha in our sympathies for Russian music. According to him he worshipped Tchaikovsky no less than we did, but as soon as we began to discuss some of the works of our favourite composer our opinions would clash. Some of our favourite works contained passages that we considered so trivial and banal that we would have liked to stop our ears when they were played. Those were precisely the passages that Seriozha chiefly admired. In them he found the "broad melody" that he adored. Indifferent to their quality, he was provoked to almost physical ecstasy.

Seriozha had, however, one first-class trump-card

and that was Mussorgsky. We had heard a lot about Mussorgsky, but at that period it was not so easy to get to know his music. His works were not given in either theatres or concerts. We accepted on credit the fact that he was the real genius of the "Great Five," for he was considered as such by "old Stassov," whom we now considered an authority in spite of our elders. Seriozha, on the other hand, actually *knew* Mussorgsky's music and not only his songs but even the piano score of *Boris Godunov*. The fact that Seriozha had such real knowledge of Mussorgsky's music would have done much in his favour, had he again not raved chiefly about Mussorgsky's "broad melody." His favourite part in *Boris* was the scene at the fountain, which was just what we liked the least, considering it to be far from the conception of the "ideal Mussorgsky" which we had formed for ourselves. At that period Seriozha himself was cherishing the hope of becoming a composer (it was to this end that he was taking a course at the Conservatoire) and it is interesting to note that when he sang his first effort in opera to us, it turned out to be a new version of the same Fountain Scene with a lot of extra "pathetic lyricism" added to it.

The reader will no doubt be interested to know about Diaghilev's attitude towards the ballet—the region of theatrical art where he gained his well-deserved fame in later years. The answer must be that Diaghilev showed no interest whatsoever in the ballet during his first years in St. Petersburg and if he did, from time to time, attend ballet performances with us, it was only for the sake of Tchaikovsky's music. Incidentally he considered the scores of *La Belle au Bois Dormant* and *Casse-Noisette* to be far inferior to *La Dame de Pique* and *Eugen Onegin*. It was not until considerably later that Diaghilev became attracted towards the ballet, which was not surprising for one who had spent his childhood in

Perm and had never seen a ballet before his arrival in St. Petersburg. At the beginning he even looked upon the ballet as something alien and slightly unworthy, which of course aroused many disputes, in which Seriozha was scolded for his insensitiveness and accused of being prejudiced. How great therefore was my surprise when, on visiting me in Brittany in 1897, Diaghilev suddenly confessed to me that he had become interested in the ballet during my absence—I was living then in France—and had visited it regularly with Valetchka during the last season. It must be admitted that in those days Diaghilev's interest in the ballet was of a definitely worldly and snobbish kind. The joys and delight which the ballet aroused in his friends—Valetchka, Kostia Somov and myself—were unknown to him. Bakst was another member of our group who, for a long while, remained distant to the ballet. There was no indication, in those days, of the decisive part they both were to play in the success of the *Ballets Russes*.

Seriozha's first outward sign of becoming involved in art expressed itself in the grand way in which he decided to furnish his new flat. He had just come of age and inherited a little capital left to him by his mother, who had died at his birth. The grandeur was somewhat relative, for it actually consisted in Seriozha filling his study with heavy, ornately-covered furniture and placing a dozen Jacobean chairs in his dining-room. The so-called Jacobean style was expressed by bronze stripes being glued on the mahogany. All these follies proved that Seriozha's taste was still immature, but it was significant that he should have wished to surround himself with a kind of magnificence, which did not correspond with the mask of modesty he had assumed when he first joined our group and which he retained even in the most intimate company. The walls, which had hitherto been hung with family photographs (his father's was taken in the brilliant uniform of the Horse Guards), were now adorned with pictures. His first purchase had been made at Bakst's insistence and was a good landscape by Endogurov, a young artist who died early in life. The next lot were bought after many consultations with me and consisted of a number of sketches by the unpretentious artist Kivshenko, acquired at the sale after the artist's death. It was then, too, that he paid ten roubles for a small sketch by Repin of a kneeling old woman. These pictures were not bad, though they were modest, but besides them Seriozha often bought and hung up on his walls all kinds of rubbish. It is true that all this trash disappeared very quickly at the insistence of his friends, without much protest from the young collector.

Diaghilev's first serious purchase was a set of sketches by Kramskoy. It was while he was buying this famous artist's water-colours and oil paintings that Seriozha first disclosed his passionate nature—which took me entirely by surprise. Having chosen a number of sketches from the mass of pictures owned by the artist's daughter, Seriozha used to bring them to me and stayed for hours discussing them and asking my advice as to the ones he should choose. He came about three times and at last all his walls were covered with Kramskoy's sketches. We even had to take Endogurov's picture from its place of honour to make room for a magnificently painted head of a Roman legionary in a bronze helmet. To this day I am not quite certain whether Seriozha really liked his purchases, but the fact that he now constantly had before him works that were of high technical quality proved beneficial in training his eye.

We began to visit Seriozha frequently, for his flat was on our way to the University. My natural pedagogic inclinations made me almost a daily visitor, for I felt it was my duty to watch over his purchases.

Seriozha had absolute faith in me and it was at this period that our friendship became more personal, for till then we had just been comrades belonging to the same group of friends. I was gradually becoming more tolerant towards Seriozha's "funny" sides, his bravado, his arrogance and the first signs of his despotism. Valetchka Nouvel's friendship with Diaghilev developed at the same time as mine and was founded on their common love of music. They used to play duets for hours at a time on the magnificent Blüthner piano which had arrived from Perm; Valetchka's talent for reading music was a great asset. I was not much impressed by these *auditions amicales*, for Seriozha's abrupt and very rough playing irritated me, but, being interested in the music, I was nearly always present. Nor did I often miss the improvised concerts given alternately at Diaghilev's and Filosofov's, where in addition to the recitals of our pianists, Seriozha's cousin, the kind Kolia Diaghilev, played the 'cello.

Chapter V

BIRLE AND NOUROK

GRADUALLY our company became divided into two groups or *cénacles*, as we called them, one of which was dominated by interest in plastic arts, the other in music. The first met at my house, the second usually collected at Seriozha's or the Filosofov's, but as both groups actually consisted of the same people it was difficult to divide them. The assemblies at my house, enhanced by a tradition of many years' standing, were rather more crowded than the others, the discussions on art more heated and passionate. It was the custom for the "artists" to paint and draw during the conversation; the musicians were expected to play. I literally steeped my guests in a profusion of books, journals and photographs, which they eagerly examined. Fruit and sweets used to be brought in with evening tea.

Seriozha's assemblies were of a more modest nature and sometimes, when music did not take the place of conversation, they used to become rather dull. I did not mind this, as I found pleasure in meeting the same people in a different setting. Actually the company was not always exactly the same in both cases. My special friends, Somov, Birlé and Nourok, hardly ever came to Seriozha's, while I, for an unknown reason, never invited some of Seriozha's relations, in spite of my being very friendly with them. Seriozha's delightful cousin, Pavka Koribut, Kolia Diaghilev, whom I have already mentioned, and the comical, unusually kind-hearted but somewhat cranky Visenka Proteikinsky, never came to my parties. A characteristic feature of Seriozha's assemblies was the large number of his relations; I never invited any of my family, with the exception of my nephew, Genia Lanceray, who had now grown up into a young man.

Our views on art at that period were distinctly influenced by Charles Birlé, a young official at the French Consulate. He had been introduced to me in 1892 by Arthur Aubert, who had taken pity on the young foreigner feeling so lonely abroad, having no friends. Our company proved congenial to him, for he had no interest in his work and was at heart a real artist. In fact, he was the same kind of art-maniac as Somov, Bakst and myself. It very soon became evident that not only could we give Birlé the atmosphere he was pining for, but that he too could be extremely "useful" to us. During his student years in Paris, Birlé had been entirely immersed in the intellectual life of Paris, studying all its aspects and sharing in all its infatuations. He worshipped impressionism—Gauguin, Van Gogh, Seurat—about whom our knowledge had been extremely vague before meeting him. In poetry he gave the first place to Mallarmé, Verlaine and Baudelaire, whom we again knew only by name (*Les Fleurs du Mal* was prohibited in Russia). Birlé also subscribed to a number of advanced reviews and magazines, like *Le Mercure de France, La Plume* and *La Revue Blanche*.

Birlé's views and opinions were far from being mature—in fact, the most contradictory ideas seemed to exist in his mind—but it was perhaps this that drew us towards him. Thanks to Birlé's influence (of which he was quite unconscious), we began to see what provincials we all were. Instead of being advanced as we imagined, we were actually quite backward.

We also began to realise how much we still had to learn and how many prejudices to get rid of. This development and rejuvenation of ours was not the pursuit of the latest fashion. On the contrary, any *dernier cri* dictated by the snobbery of fashion was hated by us with all the sincerity of our young hearts; we only gave up our old positions for new ones when we were thoroughly moved and convinced. Birlé, in his turn, thanks to being in contact with us and our sincerity, seemed in a way to become purified from the tarnish of snobbery with which he had been infected in Paris—the world centre of fashion. This interchange of influences, which expressed itself in passionate discussions and arguments, merely strengthened our friendship with Birlé. Although he only remained just under two years in St. Petersburg before he was appointed to a new post in Vienna, our friendship had become so strong that his departure was deeply felt by us all. I especially was inconsolable at the departure of the friend who had been so congenial, so indispensable to our circle, and for many years we kept up the most active correspondence. I sent him long letters containing innumerable new ideas and describing all the events of our circle and received similar ones in return from him, full of philosophy and frequently illustrated with delightful water-colours. On the strength of these paintings I persistently advised Birlé to break with his "vulgar Philistine" service and give himself up to his real vocation—painting. But alas, my friend did not follow my advice and I think he must regret it now.

It was Birlé who introduced Nourok to us and the latter soon became an indispensable member of our gatherings. Several years later, Nourok became one of our chief collaborators in the *World of Art*, where he was in charge of the Musical Chronicle and of the Satirical Sketches. Alfred Pavlovitch Nourok was one of the most curious and charming personalities that I have ever met in my life. The fact that he was a genuine and distinguished musician—I still remember some of his charming compositions—was one of the chief links between us, as was also his cult for E. T. A. Hoffmann, whom Nouvel, Somov and I had worshipped since the days of our youth. Hoffmann had once been the idol of Russian literature, but was now completely forgotten. It was Nourok, too, who gave the first practical impulse to our journal. For some years before he became acquainted with us, he had taken an active part in the comic paper *Pipifax* (founded in the 'eighties and published in St. Petersburg in German), to which he contributed humorous stories and biting anonymous notices. He generally favoured the periodical Press, being a firm believer in its reaction on the masses. His sophistication and love of paradoxes made him delight in puzzling people and he particularly enjoyed shocking the bourgeois.

In some ways Nourok took the place that had been formerly occupied in our circle by the positivist and materialist Skalon. His attitude at times slightly annoyed us, for we were much more inclined towards "everything mystical," whereas Nourok impersonated the ultra-critical and negative first principle—*den Alles verneinenden Geist.* He was also rather fond of posing as a cynic and even as a lover of refined depravity. Huysmans' *A Rebours,* which was in those days forbidden by the Russian censor, a collection of Verlaine's erotic poems and novels by the Marquis de Sade were Nourok's favourite books, and one of these volumes was usually to be seen peeping out of his pockets, which were always bulging with newspapers. All this was, to a large extent, nothing but a kind of affectation and a rather naïve pose which amused us all greatly. In reality, Nourok led a very quiet, decent and orderly life, worked as official in the Naval Ministry, and took tender care of his old mother with whom he lived. He was also anxious to be considered a drug addict or a Don Juan. This last, however, was not very easily believed, for his extraordinary outward appearance did not make it very probable: his bald head, inflamed, bespectacled eyes and funny little goat-beard had little in common with one's idea of the conqueror of hearts. His queer, mysterious ways were alluded to by us rather at random—by the Hoffmann expression *Skurrilität*. Nourok was the first to acquaint us with the drawings of Beardsley and T. T. Heine, which were later to have an important influence on our artistic creativeness.

Chapter VI

DIAGHILEV'S GRAND TOUR

BEFORE my marriage and during the first few months after my wife and I had returned from our honeymoon abroad, the members of our circle continued to assemble in my parents' home, where my sister Catherine Lanceray had been keeping house since my mother's death. In the autumn of 1895 we moved into our own apartment. Among the numerous pictures that adorned the walls of our flat there were very few of my own work, for the simple reason that I still could not quite make up my mind to consider myself a painter. In 1895, however, thanks to the fact that I had finished the University, was married, and had in August, 1895, even become the father of a delightful little girl, I felt obliged to "choose a profession" at last and therefore began to study painting seriously, giving up practically all my time to it. This drew Somov and me even closer together. He had finished the Academy and was surprising and delighting us all with his success.

Kostia and I began painting a portrait of my wife in a Directoire costume and also to illustrate some of Hoffmann's tales, but unfortunately nothing serious ever came of this.

During the first season of our independent life, my acquaintance with the artistic and literary world had grown considerably. Among the celebrities who often came to see us was the venerable painter Ilya Repin, the writer Merejkovsky and his wife, the poetess

Zinaida Hippius, the poet and philosopher Minsky, and several others. The international exhibition of the year in Munich gave me the occasion of coming into contact with the best Moscow painters: Serov, Korovin, Levitan, Archipov, Nesterov, for I was commissioned by a German promoter to form a section of the exhibition of young Russian painters. Through me the Muscovites became acquainted with my own friends and this proved to be most significant for the future stage of our collective activity.

At that time there was as yet no talk of any such active work, and we had even almost abandoned the idea of a collective publication in which we had sometimes indulged and which expressed itself in the shape of a more or less concrete dream about an art review.[1] Each of us had decided to step forward into the arena of art and some of us had already made a move towards this end. In 1893 I greatly surprised all my friends by writing without warning in the empty summer months the chapter on Russian painting for Muther's *History of Painting in the Nineteenth Century*—a book which created a sensation everywhere and was a real revelation to us. About the same time Bakst started working on an enormous historical picture—*Russian Sailors being Fêted in Paris*—which was an order from the Grand Duke Alexis. Both of us contributed regularly to the Exhibition of Watercolours, and in 1896 I celebrated my first definite success in the Spring Exhibition at the Academy.

The famous Moscow collector, P. M. Tretiakov, bought my picture *The Castle* (inspired by reading Maeterlinck) for his museum. This was extremely flattering to me and raised my authority as a creative

---

[1] Nouvel and I had started to talk about founding our own journal when we were still at the University, and I had even consulted my cousin Eugène Cavos about it, for he was then very enthusiastic about the idea of artistic publications. However, we soon got disillusioned with our plan and forgot all about it until, in February, 1897, it finally took a more concrete form.

artist among my friends, though in my heart of hearts I knew that my naïve and absurd picture did not deserve the attention it had received from so enlightened a patron of art. At the same period—the beginning of 1896—Diaghilev made his first attempts at art-reviewing in the rather independent newspaper *Novosti*, to which old Stassov was also a contributor. Seriozha was then thoroughly inexperienced in writing and his task was not an easy one. His rough draft was usually entirely re-modelled by me; our talks during these corrections were, I presume, useful in helping him to distinguish and formulate his own ideas and opinions.

Several months earlier Seriozha had undergone a change which one might compare with the turning of the chrysalis into a butterfly. I have already spoken of his gradual spiritual communion with our circle. In the summer of 1895, after having finished the University—a year later than we had—Seriozha, who had previously been twice abroad, but only for the sake of pleasure, now departed to travel "all over Europe" for the definite and unconcealed purpose of filling in the gaps in his artistic education. Before his departure, he came to ask for my blessing and advice, and I gave him several letters of introduction, among which was one addressed to the then famous Munich artist, Hans von Bartels, who was a distant relation of mine. Hans proved very useful to Seriozha by acquainting him with the artistic world of Munich and by helping him to acquire a number of important paintings.

The following letter which Seriozha wrote to us both from Antwerp on 15th June, 1895, is an unusually characteristic document:

"Dear Anna Carlovna and my dear friend Shura! For a long time[1] now I've been wanting to drop you a

[1] A "long time" meant a couple of weeks in those days.

line to remind you of my existence, but could not manage to write anything worth sending, because there simply hasn't been time to extract the quintessence of all I've seen and felt, what with visiting four and twenty museums and calling on fourteen painters in their studios. For that reason, too, I must put off, till we meet, any real discussion of certain artistic problems, of the greatest interest, which have cropped up in the last month.

"But here and now I swear that next winter, I shall put myself in Shura's hands, and solemnly declare him curator of the Diaghilev museum. I mean this seriously: who knows, a few years hence we may really have something worth-while. But whatever happens, the foundations will have been well and truly laid; however . . . silence! I refuse to reveal all the acquaintances I have recently made, lest I should spoil the effect. . . . I hope Shura will hearken to my call and agree to become curator of the museum, for I am now firmly convinced that so long as one does not attempt anything too ambitious, it would be possible to create something quite decent with three or four thousand roubles a year. There you have the practical side of my trip. Forgive this disjointed letter.

"Your friend,
"Seriozha Diaghilev."

A month after this letter Seriozha suddenly appeared at our country house near Peterhof. He was in the same mood of excitement as he had been when writing his letter. He nearly crushed me in his arms and presented me with an excellent drawing by Liebermann. Everything seemed to indicate that he had at last "found himself," and had begun to believe in his vocation. Of course nothing ever came of his "museum" (he was never really serious about it or about my "management"—it was merely one of our boyish jokes), but from that moment Seriozha began to be on the same footing with us all. The "Salon" that he started in his new flat, embellished with all the curiosities he had brought from abroad, now began to compete more seriously with mine; but this rivalry never became a petty competition.

My inclination for "free teaching" continued to find unusually fertile soil in Seriozha. One of the most valuable features of my "pupil" was his capacity for absorbing everything that could serve to develop his personality and his chosen work in life. Seriozha's attitude towards me remained for many years something like that of a pupil. It is true that the teacher (who was only two years older than his pupil) used sometimes to get annoyed with his pupil's incoherence, his daring and a certain lack of taste; but, on the whole, annoyance was easily outweighed by pleasure in his progress which was, indeed, far beyond anything that one could anticipate.

To return to Diaghilev's first ventures in criticism in the *Novosti*, I must add that, as soon as he felt he had the power of influencing people and experienced the rapture of talking to the masses, Diaghilev became and remained a promoter, a man who had a definite mission in life.

G

Chapter VII

MIGRATION TO PARIS

WE have again digressed from the subject, but it was necessary to acquaint the reader more closely with the principal members of the circle which was to become the society of the *World of Art*, its editorial staff, and later on a sort of laboratory for theatrical productions. We must now get to know the chief events which had taken place amongst us.

Several had migrated to Paris and settled there for a considerable period. My nephew Eugene Lanceray had been the first to leave in 1895. He had now become an excellent artist and had decided to complete his education in Paris, where he remained for three or four years. Genia was followed by L. Bakst, who needed Paris for the painting of his picture *The Reception of Admiral Avelan*. In the autumn of 1896 I brought over my small family and we settled in the Rue Delombre on the Mont Parnasse. In the spring of 1897 our dear friend Arthur Aubert and his young wife joined us in Paris and in the following autumn C. Somov became our neighbour. Diaghilev, Nouvel and Nourok would arrive from time to time and temporarily form a part of our colony.

Our "emigration" (which had nothing in common with politics, being purely and wholly artistic) had great significance for each of us individually and for our whole work, which was now defining itself as our own collective work. The mere fact that we had come into close contact with the artistic life of Paris, and personally established relations with several excellent French artists,[1] did much to reduce the slight taint of provincialism which was still inherent in me in spite of all our self-education in St. Petersburg. This was of particular importance, as our tastes had always shown a definite inclination towards the West, and each of us felt a spiritual necessity to come into closer contact with all that had charmed and attracted us for so long. We had no need to "discover Europe," as was the case with so many of our compatriots. We were already fairly well acquainted with it and were longing with all our hearts to participate actively in the life of the Western community. It was fortunate for us that all our circle had known French and German from childhood. Nothing we saw in Europe could confuse us by its novelty or unexpectedness; we seemed immediately to assimilate all that was new to us and none of us ever experienced any painful break or any embarrassment.

It was the same with our art, which was Western to its very foundation. It was only now that Somov, Bakst, Lanceray, Ostroumov and I were at last beginning to feel our wings. This proved of great importance to those of us who had the inclination or even the vocation to play a part in public life. Somov, Lanceray and Ostroumov abhorred any public function and even seemed to suffer from a certain form of misanthropy or agarophobia. Diaghilev, Filosofov and, to a certain extent, Nouvel and Nourok were not creative artists; only Bakst and I combined in ourselves both artistic creativeness and an inclination to "serve society"—and in me the sense of public duty was even stronger than in Bakst.

In spite of our *rapprochement* with the West, none of us ceased to love our own country. And it was in

[1] R. Ménard, L. Simon, Dauchez, Gaston Latouche, Charles Guérin, Valloton, etc.

the years just preceding our immigration to Europe that this love had reached a level of specific and passionate infatuation. It was expressed most vividly in our artistic enthusiasm. Those were the first years of our adoration for Tchaikovsky, Borodin, Rimsky-Korsakov and Mussorgsky, and I personally had combined my cult for Tchaikovsky with a passionate interest and study of St. Petersburg and its surroundings, where the sad and lovely poetry of our northern nature was so wonderfully and romantically blended with the sumptuous splendour of the Tsar's residences and Court life. I was deeply engrossed in research into the past of Russian Art and my chapter in Muther's book had been an outline of the History of Russian Painting in the Eighteenth and Nineteenth Centuries. My passionate enthusiasm acted on my friends and even infected them. Some of them tried to resist and to argue with me; they assured me that all my exalted ideas were nothing but dreams and illusory images born of a sentimentally morbid predilection. Others fully agreed with me and shared my enthusiasm.

Our conscious love for our country was closely related to our association with the West. When admiring the singular beauty of Peter's city, it was indeed impossible not to feel everywhere the power, the forethought and design of the founder. My adoration for Pushkin led me to share his cult for the grandiose figure to whom he had dedicated two beautiful poems and who was to be the subject of his unfinished historical novel. Besides, at that time, for many of us—and especially for me—our love for our country was united to a desire to serve her absolutely, and the service was somehow to be in the direction which had been given to Russia by her great Reformer.

In Russia much that was characteristically Russian annoyed us by its coarseness, triviality and unattractive barbarism. It was this coarseness that we longed to fight and to uproot. But the problem had to be solved with the greatest care so as not to harm or break what was really precious; for the good and the bad often lay close together. It was indispensable to save all that was being threatened by the levelling spirit of time, or by false nationalism.

I must again repeat that our Western orientation had nothing to do with politics; nevertheless we were all more inclined towards what is customary to call conservatism. Although, when the young Emperor, Nicolas II, ascended the throne in 1894, we shared with great masses of Russian people a foreboding of something evil, we had a genuine cult for the principle of monarchy. Our favourite figures in the past history of Russia were the representatives of enlightened monarchy: Peter, the Empress Elizabeth, Catherine II, Alexander I and Nicolas I. Even the insane Paul fascinated us by the tragic way he endeavoured to carry out the same principle, although, by nature, totally unsuited for the part. Correspondingly, in Western history, our sympathies were with Louis XIV, Frederick II and Queen Elizabeth of England.[1]

[1] If we were to divide the members of our group not according to our political views (which we lacked and even did not seek to possess) but according to our political *tastes*, Diaghilev, Bakst and I would have to be placed on the right wing, Somov and Filosofov would occupy the centre, Nourok, Lanceray and Ostroumov the left wing. Later on, when we were joined by Serov, Argutinsky, Yaremitch, S. S. Botkin, they reinforced *our* party; Argutinsky and Botkin were convinced monarchists.

Chapter VIII

THE WORLD OF ART

I STAYED in Paris for almost three years with my family (which had grown, as another little daughter had been born in 1898) and several of my friends, but in the spring of 1899 all the "St. Petersburg Parisians" were home once more.

In our native St. Petersburg and in our own circle, we found that important changes had taken place. We had already been informed about some of them, as the contact between our Paris group and our St. Petersburg friends had never been interrupted. Those were the days when people, and especially young people who were free, still knew how to write letters. There was an almost daily exchange of long letters flying backwards and forwards from Paris to St. Petersburg. Besides, I myself paid a yearly visit home. Thus, in January of 1897, I came back from abroad for a month and a half to organise an exhibition of Princess M. K. Tenishev's collection, of which I had charge, and in 1898 I spent three months in St. Petersburg in order to instal the Russian part of her collection in the new Russian Museum of Alexander III, to which it had been presented. At the end of 1898 I returned again to St. Petersburg for a very sad reason—the death of my beloved father on the 11th December (old style). Every time I returned to my native city I had the feeling that I had never been away; but I could not fail to notice certain changes that were taking place in our group of friends.

It was Seriozha who surprised me in a particularly agreeable way, for he had already begun to take his part as leader.

Diaghilev had got up his first exhibition of Scandinavian art in the autumn of 1896, and January, 1897, he was busy arranging the exhibition of British and German water-colour painters. In the following year I found him engrossed in the organisation of our first exhibition, which he was combining with that of several Finnish painters. At last, in the autumn of 1898, the same circle of friends had become the editorial staff of *Mir Iskusstva*, the *World of Art*. Financial support was provided by two patrons of art —Princess Tenishev and the manufacturer Sava Mamontov. The first number appeared in November, 1898, edited by its founder Diaghilev in close collaboration with Filosofov, Bakst, Nouvel and Nourok. I felt rather sad that, owing to my absence, the part I took in our review was limited in the beginning to the advice and criticism expressed in my letters; still, I could not help regarding the new-born publication as *my* child, for it was the realisation of what I had dreamed of for a long time, the fulfilment of my own "programme."

This is not the place to discuss our review, for its fate and character have no direct relation to my theme. It is remarkable that during the first two years of its existence there was never a line concerning ballet, and that even later on ballet was mentioned very seldom, and then only apropos a production that was being discussed, more often than not, by me. It is indispensable, nevertheless, to make quite clear what our editorial staff represented, for it survived, practically unchanged, throughout the six years of the journal's existence, and in 1905 became the unofficial committee of the great Portrait Exhibition of that year, and later was transformed, again unofficially, into the "directorate" of a new theatrical enterprise, from which originated the famous Russian Seasons in Paris, and, as a component element, what later became known as the *Ballets Russes*.

During my stay in St. Petersburg from December to January, 1899, I had a difference of opinion and very nearly quarrelled with my friends about certain tendencies of theirs in the choice of material. I was personally affronted in particular by Filosofov, who, being in charge of the literary department, had, "for tactical reasons," refused to accept one of my articles on a subject which remains vital to this day. This article was inspired by what has always played a dominating part in my attitude towards art—my fundamental aversion to all preconceived formulas, and to those in particular that were pernicious to what I thought valuable. Taking as a pretext an enthusiastic description of a picture by Peter Breughel (an artist I had grown to love ever since my first visit to Vienna in 1890), I undertook to defend not only "subject" painting, but even—*horribile dictu*—*genre* painting, whose preponderance in the Russian School I had hitherto attacked in the name of "absolute" and "pure" painting. Filosofov was afraid that my appeal for the eradication of certain prejudices would be taken as "yielding to the generally accepted opinion. Our disagreement took rather a serious turn. Nouvel and Bakst supported Filosofov, and at last I even announced my refusal to take part in the journal. Somewhat later, thanks to the influence of my friends, who could not admit the idea of my not taking part in what had become the common work of the circle, our difference was settled, and in the spring of 1899, when, on my return, I rejoined the staff, I felt perfectly at home and helped our review to get rid of certain compromises and show its real face.

It is possible that when I speak of "our editorial office" and "editorial staff" the reader may imagine a business-like office with special secretaries, desks, typewriters, files and so on. Such a picture would be entirely false. The editorial office of the *World of Art* was Sergei Diaghilev's apartment on the top floor of a big house at the corner of the Liteiny Prospect and the Simeonevskaya Street. Later on, in 1901, he moved to the second floor of No. 11 on the quay of the Fontanka, a house which stood next to Countess Panina's residence, and opposite Count Sheremetev's palace. Both these apartments were spacious, but on the whole quite ordinary. They differed from numerous similar apartments by having a more distinguished air, thanks to the good period furniture, pictures and sculptures which adorned them. These art treasures were the "foundation of Sergei Diaghilev's museum," but since 1895 the only additions to the "museum" had been a rather dull landscape by Verenskjöld and two unimportant landscapes from the exhibition of Scandinavian artists. The place of honour was occupied by three portraits by Lenbach (obtained in 1895), two drawings by Menzel, some water-colours by Hans Herrman and Bartels, a pastel portrait by Puvis de Chavannes and several sketches by Dagnan-Bouveret. The less important places were taken by the remains of Seriozha's first purchases—studies by Kramskoy and Shishkin and a small sketch by Repin.

The Jacobean chairs stood as before in Seriozha's dining-room. The drawing-room, which served our editor as study, contained, besides the Blüthner piano, several heavy, gilded, velvet-covered armchairs, a large velvet ottoman and some small antique Italian cupboards on which stood an excellent copy of Donatello's bust of Niccolo da Uzzano, several casts of Pompeian bronzes and numerous photographs of artists, authors and musicians, all autographed for Diaghilev. Here stood in close proximity Gounod and Zola, Menzel and Massenet. These were the

G*

trophies of 1895 when the young Diaghilev had found it necessary to convey his respects to a number of celebrities, although it was often not so much his reverence for them that prompted him to call on them as the impression he hoped to make on his friends by means of such "acquaintances."

A handsome, large, black, sixteenth-century table served as the "editor's desk." It had been brought by Seriozha from Italy, and was said to have aroused the envy of Wilhelm von Bode himself. Seriozha sat at the head in a very imposing armchair upholstered in old velvet. In front of him lay writing materials and among them a pot of glue and a large pair of scissors which served as a favourite distraction for him— Diaghilev was passionately fond of cutting out photographs from which reproductions were made in the review. . . . The rooms overlooking the yard were dull and dark and really rather resembled one's idea of a business office. Here were heaps of papers, kept in order by poor Dima Filosofov, who had voluntarily taken upon himself the ungrateful jobs of being simultaneously office manager, chief of staff, tutor and general secretary who had to receive all visitors. The large packages of reproductions sent from abroad were unpacked in these back rooms, where it was again Filosofov who sorted and numbered them before putting them away in the cupboards. It was here also that our other martyr—the next victim of Seriozha's despotism—Levushka Bakst spent whole days in inventing elegant titles for the drawings and retouching the photographs, in an attempt to give them a more artistic character. Sometimes the good-natured, easy-going Levushka would have sudden fits of rebellion and indignation, but more often he willingly—and, oh, how artistically!—spent his time manipulating Indian ink and Paris white. This work also helped him to earn something, for he was still in rather difficult circumstances.

The meetings of the editorial staff invariably took place in the dining-room, but they were entirely unlike those of other papers. The mere fact that they took place during tea-time, to the accompaniment of the hissing samovar, gave them a very homely, unofficial character. Seriozha's old nurse, who had taken the place of his mother during the first years of his life and was sincerely and tenderly loved by him, usually poured out tea. It was the custom for each of us to approach her and shake hands; I myself usually kissed her, for I had a real feeling of love for this venerable old woman with her faded and somewhat sorrowful face. His love for her did not prevent Seriozha from treating her in the "traditional rather masterly way." Without, however, really hurting her feelings, he used to scold and shout at her in fun; this she easily forgave, indeed, she was ready to forgive her favourite far graver pranks than those. How delighted the old woman would be when her former charge would suddenly begin hugging and pulling her about during one of his teasing moods. The nanny never took part in our conversation, and she probably couldn't make out what these noisy young people were up to, who disputed ceaselessly and sometimes laughed so un-restrainedly. What could she, an illiterate peasant woman, understand about painting, music, religion, philosophy or æsthetics? Nevertheless, it was clear that in her own way she really enjoyed being with us. She enjoyed seeing that Seriozha had so many friends and she probably felt that he was gradually becoming a person of importance, almost as important as his Papa, the General Diaghilev. Tea was always served with *krendeli* and *soushki*[1] and lemon cut in rounds. On the very rare occasions that Diaghilev entertained ladies, sandwiches of minced salt beef—*specialité de*

---

[1] *Krendeli*: biscuits in a figure-of-eight shape, *Soushki*: biscuits, shaped in rings, and made of different dough, strung on a stick.— *Trans.*

la maison—would be added to the usual fare, but nothing else was considered necessary. Diaghilev seldom took his meals at home and never invited his friends to lunch or dinner. If he found it necessary to entertain anyone, he invited them to a restaurant, for in St. Petersburg's French restaurants one could eat and drink exceedingly well.

Besides the old nanny, there was yet another figure who was a characteristic part of Diaghilev's household, his manservant Vassili Zuikov. In those days still a young man, he served Diaghilev till old age and now, by a strange freak of fortune and thanks to his devotion to his master's work, is ending his days in Paris. Vassili's appearance was not as picturesque as nanny's. He was small, and had an ordinary but rather clever face, to which a black moustache gave a rather military air not quite proper in a servant. Yet Vassili was what one might call the *perfect* servant; not that he was servile towards his master or other people in general; on the contrary, Vassili was very "independent" in his attitude and even, at times, verged on impertinence. Vassili's "professional" talent expressed itself in unlimited devotion to his master, a capacity that Diaghilev perceived at once, for he possessed a wonderful gift of detecting all kinds of talent. He immediately understood that Vassili was just the servant he needed, although from the purely decorative point of view he was not quite the thing.

Little by little, Vassili began to improve his position, while still technically valet to his master. When Diaghilev became "director of the travelling company," the manservant Zuikov turned into the "manager of the costume-department" and even became something like an assistant director and manager for the artists. He was also entrusted with various "secret" missions, which he performed zealously, always guarding Sergei Pavlovitch's interests. Vassili treated us all with varying shades of familiarity—some with more, others with less. He had a special respect for Serov, who, in his turn, was very fond of him—so fond indeed that the great artist once made him a present of his excellent water-colour sketch for Alexander III's portrait, predestined to be destroyed.

Chapter IX

FRIENDS OF OUR CIRCLE

IT is high time to acquaint the reader with Valentin Alexandrovitch Serov, who for some unaccountable reason his friends called "Anton" or "Antosha." Serov did not play an active part either in the *World of Art* or in our theatrical activities. He seemed to keep in the shade, but his significance in the inner life of our circle was enormous.

Serov, after Nourok, was the eldest of us and was already renowned as a famous artist when we all had barely started our careers. We were still schoolboys in the days we used to visit the Peredvizhniki[1] Exhibitions (where the leading elements of the time were grouped) and enthusiastically admire the portraits and landscapes by Serov. . . .

I was the first of our company to become acquainted with Serov in the spring of 1896, and soon after I introduced him to my friends. During my stay in France, Serov and I saw each other very rarely, for we could only meet during the short periods of my visits to St. Petersburg, but by that time the friendship between him and my friends had much progressed. During the exhibitions of British and Scandinavian Art arranged by Diaghilev, Serov had begun to trust in Seriozha's taste, in his culture and his energy, and therefore, although a member of the Peredvizhniki,

---

[1] Peredvizhniki, the "vagrants," insisted on the social significance of art; they organised travelling exhibitions—hence their name—to introduce art to the people.—*Trans*.

willingly agreed to take part in the first exhibition of the group arranged by Diaghilev in 1898. This in itself gave our beginning great weight, more weight even than the fact that Levitan, Nesterov and the best Finnish artists had also agreed to join us. From that moment Serov was *with us*, although it was not until some years later that he left his former colleagues.

It so happened that my family was spending the summer of 1899 in Finland, and that we found ourselves close neighbours with Serov, who was staying there with his old friend, V. V. Mathé, an excellent engraver on wood and brass.[1] It was there, during the summer months, that my acquaintance with Serov began gradually to turn into friendship, a friendship which never ceased to grow stronger, and was interrupted only by Serov's sudden death in the autumn of 1911. His loss was so deeply felt by us all, and caused us such sorrow, that it was in fact a calamity that affected our very lives. Twenty-seven years have passed since the ill-fated day when I received the grievous news of Serov's unexpected death in Moscow, but when I recall that moment I still feel the same blow, I experience the same deep, bitter feeling of resentment against fate. We all of us—and I especially—*needed* Serov. We needed him, not as a famous artist, an undisputed authority, whose friendship was at times not only flattering but even useful—by that time we were ourselves sufficiently known and did not need any support—but for the care of our *souls*, for the souls of each of us separately, and for the "collective soul" of our circle.

It is not easy to explain the strength of Serov's influence over us, but his influence was so great that in his presence the whole tenor of our intercourse was changed. At the beginning of our acquaintance I personally used to experience something I hated and

[1] Two years later Serov bought a site in Finland and had a timber house built there after his own design.

despised in myself. I used, involuntarily, to adapt myself to him and change my usual manner, and refrain from a certain inclination to buffoonery which I had probably inherited from my Italian ancestors. In our company we had adopted a sort of gay and jesting tone, which was not dropped even during conversations on the most abstruse subjects. This gaiety consisted of a good deal of teasing, a remnant of our school-days; it had become so habitual that we frequently indulged in it in the presence of strangers, often realising too late that we were behaving in an "unworthy" manner. At first we used to pull ourselves together in Serov's presence, but as we gradually got accustomed to him our inhibitions began to disappear, and at the same time, to our surprise and delight, a corresponding change took place in him. He began to be infected with "our manner" and we then saw that under the cover of moroseness and seriousness he concealed a very ready sense of humour that was quick to see the funny side of everything. Serov's jokes had a unique flavour and were presented in the manner for which the French have the excellent expression, *pince sans rire*. It was only when our fun transgressed beyond certain limits—as happens among schoolfellows—that Serov would show faint disapproval. He was not very fond of spicy stories, especially when they erred on the side of cynicism.

Serov did not in fact play an important part in the creation of our theatrical productions, but in 1909 it was he who made a beautiful drawing of Pavlova. The drawing was used for the poster which adorned Paris, announcing our first season. In 1911, when he was engrossed in Persian miniatures, he offered to design the curtain for *Schéhérazade*, which up till then had been given without any special "frontispiece." This work was beautifully done. In addition to this Serov had painted for the Imperial Stage the sets for his father Alexander Serov's famous opera *Judith*.

One of the scenes from this production was included in the programme of our first season. Serov was not very anxious to take a more active part in our theatrical work, as he could hardly find time to fulfil all the portrait orders which were showered on him. His portrait work did not prevent him from following with intense interest the work of his friends; we, on our side, had the greatest respect for his opinion, and valued it above everybody else's. When Serov approved of anything, it was a great joy. If he disapproved, even though other friends may have been pleased and perfectly content, our conscience was not clear and nothing seemed to remain but to re-make all that had been created, or rather, to search more intently for a more vivid and definite solution. Serov never pressed any of his personal views on anybody, but he seemed to demand from each of us that our ideas should be expressed fully. When we succeeded in this, his eyes alone, or a single word, dropped as if by mistake, or sometimes even just his characteristic silence, would make us feel that "the goal had been reached, the business done." In general, Serov was the only arbiter to whom we all submitted, including our leader Seriozha. I would even say that had Serov lived longer and been in contact with Diaghilev during the period when, owing to the war, he had lost all his original environment, Diaghilev would never have been allowed to follow so blindly the demands pressed on him by the snobbishness of Paris.

There were several other people who were in more or less close contact with the nucleus of the *World of Art*. Some of them were, in a way, our forerunners in the theatre; others, though they did not take a creative part in the general work, were nevertheless our friends and comrades—so much were we of one mind with them and in need of their moral support. Constantin Korovin and Alexander Golovin belong to the first category, Prince Vladimir Argutinsky-

Dolgorouky and the physician in ordinary, S. S. Botkin, to the second.

C. Korovin as a painter was greatly esteemed by us for a long time before we suspected in him a future theatrical artist. His pictures, or rather his sketches, of consummate artistry, nobly painted in strong, vivid colours, had often appeared at the Peredvizhniki Exhibitions, enchanting us as much as Serov's portraits and the landscapes of Levitan. Korovin, together with Levitan and Serov, were distinguished by the exceptionally high artistic value of their aims, which were in full accord with our ideal of art for art's sake. Korovin's art had for us particular merit in that his bold technical methods reflected the work of the French progressive school, with which we were not yet well acquainted. Although we felt a certain grudge against him for his light-mindedness and a certain inclination to be *chic*, he undoubtedly remained one of our favourite Russian painters. Then, suddenly, the Muscovite Korovin emerged as a highly interesting theatrical artist and even a sort of reformer in stage painting. In Moscow, his native town and residence, he was known to be a great lover of the theatre, willing to place his talent at its disposal; but through the lack of art-journals and of what is now called publicity, the news of what was happening in Moscow did not always reach St. Petersburg.

We had got to know the work of the Moscow artists only through exhibitions, but had, more often, to be content with gossip, which frequently proved absurdly false. Rumours, for instance, reached St. Petersburg about the amateur theatrical enterprises of a rich manufacturer called Sava Mamontov. It was said that he never employed professional artists, but only outside painters—in short, *real* painters. Even Victor Vasnetzov himself did not scorn to take part in the theatrical experiments that took place on Mamontov's estate; but nobody in St. Petersburg knew anything for certain, and by many people, even by such as were interested in art, all that happened in Abramtzevo[1] was looked on as the follies of a rich dilettante of the merchant class.

Mamontov's enterprise was, in fact, very far from being a "folly." If, at the beginning, it savoured of dilettantism, as time went on Mamontov acquired more confidence in himself. Encouraged by artists, he began to understand the significance of what he had undertaken and at last decided to bring it before a larger public. He created an opera company, with the object of presenting model performances of the best works of Russian composers and employing young artists, unspoiled by success. This gave Korovin, who had long been on friendly terms with Mamontov, the opportunity to distinguish himself as a theatrical painter.

In 1898 Mamontov's company paid a visit to St. Petersburg and it was there that we all (I had just come from Paris for a short stay) were able to see for ourselves how original and interesting was Korovin's treatment of scenic painting. I did not like everything—the planning was rather poor at times, and there was a certain roughness in the technique—but these shortcomings could have been explained by the very modest means the private enterprise had at its disposal. On the whole, Korovin's décors amazed us by their daring approach to the problem and, above all, by their high *artistic* value— the very quality which was so often missing in the elaborate productions of the Imperial stage. It was obvious that the path Korovin had chosen was the right one and needed only to be developed and improved.

As a result of his first efforts Korovin became a candidate for the post of theatrical artist, and when

[1] Abramtzevo: Sava Mamontov's estate.

it was offered to him by Teliakovsky, the Director of the Moscow office of the Imperial Theatres, Korovin very soon displayed the full scope of his talent. Since that time he has presented the Moscow and St. Petersburg stages with many magnificent décors, which, so far from being amateurish, astonish one by their maturity and technical skill.

Korovin's work with Mamontov, and on the Imperial stage, proved him to be a first-class *theatrical artist*—that is to say, an artist who possesses the peculiar gift of managing all the inevitable conventions of a scenic picture, without disturbing the fundamental character of the scheme. His knowledge of perspective was of enormous help to him, as also was his ability to organise his group of assistants with the least possible delay. He was lucky enough to have as collaborator so excellent a technician as Baron Klodt. This enabled him to work with the greatest speed and deliver his orders on time. If there is any fault to be found with Korovin's theatrical work, it is only that, thanks to his continual hurry, it was not always fully thought out.

In full contrast to Korovin was Alexander Golovin, another remarkable Russian painter who became entirely absorbed by the stage, in spite of the fact that he was not a professional of the theatre and that his best works—landscapes and portraits—have nothing specifically theatrical in them. In public opinion Golovin was indissolubly connected with Korovin— evidently because his work appeared on the Imperial stage at the same time, as they were both engaged by Teliakovsky. But as a matter of fact, Golovin had essentially nothing in common with Korovin.

Golovin's first décors and costumes created a real sensation. Diaghilev, who on his way through Moscow happened to attend a performance of Koreschenko's rather mediocre opera, *The Ice Palace*, was delighted with Golovin's décors and on his return to

St. Petersburg described them to us as a revelation. Outstandingly successful had been Golovin's representation of a winter night in the snow-clad Winter Palace Square illuminated from the windows of the Palace. Golovin's décor for the scene of the "Moot" in *Pskovitianka* can still be numbered among the classical décors for a typically Russian opera. From that moment the greatest hopes were built on Golovin, and when he moved from Moscow to St. Petersburg we began to expect miracles of him. Unfortunately we were soon to be disillusioned. The Moscow successes proved to have been flukes, and never again did Golovin rise to such heights. Every new production of the master both for the Maryinsky and Alexandryinsky Theatres seemed to show more and more clearly, that he was *not* a theatrical artist. Combinations of original and beautiful colouring would appear on the stage, but these combinations expressed either nothing at all, or else something absolutely out of keeping with the problem. Golovin's methods were not essentially theatrical. His first "mosaic" manner made the stage too patchy; the effect—especially in conjunction with his highly-coloured costumes—was kaleidoscopic and tended to divert the spectator from the action. His second manner, which was supposed to be more "thoughtful," actually achieved the absurd in the 1917 production of Lermontov's *Masquerade*, in which Meyerhold collaborated. The excess of detail was tiring, while the "over-refinement" betrayed a certain lack of taste and culture; this new manner of Golovin's suffered from the same defect as the first—the artist's scenic pictures were somehow inconsistent with the action.

The contrast between the creative theatrical work of Korovin and Golovin was apparent in their personalities. Both artists possessed great charm. Korovin's charm lay in his frank and open manner, in his ability to wear his heart on his sleeve and to reach, at once, an intimate footing with everybody. It is typical that Korovin and I began to say "thou" to each other from the beginning of our acquaintance—long before I did the same with Serov. With Golovin my relations remained unaltered from beginning to end. Korovin's great friendship with Chaliapin was characteristic of him. They adored each other; both had the same tastes and inclinations: both were fascinated by the freedom and space of country life and were especially fond of fishing, both loved to go on the "spree," in pleasant company, both seemed to have something Bohemian in their make-up. It is remarkable, too, that both of them were highly gifted story-tellers. I used to be fascinated almost as much by Chaliapin's *talking* as I was by his *singing*. In this respect Korovin was in no way inferior to Chaliapin; he even excelled his friend in minute and accurate observation of nature and the frequent strokes of genius with which he distributed his effects. Korovin retained his marvellous gifts in his old age and when he became an *émigré* they proved highly useful to him. Having become a writer, he literally "treated" the readers of the *Renaissance*[1] to the most fascinating stories, either drawn from the store-house of his wonderful memory, or composed so skilfully that no one could suspect that they were fiction.

Both Korovin and Golovin were exceedingly handsome in their young days. Although Korovin had a typical Russian face, his curly black hair, thick black beard and the roguish humour that sparkled in his eyes reminded one of a gipsy. His sparkling humour and certain "cunning" mannerisms of speech made some people think of him as shrewd. In fact, no one was further from intrigue than he; his thoroughly artistic and rather untidy nature would have prevented

[1] One of the two great newspapers published by the Russian *émigrés* in Paris.

him from following any premeditated plan—had such a strategy ever occurred to him. It was our suspicion of his shrewdness that, later on, was the cause of our falling out with Korovin. At first, influenced by his strong, long-standing friendship with Serov, we had taken Korovin straight to our hearts. Our difference with Korovin (which, however, never became a complete break) occurred because he remained perfectly faithful to his patron Teliakovsky, to whom he was much indebted, instead of joining "Diaghilev's camp," which occupied—as we shall see later—a definitely hostile position towards the Direction of the Imperial Theatres as a whole. Naturally Korovin could not well remain closely connected with us; but it did not follow that he should begin intriguing against us, as Bakst has insinuated.

My relations with Golovin remained always unchanged. When I first visited him in Moscow in 1899, I was extremely surprised by the "aristocratic complacency" which he displayed. In spite of the very modest surroundings in which I had found him (at that period he had painted only decorative panels of northern landscapes and was not yet actively engaged in work for the theatre), he gave the impression of a real aristocrat, though in difficult circumstances. I was therefore extremely surprised to discover that Golovin had nothing in common with the noble family bearing the same name. His striking outward appearance was due to his height, his good manners, his voice and intonation and his handsome face with its noble profile and thick, fair moustache.

I was received so kindly by Golovin when I first visited him that I felt sure we would soon be friends, particularly as he heaped compliments upon me. At the same time I greatly admired his talent, above all his exceptional gift for colour. But nothing came of my friendship with him, nor did he become intimate with any of our circle, in spite of the fact that he moved to St. Petersburg in 1901, and that everything seemed designed to draw us together. The chief reason was, as it was for Korovin, Golovin's even closer connection with Teliakovsky, but partly it was the fault of his character, his distrust of people, his suspiciousness and his inability to become intimate with anyone. Such was his attitude not only towards us but towards everybody in general. He went nowhere and never received guests at home. All sorts of legends circulated about his intimate life, but hardly anybody had ever stepped across the threshold of his flat near the Lion's Bridge. In fact, he was seldom there himself, for he spent almost all his time in the huge studio that had been built especially for him above the auditorium of the Maryinsky Theatre. The only persons to whom he was undoubtedly devoted were the Director and the Director's wife. He was a sort of artistic adviser to her, for Guria Longuinovna Teliakovskaya was fond of "taking a hand" in the productions; the *invisible directrice* was, indeed, said to be the real source of her husband's inspiration and to surpass him in general intellect and artistic flair.

Chapter X

DIAGHILEV'S ANNUAL

I HAVE called Korovin and Golovin our fore-runners, and so they were, but this statement demands a certain reservation; both of them were essentially free artists—and not theatrical professionals —who were called upon to work in the theatre several years before we were. But here the matter ends, for their theatrical work differed from ours in character and aim. They differed from us, too, in their artistic culture and their taste. It cannot be said that they "showed us the way to the theatre."

The reader has seen how greatly, from my earliest years, I was attracted by the theatre, and how I longed to take part in it creatively; my friends were infected by the same enthusiasm. In 1899, during our University years, we attempted, all together, a sort of pantomime on the subject of *Daphnis and Chloe*; during the same period Nouvel and I tried to compose something like an opera or a "musical drama," taking as our subject the Hoffmann tale which had inspired Wagner to compose the *Meistersinger*. At one time we were much preoccupied by a symbolic drama *à la Maeterlinck*; its lengthy and extremely muddled story was to be given with the aid of a magic lantern —to produce the effect of the Chat Noir's *ombres chinoises*, or, if one strains the point, as a sort of "premonition of the cinematograph," the invention of which was not so far off and seemed already to be "somehow in the air."

It was I who usually conceived and inspired these fancies, but Bakst, Somov, Lanceray and Birlé all joined me with enthusiasm. Once again I must put on record how greatly I was impressed by the Meiningen company which had visited St. Petersburg in 1885 and 1890. Never before had the part of the stage-manager and producer achieved such eminence; it was only natural that the stormy ovations which invariably greeted the Meiningen performances should have been directed not only at this or that actor, but at the company's principal producer, Chronegk. From then on my ambition—and it survived even during my period at the Academy of Arts—was to become a "second Chronegk." I wanted to become a stage painter only in order to be able "to do everything in the theatre," to be complete master and manager of the stage.

This passion of mine was well-known to my friends, and when, in 1899, our common acquaintance, Prince Serge Volkonsky, was appointed Director of the Imperial Theatres, all our group established a closer contact with the theatre and I found myself a sort of private adviser to the directors. Volkonsky, with whom I always willingly discussed theatrical subjects, considered me to be a great connoisseur of the theatre, a dreamer of many reforms, from whom he expected to hear new suggestions. Diaghilev regarded me in the same light; he still continued to a certain extent to treat me as his "teacher," and of course considered that "Shura would now show his mettle."

I myself had no doubt that I would now be called upon to take an active part in the work of the theatre. The fact that my two greatest friends had been attached to the administration—Diaghilev for special duty and Filosofov in the important position of a member of the repertory committee—only served to strengthen my hopes and aspirations. But several months passed without anything being entrusted to

ALEXANDRE BENOIS
From the portrait by *Léon Bakst*, 1898

Facing page 204

PRINCE SERGEI MIKHAILOVITCH VOLKONSKY
From the portrait by Repin, 1893

Facing p. 205

any of us. Volkonsky kept on apologising, without concealing from us that he was rather afraid of giving work to outsiders, as it might displease his subordinates. Every conversation we had about possible projects invariably ended with the Prince's appeal "to be cautious," and he was especially fond of repeating two sentences: "Il ne faut rien brusquer" and "Nous nageons dans le tact."

It was during the first months at his new post that Diaghilev's behaviour particularly annoyed and irritated the society of St. Petersburg. Dressed in his smart, faultlessly-fitting uniform, he had a way of walking through the stalls, his head in the air, which made tongues wag and gossip about him—often unfounded—spread like wildfire throughout the town.

After a time Volkonsky summoned up his courage and gave us some active work to do. His caution did not allow him to entrust us with any significant work on the big stages, but he gave Bakst and me an opportunity of showing our mettle in the performances at the Imperial Hermitage Theatre. This was rather an honour as the performances were attended only by the Imperial Family and the court. Bakst proved to be luckier than I, for he was given the task of producing a graceful little play, *Le Cœur de la Marquise*, which enabled him to show his marvellous feeling for colour. Against the white background of the exquisite little *empire salon* the costumes stood out in a most distinctive harmony of shades. I myself was entrusted with the production of a one-act opera by Alexander Taneyev, but as the music of this statesman-composer was absolutely devoid of talent it could provide me with no material for inspiration. At first I even tried to refuse the task, but the insistent persuasion of Volkonsky made me accept the order. As was to be expected, the opera had no success and was not transferred to the big stages. Neither could

my setting be called successful, although the theme—
"a French park of the eighteenth century"—seemed
to be a suitable one for me. The sketch had not
been bad, but the execution of the work in the proportions necessary for the stage had been done by
uninspired, though very experienced specialists, and
was so dull that it made me sick to look at it, the more
so because, for economic reasons, the costumes had
been borrowed from various other plays and did not
suit the background at all. Thus it happened that
my first experience on the real stage had proved to
be *un four incontestable*!

Volkonsky also offered work to Somov, but my
witty and fastidious friend had firmly refused to take
part in any productions, and only agreed to contribute
to the Hermitage performances by making some
programmes, in which his original decorative gift was
fully displayed.

In 1900 Volkonsky at last entrusted Diaghilev with
some responsible work: he was to compile the coming
volume of the *Annual of the Imperial Theatres* of that
year. Seriozha set to work at once with his customary ardour which even made him cool down considerably towards his duties as editor of the *World of Art*.
He even forced *me* to work for the *Annual*, in spite of
all my remonstrances. From the autumn of 1900 I
was the editor of the historical-artistic journal *Art
Treasures of Russia*, which took up a lot of my time.
Besides endless consultations and the choice and
criticism of all the materials, my part in the *Annual*
consisted of an article on the Alexandryinsky Theatre
—that *chef d'œuvre* of Russian *empire*. Poor Bakst, on
the other hand, nearly perished from the labour of
retouching photographs; for it was essential for the
needs of this publication that even the unavoidable
portraits of important artists in their theatrical
costumes should be in impeccable taste. But in spite
of his grumbling, Bakst used to be rather fascinated

by his work of deftly putting in romantic backgrounds in the place of the commonplace studio settings.

Diaghilev's plan was to stagger the world with his *Annual*. He thought that after that, it would become plain to everybody that he was capable of "great deeds," that perhaps the Emperor himself would be convinced of how talented a worker he was, and that this would enable Volkonsky to make of him his chief and most active assistant. It is just possible that our friend's ambitious plans—which he did not always hide from us—included the hope that he would, in time, replace Volkonsky himself and establish in the Imperial Theatres an era which would survive for posterity as "The Diaghilev Era." It is also possible that Volkonsky was not quite blind to the dreams and ambitions of his brilliant subordinate —in any case, in his relations with Seriozha, a certain watchfulness not unmixed with suspicion began to appear. He sometimes complained to me about Seriozha, mostly about his lack of tact—which, he implied, was liable to do harm to the best intentions. I remember one luncheon with *Son Altesse Serenissime*— as we jokingly called dear Volkonsky—during which he never stopped complaining about Seriozha and begging me to use my influence with our common friend. But was there anyone alive capable of influencing Seriozha, at a time, above all, when he was possessed by hopes that he considered very near to achievement?

There can be no doubt whatsoever that Diaghilev succeeded marvellously with the *Annual*. It could hardly have been otherwise, for when he was possessed by the wish "to do a pamps,"[1] he managed to break through all obstacles; everything had to give way to his wishes, which were usually expressed in the shape of demands. The *Annual* had undergone a real metamorphosis under Diaghilev's editorship. In former

[1] To create a stunning effect—this was Diaghilev's favourite expression, which possibly may have dated from the years of his childhood.

years it had been a useful but decidedly modest publication, printed on paper of mediocre quality and bearing all the signs of economy. Even so, as a chronicle of Russian Theatres, it was of exceptional interest, and represents, to this day, an indispensable collection of documentary value. Now, from under Diaghilev's hands, instead of the usual modest and useful publication, there appeared something that was monumental and luxurious.

I remember vividly how impressed we were with the Diaghilev qualities of the *Annual*, although we ourselves had taken part in it. It was a large, heavy tome, whose cover alone was impressive, thanks to the style of the title (the letters were drawn by either Bakst or Lanceray). The contents of the volume were in keeping with its outward appearance. Every page seemed to present a treat for the eye. It even gave one pleasure to see the type, the lay-out of the page, the way the illustrations were distributed. The illustrations themselves were all chosen with taste and excellently reproduced from faultless plates. Several supplements—among which Somov's Hermitage programmes and an original lithograph by Serov were outstanding—gave the transformed *Annual* an added distinction. Nor was the documentary side forgotten. The articles on the Alexandryinsky Theatre, on Vsevolojsky and on the great decorator Gonzago, whose forgotten drawings I had succeeded in finding in the theatrical archives, were included in the text of the volume. All statistic material, administrative orders and other "undecorative" things were published in a separate supplementary volume. This made Diaghilev's edition even more impressive.

The appearance of Diaghilev's *Annual* created a sensation in St. Petersburg. It was two years since we had started publishing the *World of Art* and although our review had gained many friends and admirers during that time, the general public still regarded it as the fad of impertinent, "decadent" youngsters who only published it in order to challenge everything that was reasonable, honest and secure in Russian Society. This absurd notion about the *World of Art* made even our patroness, Princess Tenishev, withdraw her financial support. Unkind caricatures of her had appeared, showing her handing over money to us for our enterprise. Princess Tenishev's refusal to continue her patronage was felt all the more because our second patron, Sava Mamontov, had also left the ranks, having got into trouble with the law courts on account of some of his industrial enterprises. But it so happened that we were saved by the Emperor, who gave 10,000 roubles from his private funds—thanks to Serov's intercession; otherwise our review would have ceased to exist. Our failure would, no doubt, have been spitefully welcomed in many quarters, where it would have been found particularly gratifying that the principal "leader of the decadents," Diaghilev, should be "punished for all his wicked doings." The appearance of the *Annual* produced the first signs of a change of public opinion in favour of Diaghilev. Here at last was something in which there was nothing to criticise; even Seriozha's bitterest enemies were obliged to agree that this edition was the first of its kind in Russia—never before had such a book been published, and, what is more, by a government institution, where official routine had always reigned supreme.

Chapter XI

THE SYLVIA CATASTROPHE

UNFORTUNATELY the success of the *Annual* made our friend lose his head. The result was a catastrophe which had fatal consequences not only for him personally, but in many ways for all of us, and in a certain degree even for the Russian Theatre as a whole.

Just when we were united in our dream of Diaghilev becoming the head of Russian theatrical work, and when our dream seemed near to realisation, precisely at that moment Diaghilev committed a *faux-pas* that completely severed his connection with the Imperial Theatres. After his triumph with the *Annual*, Diaghilev began to over-estimate himself and his significance, thinking that his path was clear. Being in friendly relations with the Grand Duke Sergei Mikhailovitch, he had heard from him about the excellent impression the *Annual* had made on the Emperor himself, and it now seemed to Diaghilev that he could rely entirely on this all-powerful support. These dreams were, alas, soon to be shattered and, strangely enough, it was Delibes' ballet *Sylvia* which happened to be the innocent cause of the catastrophe. . . .

The reader already knows about my cult for Delibes, which dated from the time I had first seen and heard *Coppélia* in 1884. This cult had not ceased to grow since then and had even become more conscious and deliberate. Delibes was worshipped by other members of our circle—by Nouvel, Nourok and Somov—and even Diaghilev became infected with our enthusiasm. From the moment Volkonsky was appointed director and Diaghilev became his assistant, my burning desire was to honour Delibes by creating for him a supreme memorial—a perfect production of one of his works. We did not want to attempt *Lakmé* for the reason that there was nobody who could undertake the chief part. *Coppélia* was already in the repertoire and was extremely popular in spite of its very commonplace production. There remained *Sylvia*, the music of which was in parts even more inspired and poetical, and contained a greater variety of nuances than either *Lakmé* or *Coppélia*. Besides this *Sylvia* would have had the advantage of being a novelty, for it had never been produced in our theatre. We therefore began to "thrust" *Sylvia* upon Volkonsky from the very beginning of our talks and consultations. As a matter of fact, the Director raised no objections, but here again, as was his usual way, he begged us to wait, to be patient, saying that the programme was complete for two years ahead and it was impossible to introduce another new production, especially a model one. We consented to wait patiently, but reminded Prince Sergei Mikhailovitch about *Sylvia* on every possible occasion.

At last, in January, 1901, the moment came when our wish seemed likely to be fulfilled and our group was actually to create the production of *Sylvia*, while Diaghilev, to whom Volkonsky had promised full powers for this occasion, was to act as intermediary between us, the creative artists and the directors of the theatres. This, at any rate, was the way in which Diaghilev, in his great excitement, put the case to us. The news was received with great joy and we started on the spot to distribute the work. It was decided to invite the two brothers Legat to be our ballet-masters, for they were the most prominent of all the

H

young dancers; the part of Sylvia we assigned to O. O. Preobrazhenskaya, for whom we had the greatest admiration as the creator of the parts of Raymonda and Javotte. The question as to whether such a combination of unofficial people, working independently in an institution so bound by red tape, would be possible, never entered anybody's head. Seriozha was the last to have any doubts, for since the publication of the *Annual* he seemed to be intoxicated with his success and in this scheme of ours he saw the way to rise quickly to the very top, to show the world that he possessed all the ways and means— the means were us—to produce creations never before imagined. . . .

But poor Seriozha had too great an idea of his own power. He was so simple as to think that others would *wish* him to triumph and see the *chef d'œuvre* he dreamed of appear on the Imperial Stage. It is quite possible that, under the pressure of Diaghilev's energy, Volkonsky did promise him full power, but in a few days' time the Director suddenly "came back to his senses." It happened after his consultation with his immediate official collaborators, the "head of the office" and the manager of the stage properties department. These people were not in principle against our scheme; on the contrary, I well remember how attentively the latter of these two officials, Baron Kussov, followed my corrections and remarks during the rehearsals of some new productions, and even made detailed notes of them in his pocket-book. All my wishes would be scrupulously observed in the following rehearsal, and this, I must confess, greatly flattered me. An equal degree of attention was paid by both Baron Kussov and another official, Petrov, to Bakst's opinion and judgment, although Bakst, like me, had no official standing and was present at the rehearsals only as a guest of the Director. . . . This state of affairs might have gone on for a long time and without friction, till at last, by a process of gradual evolution, we had become part of the staff of the theatre. Such a process was certainly envisaged by the cautious, courteous and sympathetic Volkonsky, but was essentially distasteful to Seriozha, who was always strongly inclined towards a *coup d'état*. Such a *coup d'état* very soon took place on account of *Sylvia*, but its consequences were far from beneficial to Diaghilev; they led him to something very like a catastrophe which he needed all his vitality and strength of character to overcome.

It started with Volkonsky confessing to Seriozha that, after consulting his subordinates, he had come to the conclusion that it was impossible to take a whole production out of the hands of the general management and entrust it to Diaghilev, who was not officially entitled to it. Therefore he now came to Diaghilev, as a friend, and asked him to undertake the production of *Sylvia*, but not as its completely independent director. Volkonsky assured Seriozha that everything would remain as before, that he, Diaghilev, would, for practical purposes, be the director and that all his group could carry out what they had planned, but that officially the production would be controlled by the "Management"—that is to say, by Volkonsky himself—and then nobody could possibly be shocked. But at that point Diaghilev took the bit between his teeth. He insisted, very decidedly, on retaining the powers already given him and very soon the conversation, which had started amicably, developed a distinctly unpleasant tone. Losing his self-control, Diaghilev even resorted to a kind of blackmail. He announced to Volkonsky that, should *Sylvia* be taken from him, he would refuse to publish the next *Annual* already in preparation. Volkonsky naturally became indignant and, as often happens with easy-going, good-tempered people, suddenly raised his voice and, taking the tone and attitude of a superior, announced that in such a case he, Volkonsky, *ordered* Diaghilev to proceed with the *Annual*, and if Diaghilev did not agree to obey him, he would ask him to resign. Immediately after this conversation, Diaghilev dashed home, where he found the entire "editorial staff" at his table having the usual five o'clock tea. We were all so convinced that we were actually to create *Sylvia* that we had sat down to tea only after having worked for several hours at sketches for our production. Some of us had taken possession of the dining-room, others were busy in Seriozha's study, while even the back rooms were strewn with drawings and sketches. I distributed the work and gave directions and had just sketched the plan of the décor for the first act; Lanceray was busy with the third act, which was to be in the style of Claude Lorraine; Korovin was working at the second scene of the second act; Bakst had been entrusted with creating Orion's cave and almost all the costumes; even Serov, carried away by the general enthusiasm, had started on a sketch of the principal satyr, in which he was succeeding admirably. It was just at this moment that Seriozha returned. He came in looking preoccupied, and after several seconds in private with his cousin Filosofov, began telling us about his conversation with Volkonsky, describing everything in detail.

The effect produced was not quite what he had expected. Korovin, frightened at the thought of losing his job on the staff of the theatre, began at once to implore us to be careful. I tried to pronounce a few "words of reason." Serov became gloomy and silent as usual. But Bakst, Filosofov, Nourok and Lanceray all flared up with holy indignation at Volkonsky's "treachery," and suddenly we all decided that we must get up a punitive demonstration against Volkonsky. I started to compose a rough draft of a letter in which I reproached Volkonsky for being ready to take sides with officialdom against his own friends and supporters. Later I sent this letter from home by hand. Filosofov wrote a similar letter; Korovin, who had promised Diaghilev to send in his resignation, never fulfilled his promise.

I am certain that by then Volkonsky was already suffering from the turn things had taken on account of so innocent an enterprise as the production of a ballet. When he received Seriozha's letter confirming his refusal to edit the *Annual*, Filosofov's resignation and my own letter, he decided to make an attempt to put matters right. He was supported in this by V. A. Teliakovsky, who happened to have arrived from Moscow. When we assembled the following day, we were suddenly informed that Volkonsky and Teliakovsky were on their way to our editor's office. For two whole hours they tried to persuade Seriozha and us to let bygones be bygones, and all of us to be friends again, especially as "we were all surrounded by enemies and half St. Petersburg was only waiting for a scandal to take place during the Prince's directorship." Teliakovsky was the more insistent; Volkonsky very soon became silent and sat in the corner of the sofa, looking gloomily from side to side, his eye-lashes and moustaches trembling nervously—a sign of great agitation. When they were leaving, and we had all gone into the hall, Volkonsky took me into a corner and half-whispered: "I have received your letter, but it is a letter not from this 'World of Art' but 'not of this world,'"— a *jeu de mots* which he had probably composed before and could not keep back even at so pathetic a moment. I must confess that I felt very much inclined to answer back something like: "You are quite right, and the whole thing is really a lot of nonsense," but in view of the stubborn position taken by our "leader," and in deference to the "general discipline," I remained silent and was only filled with pity for Volkonsky, who was suffering visibly. *Le beau rêve* of which he had been dreaming for the last two years was threatening to melt away into air. . . .

Behind this dramatic incident, there was another side about which, at that moment, we had been kept in the dark, but which encouraged Diaghilev to persist on the spectacular break. The Grand Duke Sergei Mikhailovitch was active in the wings. His friend—one of our famous ballerinas—heartily hated Volkonsky. Both she and the Grand Duke passionately desired Volkonsky's dismissal, hoping that His Imperial Highness himself would then get the post of director of the Imperial Theatres. A new title had even been invented by them; the Grand Duke would not be called "Director" but the "August Manager." Diaghilev had been promised an important position. The Grand Duke—whom Diaghilev saw daily—encouraged him to resist Volkonsky, assuring him that Volkonsky would be the one to go, as the Emperor could not bear him. In any case—and this was his most convincing argument—should the position become critical, he would have no difficulty in obtaining the Emperor's support. Actually the Grand Duke left the same day in a special train for Tsarskoye Selo, where he explained the whole incident to his cousin.

It has since been said on Diaghilev's authority, that the Grand Duke went to Tsarskoye Selo about this business not once, but several times. This seems rather improbable and certainly we—at the time—had heard nothing of it. One feels inclined to suspect here a case of "stylized ornamentation"—as they say in Russia—on the part of Seriozha, who was generally prone to sin against strict accuracy in his tales. On this occasion, the fact that the person of his Sovereign Lord and Master was involved must have increased the temptation.

However, whether the Emperor was approached once or several times, he seems to have agreed with Diaghilev's point of view. The Emperor had even pronounced the somewhat puzzling phrase: "In Diaghilev's place I would not have resigned."

After hearing this, Seriozha firmly believed in his security and that the whole affair would be ended by a full confession from the arrogant Director who had dared to assume an authoritative tone with him, Diaghilev. Volkonsky was informed that Diaghilev was persisting in his refusal to edit the *Annual* and would not agree to the Director's demand that he should hand in his resignation. It was then that the miniature drama came to a climax quite unexpected by Diaghilev.

The day after the Grand Duke's visit to Tsarskoye Selo, General Rydzevsky, one of Diaghilev's personal enemies, went there with the usual report on the affairs of the Imperial Household, in place of the minister, Baron Fredericks, whose assistant he was. He had in his portfolio an order prepared for the Emperor's signature, an order for the summary dismissal of S. P. Diaghilev. We never knew whether Rydzevsky succeeded in reporting the episode in a new light to the monarch, or whether Nicolas II did not realise that his earlier statement had given Diaghilev confidence in his support, but the order was signed by the Emperor.

The following day being Sunday, there was no publication of the Government Gazette, but when Diaghilev unfolded the paper on Monday morning, secretly hoping to find in it Volkonsky's resignation, he found his own name accompanied by the disgraceful words: "according to article three." In this form the dismissal had a definitely ignominious character, as article three was only applied in exceptional cases and only in connection with disreputable behaviour.

One can imagine Diaghilev's horror, shame and grief. All his hopes and plans had collapsed in one minute, and he, who had dared to hold out against a very high dignitary, who had had the support of the Grand Duke, and even, as it seemed, that of the Monarch himself; he who had seen himself in Volkonsky's place, reaping triumph after triumph, was now cast out and was "finished" when still at the height of his strength and capacities.[1] The position seemed to be absolutely irreparable. Diaghilev's despair turned to fury when he thought of the triumph of all the "worthless officials"; when he realised that Volkonsky's position of genuine *grand seigneur* was of some use to him, whereas his own position of a gentleman *tout court* had turned out to be a broken reed. . . .

[1] It was only later that the Emperor realised the injury done to Diaghilev by his "ignominious" dismissal. When he became aware that Diaghilev would be forever banned, by law, from any kind of State service, he is said to have expressed himself in the words: "What a stupid law!"

Chapter XII

WE ATTACK TELIAKOVSKY

THE consequences of the *Sylvia* catastrophe were innumerable and of immense significance not only for Diaghilev, whose career had undergone a complete change, but also for all our circle. It is true that we were united by our review, which continued its existence during three more years, and it is true also that Diaghilev continued to arrange our exhibitions, and that each of us went on with his own personal job. I myself, for instance, continued to edit my *Artistic Treasures of Russia*, to illustrate books and to bring back a number of sketches after every summer. But all this did not alter the fact that our group, and especially our leader, Diaghilev, had ceased, as far as the theatre was concerned, to have any importance whatsoever. Nevertheless, for the Russian ballet, the results of our catastrophe were of actual advantage. Had Diaghilev remained on the staff of the Imperial Theatres and we become his chief advisers, the Russian ballet would hardly have achieved its world renoun.

Diaghilev's despair and confusion after the "*Sylvia* episode" did not last very long. The fact that Volkonsky himself handed in his resignation a few months later was a certain consolation. The incident with M. F. Kshesinskaya, who refused to obey the Director's orders, served as pretext, but the real reason was that, having lost all his collaborators and supporters, Volkonsky was unable to carry on. No

H*

doubt, too, he was uneasy at the thought that he was the cause of his friend's having received so severe a lesson. This became clear to me some years later when I had with Volkonsky one of those heart-to-heart talks in which Russians are apt to indulge. It is curious that the two enemies made it up years later, and even began to "thou" each other. . . . But in 1901 there could be no talk of a reconciliation, for Diaghilev hated Volkonsky with all his heart and wished him every misfortune.

Teliakovsky's appointment to Volkonsky's post revived Diaghilev's hopes. He had appreciated Teliakovsky when he was just beginning his career in Moscow as director of the Moscow department of the Imperial Theatres, and had been delighted with some of his productions. Every time Diaghilev went to Moscow he made a point of calling on Teliakovsky and made friends not only with him but also with his wife. Finally, the fact that Teliakovsky had come with Volkonsky on the memorable day of the unsuccessful peacemaking, and had used all his powers of persuasion to induce the enemies to make it up, gave Diaghilev cause for hope.

Unfortunately Diaghilev was to be disappointed. Teliakovsky was very different from the kind, noble-minded but rather inconsistent Volkonsky. Teliakovsky was a retired officer of the Household Cavalry, and had retained all his military ways, in spite of his new post; nevertheless, under his mask of rough good-nature was concealed what the French call *une fine mouche*. It was only natural that it did not at all suit his plans to have in his department a man as ambitious, cultivated and attractive as was Diaghilev. He was quite ready to use us—"Diaghilev's artists"—but he did not want us to act as a sort of board of trustees for him. All this soon became manifest.

It had been decided during Volkonsky's time that

Bakst should undertake the production of two antique tragedies and of the one-act ballet *Die Puppenfee* for the Hermitage Theatre. The order remained in force and gave Levushka the opportunity of creating a brilliant display in two absolutely different domains. At the same time I was entrusted by Teliakovsky with the production of *Götterdämmerung*, which was to be given at the end of 1902. Once more I was reluctant at first, for in spite of my love for Wagner I could not quite *see* how this work of genius could materialise on the stage. Nevertheless I was induced to take on *Götterdämmerung* and, having once started, became utterly absorbed in the task.

Our taking part in the theatre infuriated Diaghilev. He looked upon it as a betrayal, as "a disgraceful compromise." His bitterness was reflected in his criticism of my *Götterdämmerung* in the pages of our *World of Art*. We, both Bakst and I, often had very disagreeable conversations with him on the subject, but luckily Serov took our side; he considered that neither Bakst nor I had the right to refuse any chances of expressing ourselves in what was our vocation. In the case of Korovin there was no change, he and Golovin remained with Teliakovsky as "his artists," with the result that their relations with Diaghilev had become still more distant. The *World of Art* was gradually becoming a citadel from which Teliakovsky's management was continually bombarded. It would have been unwise of Korovin to keep up friendly relations with people who did not spare either him or Golovin and raised all sorts of accusations against their patron.

I must dwell a little on the campaign against Teliakovsky conducted by the *World of Art*. The most destructive shells were fired by me. It was I who unmercifully demolished the new productions of the two ballets *Don Quichotte* and *The Magic Mirror*. In so doing, I was, however, absolutely sincere. I would have preferred to praise these productions that had been created by artists—Korovin and Golovin—with whom I had friendly relations, and it would have been far more "profitable" for me not to annoy one who now was in full control of the Imperial Theatres. If, nevertheless, I cruelly attacked these productions, it was because I was bitterly disappointed by them. On both occasions I had gone to the theatre anxious to enjoy, if not the ballet, at least the spectacle. There had been rumours that the Moscow production of the old ballet *Don Quichotte* was a masterpiece, and that its producer, the ballet-master Gorsky, had revealed new horizons. This proved to be untrue. Gorsky's new version was vitiated by the abhorrent lack of organisation that is typical of amateur performances. His "novelties" consisted of making the crowds on the stage bustle and move about fitfully and aimlessly. As regards the action, the dramatic possibilities and the dancers themselves were depressed to a uniformly commonplace level. *Don Quichotte* had never been an adornment to the Imperial Stage; now it had become something unworthy of it and almost disreputable.

The blame for the unsuccessful production of *Don Quichotte* lay chiefly with Gorsky. *The Magic Mirror* —a choreographic version of Grimm's charming fairy tale *Schneewittchen*—was produced by the old Petipa, and was given in fact at his benefit performance. In spite of this, it was even more of a failure than *Don Quichotte*. Both the composer, Koreschenko, and the artist, Golovin, were disappointing. But the chief defect of the production was the absence of unified control—the control that had been so apparent during Vsevolojsky's time, even in his less successful experiments. That is why my criticism, though dealing principally with Golovin's contribution, was in reality directed against Teliakovsky.

To show the general mood I was in, I will quote

a passage from my article in the "Chronicle" of *World of Art*: "Certainly the coarse and absurd attacks made by the newspapers and the public against the production of *The Magic Mirror* are to a great extent unjust. There is much in Golovin's sets that is beautiful. But where is the ensemble? Where is the central idea? Everything seems so badly patched together, so little thought out. Of course Golovin's genuinely artistic manner and his remarkable range of colours are a great treat for the eye. His sets are like a very refined gastronomic dish, beside which our usual décor is no better than an ordinary *plat du jour*. And yet, in the theatre, these dull *plats du jour* are perhaps more in their place than a dish served at the wrong moment—however refined it may be. It seems to me that the chief object of a production should be to interpret its subject . . . that the décor should be painted by first-class artists is less important. The productions of Chronegk, Vsevolojsky and Stanislavsky must be considered as *classical* in spite of the fact that their sets are executed by mediocre artists. There is sense in them, and in some there is even genuine poetry . . .

"Decadence is now the name for all that rises above triviality and lack of taste. Still, I cannot refrain from using this epithet in connection with the present production of *The Magic Mirror*. It is decadent in the literal sense; it has revealed the paralysis of artistic *will* that is the normal attribute of epochs of decadence—when great talents, stultified by apathy, neurosis or despair, are so prevented from realising their full possibilities."

Chapter XIII

A BALLET OF MY OWN

THE reader will recollect how eager I had been to create a ballet of my own in the days when I was still a schoolboy and had composed the music and part of the sets for my *Kette der Nixe*. Afterwards the *Kette der Nixe* was put aside, together with other childish fancies. Yet the desire to create something of my very *own* in the domain which was nearest to my heart still persisted. When Volkonsky was appointed director in 1900 my ambition seemed nearer fulfilment. This time I did not intend to appear as the composer; yet I definitely wanted to take an active part in the music—if only I could find a man of talent who would agree to a close collaboration with me. At one time I tried to persuade my friend Nouvel to collaborate with me, but he was either too lazy or had too little confidence in himself to attempt it. Nourok also refused, although his work had undoubtedly an individual fancy which, from my point of view, was highly desirable. Nourok suffered from a kind of paralysis of creative will, and was further handicapped by being a real dilettante. His lack of technique was a serious drawback to him when developing a good musical idea. Of our circle there remained Tcherepnine, a young composer, one of Rimsky-Korsakov's "most promising" pupils at the Conservatoire. Tcherepnine had been married for several years to my niece, Marie Benois—the "Mashenka" who used to take part in my ballet improvisations to her father's (my brother Albert's) music.

It is true that I was not very much impressed with what he composed, although it was approved of in Conservatoire circles. I found his first efforts too academic, too reminiscent of good, conventional music—in other words, it was typical "Conservatoire" music. But I appreciated Tcherepnine's society; I loved talking to him on different subjects— among others the ballet, which attracted him strongly, although, at first sight, hardly a suitable domain for a composer poisoned by academic principles. My two other musical friends were even more critical of Tcherepnine; they used to scold me for my friendship with him and for my leniency towards his compositions. Nor had Diaghilev any confidence in him. Still, Tcherepnine was the only serious musician in our group, if not a member of our intimate circle.

During 1900–1901 the idea of my ballet began to take a somewhat more definite shape. I had found a subject. At Somov's advice I read a volume of Théophile Gautier's tales and was struck in particular by a fantastic story called *Omphale*. It was a mixture of reality and fancy. The hero finds a lock of hair in an old chest of drawers and falls in love with the beautiful woman, portrayed on an ancient Gobelins, whose lock it turns out to have been. The story was written in my favourite "Hoffmann" style, and I decided that it was an excellent subject for a dramatic ballet, for my ballet must be dramatic. The dramatic quality of *Omphale* would give my ballet sufficient seriousness to save it from being merely commonplace and gay as the fashion of the times prescribed. At the same time, I wanted it to have all the sparkle, the sumptuousness, the importance, of former ballets. It was to be in three or four acts so as to occupy an entire evening. I also wanted it to express my admiration for the baroque and rococo periods. The figure

of the crafty, designing abbé, the wicked genie who
entices the lovers into the snares of Satan, was to be
in the foreground. The ghostly beauty from the Gobelins was to enter into real life, take part in the great
ball, cause the hero to fall in love with her, etc. At
the end the hero would realise that he had forsaken
his beloved for a phantom and thus bring about his
own destruction.

I described the subject to Tcherepnine, and after
our first talk I was convinced that, being a true
admirer of the author of *Kreisleriana*, he had immediately grasped the whole essence of my idea. He
had even become enthusiastic about it. Very soon
his first musical sketches appeared, illustrating certain
moments and some *entrées*. To my great joy I found
that there was nothing academic in them; on the
contrary, they were full of delightful musical *trouvailles*. From that moment I began to believe that
my ballet might come into being. When my friends
made fun of my confidence in the composer, I could
now parry their attacks with conviction. My talks
and consultations with Tcherepnine became more
frequent, his sketches began to acquire definite shape,
and the result was a thoroughly presentable piece of
work.

At that time my relations with Teliakovsky were
still good. I had just emerged with honours from
the ordeal of producing *Götterdämmerung*, and the fact
that Diaghilev, who had already become the *bête noir*
of the new director, had criticised it unmercifully in
the pages of the *World of Art*, had only established me
still more firmly in his favour. I told Teliakovsky
about my enterprise with Tcherepnine and he seemed
interested, though the idea of three acts made him
frown. It rather amused me when, speaking in his
barrack-square voice, he expressed the wish that there
should be more waltzes—"waltzes create the success of
ballets!" This, to my mind, was far from appropriate

to my plan of reviving my favourite eighteenth century. What waltzes could there be in the epoch of panniers and minuets? But I knew that it was no use arguing with Teliakovsky, for he would stand firmly for his opinion as a "practical business-man," and the fate of our ballet would depend upon whether we succeeded in satisfying his demand. Luckily Tcherepnine was less upset than I was by the director's wishes. He had already a theme for a *valse noble* in mind. When he had composed another, we asked Teliakovsky for an audition. He met us with the words: "Are there any waltzes? It is most important to have waltzes." The waltzes were immediately produced, Teliakovsky was pleased by them, and our ballet was accepted. I was even paid a fee without delay for the libretto of *Le Pavillon d'Armide*.

But that was as far as it went, for soon after that Teliakovsky and I fell out. I took great offence because he did not himself answer some observations of mine sent from Rome, but sent a reply through a subordinate. After that I decided it was not worth while having anything to do with him—that it was not for me to improve the manners of so ill-bred a boor! ... On my return from Rome, I did not renew my relations with him, and ceased thinking about my ballet. Just at this moment, the production of *The Magic Mirror* forced me to criticise it with extreme violence, after which, of course, all hopes of ever being invited to take part in the Imperial Theatres had to be abandoned, and so the first chapter of the history of my ballet came to an end. Tcherepnine, however, continued the work in which he had become absorbed and gradually composed a whole suite, which he orchestrated with his usual skill. It was given in concerts with notable success. Some years later, the existence of this suite greatly helped our ballet to "reach the footlights"—but that was in 1907, in the days when Fokine's star was just rising.

Chapter XIV

DIE PUPPENFEE

THE most important events that took place in the realm of the ballet before the arrival of Fokine were the productions of the *Die Puppenfee* and *The Magic Mirror*. I have already spoken about the second of these ballets and now, before I go on, I must say a few words about Bakst's undisputed masterpiece, *Die Puppenfee*.

Le Cœur de la Marquise in 1900 was Levushka's first theatrical production and was, at the same time, one that was really characteristic of him. He had somehow managed immediately to form his own style and exceptional harmony of colour, but *Le Cœur de la Marquise*, which had been given in the Hermitage Theatre, had passed unnoticed by the general public. His next two productions were Euripides' *Hippolytus* and Sophocles' *Œdipus* for the Alexandryinsky Theatre.

The severe and noble colouring of Bakst's costumes and his highly intelligent interpretation of classical dress were unique; nothing of the sort had been seen either in the Russian Theatre or in any other theatres in the world. But as a whole these productions could not be held successful, for the décors were distinctly weak. Both the attempt to re-create the ancient stage in *Hippolytus* and the more realistic and "romantic" treatment of *Œdipus*, with elements borrowed from Preller and Böcklin, were unconvincing.

Die Puppenfee was of a quite different order. The

ballet is a trifle and the music mediocre, but Bakst was delighted when he was commissioned and, feeling at once that it was something of which he would make a success, set to work in a kind of frenzy—unusual for him in those days. His enthusiasm and love for our native city, St. Petersburg, and personal recollections of his childhood, gave Bakst the happy idea of transferring the action to the St. Petersburg Arcade, known to every St. Petersburg child because of the toy-shops that were concentrated there. Here, too, during the sixth week of Lent, was held the famous Palm Week Fair, in which toys played a most prominent part. These memories formed the foundation of the scenario as adapted by Bakst, and luckily he found the friendliest support for the idea in his two ballet-masters, the brothers Legat.

Bakst worked at *Die Puppenfee* with enthusiasm, but partly for a sentimental reason. Our friend was in love with a young widow—Lubov Pavlovna Gritzenko, the daughter of the famous Russian patron of Art, P. M. Tretiakov—and his feeling was reciprocated. Their meetings usually took place in studios of the Maryinsky Theatre under the curious pretext of Bakst having chosen to paint his beloved in these strange surroundings. The result of these séances was still more curious. Bakst really did paint Lubov Pavlovna, but the "portrait" proved to be one of the dolls in the toyshop, and this doll was suspended from the ceiling, among all sorts of other toys, drums, hoops, carriages, clowns, etc. The Imperial Family had noticed this detail during the performance at the Hermitage Theatre and indeed it was impossible not to notice it, for "Lubov Pavlovna," smiling gracefully, was dangling in the very foreground.

Later, when the ballet was transferred to the Maryinsky Theatre, those who were initiated into the mystery of the strange doll in the black Paris dress and huge hat, so out of place among the other toys, were tremendously amused at the infatuated artist's invention. Lubov Pavlovna's brother-in-law, our great friend S. S. Botkin, was the one who especially enjoyed the joke. "Look, look at Luba dangling there!" he would repeat, choking and almost weeping with laughter. Soon after this, we learnt that the lovers would be united. After many complications from both sides, the wedding took place. Lubov Pavlovna had to overcome the indignant resistance of all her purely Muscovite relations at the idea of her marrying a "Jew," while Levushka could not make up his mind to change the faith of his fathers, as was demanded by the Russian law of that time of Jews who married Christians.

The happy atmosphere which reigned during the work on *Die Puppenfee* found expression even in the set representing a shop in the Arcade, whose wide windows overlooked the principal thoroughfare of St. Petersburg, the Nevsky Prospect. But Bakst again scored his chief success with the costumes; every entrance was a fresh enchantment for the eye. Furthermore, the whole ballet had been decked out with the most graceful choreographic detail by the brothers Legat. The "trifling" little ballet became a real "theatrical treat." Outstandingly successful was the added number, *The Wooden Soldiers*—to Tchaikovsky's music—for which Bakst was inspired by my collection of folk-toys.[1] The same collection served him as material for the décor of the apotheosis of the Fairy Doll. It consisted of the slightly coarse but infinitely attractive and amusing objects which delighted us in our childhood and which were far more beloved by us than expensive foreign toys. Little country houses with trees made of birds' feathers,

[1] This number served afterwards as prototype (to infinitely inferior music) for one of the chief items of Balaieff's *Chauve-Souris*. Since then, these *Wooden Soldiers* have had a great success on many a stage of Europe and America.

windmills, fantastic figures, striped sentry-boxes, and
even the cathedrals, towers and belfries of the Troits-
kaya Lavra Monastery—all this was piled up by
Bakst in fantastic disorder, giving a real picture of
that wonderful world of childhood that many of us
look back upon as a lost paradise.

Chapter XV

ART EXHIBITIONS

WE are now approaching the moment when, from a simple spectator of the ballet, I became a creative agent and produced my own ballet on the stage of the Maryinsky Theatre. But this happened in 1907, and *Die Puppenfee* was produced in 1903. Before passing over to 1907, I feel compelled to give a short account of what happened to us all during the four intervening years.

During the period of 1903–1904, Diaghilev and I were chiefly absorbed in preparations for the Historical Exhibition of Portraits in the Tauride Palace, opened in the beginning of 1905, unfortunately a most unsuitable moment. The idea of such an exhibition was originally mine and its first realisation was the so-called "Exhibition of the Blue Cross" arranged in 1902 by Baron N. N. Wrangel, who then had just begun his public activities and had tackled the task with all his energy. At the time Diaghilev had refused to take part in our venture on the pretext that it was not on a sufficiently serious footing.

Immediately after the Wrangel exhibition, Sergei began preparations for his own. He secured the patronage of the Grand Duke Nikolai Mikhailovitch, famous for his historical works, and thanks to him received a very substantial subsidy from the Emperor. Diaghilev became so absorbed by his new work that he neglected everything else. At the end of 1904 we decided to cease publication of the *World of Art* and

ANNE BENOIS, NÉE KIND
From a photograph by Alexandre Benois, 1903

Facing p. 232

ALEXANDRE BENOIS AND HIS FAMILY AT PAVLOOSK
From a photograph by M. Risnikov, 1902

Facing p. 233

one of the main reasons for our decision—besides some other unfavourable circumstances—was that Diaghilev had become completely indifferent to his creation. He was now entirely engrossed in his new undertaking, which was to surpass any exhibition yet held.

Diaghilev spent the whole summer of 1904 in ceaseless travelling all over Russia, visiting provincial museums, country seats and private collections, in his search for everything of historical interest. I, too, made several trips, but my contribution was modest in comparison to Seriozha's gigantic efforts. I only visited a few estates near Moscow and St. Petersburg and studied the palaces of St. Petersburg and its surroundings, which I already knew. Seriozha's furious activities were almost frightening at times; one could only marvel at his energy, patience and firmness.

The result surpassed even his own expectations. The enormous building of the Tauride Palace was filled with thousands of portraits, statues, busts, watercolours, bas-reliefs, miniatures and drawings collected from every corner of Russia. All Russia's past seemed to have been resurrected in the halls of the former residence of the Magnificent Prince of Tauride. The effect was greatly enhanced by the way in which the most important portraits were grouped together. In the centre of each group, under a special canopy, hung the portrait of the Emperor or Empress indissolubly identified with the epoch.

Seriozha and I were responsible for the grouping and the distribution of the innumerable masses of exhibits, while Bakst had been entrusted with the arrangement of the "Winter Garden" in which stood the most important sculptures, a task that he had accomplished with great success. The green trellis occupying the middle of the colossal colonnade and the hot-house plants brought from the Imperial conservatories formed an enchanting background for the white marble statues, immortalising eminent statesmen, soldiers and wealthy magnates, as well as court ladies and favourites.

To my great disappointment, I was unable to attend the opening ceremony. Towards the end of our work, when everything was ready and in its place, I was obliged to leave St. Petersburg. It was only from hearsay that I learnt that the opening of the exhibition had been a real triumph, in spite of the fact that at that moment Russia was passing through a period which was far from happy—it was but a few weeks after the tragic 9th of January, 1905 (old style). What could the thoughts of the unfortunate monarch have been on that day, as, surrounded by his family and suite, he passed through the endless portrait gallery—a portrait gallery, to a great extent, of his own house, his ancestors and his predecessors? The Emperor was a lover of history; he presided personally at the meetings of the Imperial Historical Society and willingly consented to become the patron of our exhibition when his cousin, the Grand Duke Nikolai Mikhailovitch, asked him to do so. If the Emperor had a feeling for history as keen as his interest in it, if this representation of the past was, for him, not merely a museum curio, but something that regarded him personally, something from which he could draw advice and counsel—then the visit of the Autocrat of all Russia to our exhibition must have moved him to the very depths of his heart. But there were no outward signs of this. Everything passed with the usual official dullness and the questions addressed by the monarch about this or that portrait did not rise above the pitch of ordinary curiosity. Diaghilev told me afterwards how disappointed and hurt he was, in spite of the gracious attention with which Nicolas II had listened to his explanations.

The reason why I was unable to be present at

the festive opening of the Portrait Exhibition at the Tauride Palace was a family one. Our little son had been failing in health during the last years and we were extremely worried about him. He had managed to catch malaria during the summer of 1903, which we spent in the vicinity of Rome, and the effects of it were felt more and more; it was indispensable that the child should be taken away from St. Petersburg as soon as possible. As our city is built on a bog and the climate very changeable, it cannot be considered a healthy place, and I imagine that nowhere else in Europe are parents so anxious about their children's health as they are in St. Petersburg. Since the autumn of that year, when we had come back to town from the country, our little Kolia had been suffering from attacks of fever which were steadily increasing, and when 1905 set in we began to think seriously of taking our three-year-old child away from the atmosphere which was so harmful to him.

There could be no question of remaining in Russia and taking him to the Caucasus or the Crimea, for the whole country was enveloped by a wave of disturbances since the fatal 9th of January and there was every likelihood of our being cut off. There remained only to go abroad.

I decided to accompany my wife and children on their journey and we had to hasten our departure as threatening rumours were circulating about a coming general strike. In such a case, the railways would be the first to cease work. Pessimists assured us that a revolution would surely follow, after which we would lose all chances of leaving Russia.

Thus it happened that I left St. Petersburg just before the opening of the exhibition in which I had taken so active a part. We had to leave the beautiful new apartment we had recently taken on the Vassilievsky Prospect—for we were going away for a year, at the very least. The financial side of our life abroad was provided for. I still had some money left to me by my father and I was to receive quite high pay as correspondent of the very popular newspaper *Russ*, which I had just joined, having started my journalistic career some time before in the very moderate and respectable newspaper *Slovo*. We had not made up our minds as to where we were going to live abroad, but my journalistic work demanded that I should be in a large cultural centre, so we wended our way first to Paris, with the intention of afterwards choosing some suitable spa to live in. To our great joy, even Paris proved to be very beneficial for our boy. The attacks of malaria ceased, and in a few weeks our child was unrecognisable: the pale, apathetic little creature we had brought to Paris now rivalled the lively, rosy children in the Luxemburg Gardens with whom he played games and sailed boats.

Our old French doctor was excited by this metamorphosis and the only explanation he could offer was the sudden and complete change of air. We had left St. Petersburg during severe winter weather and had arrived in Paris in the first days of spring, which was exceptionally mild and pleasant that year. Next summer we spent in Brittany and stayed in Primel, the delightful, remote little place that we had discovered in 1897.

We passed 1905, 1906 and part of 1907 in Paris, Brittany and Versailles; once more I found myself for nearly three years torn away from my native St. Petersburg and from my old circle of friends. This severance became almost tragic in October, 1905, when it was temporarily impossible to communicate with Russia, as a result of the first throes of Revolution, after the disastrous Japanese War. But on the whole those years abroad passed rather successfully for me. I gave myself up entirely to painting and sketching in my beloved park of Versailles and to creating a series of pictures on themes from my favourite epochs, the seventeenth and eighteenth centuries. At the same time I finished writing my book, *The Russian School of Painting*, published a monumental volume dedicated to the Russian Museum of the Emperor Alexander III, collaborated in several newspapers and in the Moscow art journal, *Zolotoye Runo* (*Le Toison d'Or*), which aspired to be the successor of the *World of Art*. Nor did my relations with my friends cease. I corresponded with some of them and had personal intercourse with others, for two of my friends —S. P. Yaremitch and Prince A. K. Shervashidze— were also in Paris, besides many other compatriots and friends.

During these years Diaghilev came to Paris several times. He had undertaken to arrange a grand exhibition of Russian Art, and it was quite natural that I should do a good deal of the work, not only in the choice of exhibits and in the planning, but also, together with Bakst, in the hanging of the pictures in the ten halls of the Grand Palais, which had been placed at our disposal by the directorate of the Salon d'Automne. Besides this, I prepared a lavishly-illustrated catalogue of the exhibition and, at Seriozha's insistence, mastered my dislike of appearing in public and delivered a lecture on Russian Art. I must confess that, while doing so, I secretly cursed Seriozha's despotism and my own compliance.

As the Emperor had allowed Diaghilev to take abroad many priceless works of art from the Imperial Palaces, and owing to the ready response of those of our friends who were art collectors and patrons, the exhibition in Paris of 1906 proved to be of exceptional interest and brilliance. Bakst repeated his charming *bosquet* garden as a background for the sculptures; the marvellous ikons—from Likhachev's famous collection—were hung on the brocade-covered walls of two of the halls, and the rest of the suite was decorated and furnished with the most perfect taste and elegance in keeping with the character of the different periods. I shall not indulge in any further detailed description of this *véritable événement parisien*, as I am going to write about it in my general memoirs, but I must add that the exhibition of 1906 had great significance for us, for, through it, Paris became acquainted with our group and in this way we formed connections with a number of people who became our friends. This proved very useful later on. Among our new friends, gained through the exhibition, were Georges Desvallières, Maurice Denis, Maxime Dethomas, Jacques Emile Blanche, Comte Robert de Montesquiou, Comtesse de Greffulhe; refined, benevolent, highly-cultured and intellectually alert, they helped us to gain a firm footing in Paris. They were the first to appreciate all we had brought to show from our distant country, and after their appreciation followed that of wider circles, and lastly, that of the popular masses.

The Russian Exhibition of 1906 was the first important step in what might be called our "export campaign of Russian art," or rather our endeavour to acquaint the public abroad with what we especially loved and had the right to be proud of in our native land. We had already tried to make propaganda for Russian art abroad. Thus, in 1893, when still at the University, I had written my chapter on Russia for Richard Muther's *History of Painting in the Nineteenth Century*. It was for reasons of propaganda that, when I edited my *Artistic Treasures of Russia*, I insisted on a French text as well as the Russian. In 1896 I organised a section for Russian painting at the Exhibition in Munich. But all these were the timid, unimportant endeavours of a "beginner," whose possibilities were very limited. Now, feeling firmer ground under our feet, we decided that the time had

come for the "second part of our life programme"—
the serious export of our art abroad.

Diaghilev, who was our chief promoter and the only
really enterprising and courageous one among us,
understood that he was now equipped for the fulfilment of such a difficult and responsible enterprise.
The fact that I was living abroad helped to give our
"export programme" a stimulus. I never ceased
repeating to Seriozha, both in my letters and in my
talks with him, that it was necessary to show Russian
art to the West, and he welcomed my insistence. He
welcomed it because he himself was now anxious and
keen to develop his activity on a larger scale, being
disgusted with what he called "the incorrigible provincialism" of our compatriots. In moments of
weariness and depression, it seemed to Diaghilev that
nothing more could be achieved in Russia and therefore it was indispensable to transfer his activity beyond
her borders. We did not need to worry about Russian
literature, for during the last thirty years it had gained
universal recognition (due principally to Tolstoy),
but there remained music, which in our opinion was
not yet sufficiently appreciated, and, above all, the
pictorial arts and the Russian Theatre, which were
almost unknown to Western Europe.

The first step in our systematic campaign was the
exhibition of 1906 that I have described; the second,
a series of Russian Concerts arranged by Diaghilev in
the Paris Opéra in 1907; the third, a series of performances of *Boris Godunov* at the Opéra in 1908; and
at last, in 1909, we presented our productions of
ballet and opera for the judgment of Europe.

Strange to say, of all these "export" items, the
most decisive, stable and universal success fell to the
Russian ballet, while our endeavours to "export"
Russian pictorial art did not get the success it deserved.

Nevertheless, after the music, it was the painting
that had the predominant part in our productions.

Chapter XVI

RESURRECTION OF MY BALLET

IN the spring of 1907, after the French concerts with which I had little to do as I thought I had not yet exhausted the beauties of the park of Versailles, I started a series of pictures with the intention of remaining in Paris yet another year. But an event of the first importance occurred which made me alter my plans and hasten back to St. Petersburg.

It was Tcherepnine who brought me the pleasant news that our ballet, *Le Pavillon d'Armide*, now had a chance of being produced. This was indeed a surprise, as I had almost forgotten about it, and in view of my bad relations with Teliakovsky I considered there was no likelihood of it ever reaching the footlights. It appeared that the young artist Fokine, whom I had known as a dancer, but who was regarded now as a choreographic genius by the young group of the ballet company, had become interested in my ballet and wished to produce it. He was supported in this by A. D. Krupensky, the new manager of the production department, who had gained great influence in the Imperial Theatres.

It had happened in the following way. Fokine had been entrusted with producing something for the annual final examinations of the Theatre School. He turned for advice to Tcherepnine, then one of the conductors of the Maryinsky Theatre. Tcherepnine told him of the existence of a ballet composed by him that had been pigeon-holed, though accepted by the Directorate some time ago. It was not quite complete, but the central scene—the magic coming to life of the old Gobelins—was already orchestrated and could easily be used. Fokine liked the idea and both ballet-master and composer started to work out the scene in the intimate surroundings of a school performance, without any official noise. The scene was produced at the examination and had considerable success. This encouraged Krupensky to try to get *Le Pavillon d'Armide* produced in all three acts, with the condition, however, that it should be shortened. The fashion for short ballets had started just then, and the Directorate counted on their having a greater success than the interminable, heavy ballets of tradition.

Tcherepnine agreed to this abbreviation and there remained only to obtain the sanction of the author of the scenario—that is to say, me—whom he found in Paris. I am under the impression that Teliakovsky was not even consulted on this occasion—the Director had lately ceased to take an active part in the affairs of the theatre and was perhaps contemplating his resignation. Krupensky, on the other hand, was a very ambitious man, and perhaps hoped to occupy in time this high position himself. . . .

I cannot say that I at once welcomed the idea of having *Le Pavillon d'Armide* produced. During the past years I had considerably cooled down towards my "progeny," I had begun to see its defects more clearly and in general my ideals now lay in a different direction. More than that, I had rather lost interest in the ballet in general, probably because the ballets I had seen on the Paris stage had nothing in common with what I had so loved and admired in St. Petersburg. The performances lacked both taste and talent and many of the things which were looked upon in Paris as being *le dernier mot* were really *du dernier ridicule*.

What displeased me especially in Tcherepnine's proposal was the fact that the ballet had to be abbreviated—*conditio sine qua non*. When composing my complicated choreographic story, I had intended to create something imposing, something that would resurrect the tradition of the former ballets, so beloved by me. The very fact that the ballet was to take up the *whole* evening was to show what significance I attached to ballet action in general. I was averse to short ballets, because the fashion for them revealed a somewhat unworthy attitude towards ballet, which at the time was gathering strength, probably under the influence of music-hall and variety numbers. Short ballets were included in the programmes only as gay and frivolous entertainments.

However, it was an offer which was *à prendre ou à laisser* and Tcherepnine's persuasion overcame my reluctance. For me the essential was the *dramatic* side —if that was preserved, I felt satisfied that the ballet would not fall to the level of a cabaret item. It was precisely the dramatic pantomime in connection with the dancing that imparted to the old ballets their peculiar and original charm. One had only to think of *Giselle*, *Coppélia* and *La Belle au Bois Dormant*. All the great ballet-masters, from Noverre to Petipa, had insisted on the dramatic side. The new version of *Le Pavillon d'Armide* that was coming to my mind would allow me not only to preserve the dramatic sense, but even to make it predominant. It was necessary to concentrate the essence of the subject by expressing it in three scenes, that should follow without interval. The middle scene, where the sleeping hero finds himself in the enchanted garden of the " Gobelins " beauty, was all given up to dancing; the first scene represented the arrival of the hero in the fatal *pavillon* with the Gobelins; the third and final scene showed his awakening, when he becomes convinced of the reality of the strange things he had taken for a dream. . . . The question as to how the hero would meet his doom I preferred to leave open. I did not know myself whether my poor René de Beaugency dies from the shock of this revelation or becomes insane, or just remains injured for life. The important fact was that contact with the phantom world had proved fatal for him. A few weeks after my discussion with Tcherepnine in Paris, I found myself back in St. Petersburg, becoming acquainted with Krupensky in his office-room that overlooked the Alexandryinsky Theatre Square. I must say that my first impression of Krupensky was a very agreeable one: he was a young, pleasant and rather portly man with a dark Assyrian beard and charming manner. I had been warned that one could not trust him, that he had the ways of a *parvenu*, but our first interviews did not give me that impression. On the contrary, Alexander Dmitrievitch charmed me by his courtesy, his open manner and the readiness he expressed to fall in with all my ideas, putting at my disposal all the technical means necessary to produce *Le Pavillon d'Armide* exactly in accordance with my wishes. He was most of all concerned that it should be produced in the "real Gobelins shades," which I readily promised to arrange, although I did not quite understand what he actually meant. My own conception of "Gobelins shades" was of something far from pale, faded or dim. The beautiful, vivid colours of tapestries woven after pictures by Detroy and Boucher still lived in my memory, and it was them that I had in mind when I agreed with Krupensky.

It was very soon clear that Krupensky meant to make *Le Pavillon d'Armide* into his own "show-piece." A week had hardly passed before an enormous studio on the Alexeyevskaya Street had been assigned to me. Usually this studio was at the disposal of the scene-painter Allegri; with the studio, Allegri's assistants and

I

all his staff of artisan scene-painters were also assigned to me.

There are two sets in *Le Pavillon d'Armide*, one of which appears in the first scene and is shown again in the third. The first scene takes place at night, the third in bright daylight. It would certainly have been better for the two contrasting effects to have been produced in the painting. Economic reasons, however, triumphed over artistic and the same décor had to be used for the third scene as for the first. Having this in mind, I tried to spread the whole system of painted shadows and reflections in such a way that it could serve both for night, when the sumptuous *pavillon* was lit by candles, and for day, when sunshine penetrated the windows.

The *pavillon* was to represent the quintessence of baroque architecture and decoration. Tall windows with an ornate *œil-de-bœuf* over each of them alternated with columns of polished marble, while the plastic modelling above the central niche represented allegorical figures resting on clouds and supporting a sumptuous canopy adorned with feathers that overshadowed the magic Gobelins. It took me some time to get this composition right, but at last I succeeded. My chief problem was how to make the niche of the Gobelins dissolve before the eyes of the audience into its component parts and disappear as the action of the play demanded, so that, in the end, all that would be left visible would be the central group of the Gobelins, the beautiful Armide surrounded by her handmaidens.

While working at the décor, I was in continuous consultation with Tcherepnine, trying to improve the scenario. There were points on which we were at variance. My plan was to have the beginning worked out in great detail—the incident in which the young René seeks shelter in the old, mad marquis's castle and is led by him to the neglected *pavillon*. I wanted all the terror of that night to be fully expressed in the music, but Tcherepnine refused to add a single bar to what he had composed, which, in my opinion, expressed neither storm nor terror. I was obliged to console myself with the thought that the next scene was very successful and that the spectator was really "prepared" by the music to enter the fantastic world in the way that I had wished.

Delightful was the "March of the Hours"—imagined as a procession of lanterns emerging from the momumental clock standing under the tapestry. The golden figures of Cupid and Saturn which adorned the clock began a struggle, which ended in Cupid's victory—this meant that Time had ceased to exist, for Love had stepped into his right. . . . Marvellously illustrated by the music was the transition into the fantastic world of dreams. The composer had had the happy idea of introducing into the orchestral ensemble soft choral singing *à bouche fermée*, which gradually grew louder. This fully expressed the mysterious horror René must have experienced when he was awakened by the strange noises and, running out of the alcove, suddenly saw what was happening.

For the first weeks our work had been going on without the ballet-master, but in the middle of the summer Fokine came back from his leave. My meeting with him took place in the studio. I already knew from Tcherepnine that Fokine was a pleasant young man (he was not yet thirty) who was ready to give himself up entirely to the realisation of my plan, and our personal acquaintance fully corroborated this. What appealed to me at once was his gaiety. There was absolutely no affectation or pose about him, no pretence of being a genius; on the contrary, he possessed the simplicity and a certain youthful charm that I consider to be the undoubted sign of real talent. One could see that he was captivated by the problem entrusted to him. We agreed with each other at once. He told me about the way he had produced Armide's dances for the performance in the Theatrical School and all his ideas fell in with mine. It became clear that I could trust and depend on him.

Other conversations, in the presence of Tcherepnine, soon followed our first one. We all three proved to be possessed by the same idea and were in full agreement about the endless details of which our work consisted. There were, however, some points of disagreement in which I had to insist on having my own way and to convince my collaborators, especially Fokine, who was rather stubborn where miming was concerned. He was afraid that it would degenerate into the ostentatious and senseless "thrashing of arms" which, in the Theatre School, had gradually superseded the consciously and very finely worked out system of mimic gesture. In Fokine's somewhat disdainful attitude towards miming one felt the spirit of the times which was tending to transform the ballet into a disjointed sequence of dance-numbers. But Fokine was too great an artist to be governed by these new ideas and he understood perfectly what constituted the fundamental charm of the old ballets. In fact, one could say about him that *il ne demandait pas mieux que de se laisser convaincre.* Wishing, no less than I did, to save the ballet from cheapening influences, and to give his art a new lease of life, he understood that by standing up for miming I was only defending the principles that were equally dear to him.

Thus Fokine, Tcherepnine and I were collaborating in full harmony when suddenly, for no visible reason, the atmosphere of our work changed. I had been warned about Krupensky's unreasonably capricious character, but I had not believed these insinuations, especially as Krupensky expressed full respect for my creative work and was helping me in every way to realise my dream. But, abruptly, Krupensky dropped his pleasant and affectionate ways and ceased to converse in the tone of the society to which we both belonged. Adopting the attitude of a superior, he became arrogant, overbearing and insolent, putting silly obstacles in my way over every detail. I did not fail to pay him back in the same coin. As a rule I am a peace-loving and rather benevolent person and when necessary am capable of agreeing with the greatest cranks, knowing how to close my eyes to absurdities. Sometimes I even enjoy the task of bringing the unreasonable to reason. But to do this I have to preserve my self-control, which, alas, I am apt to lose when I come up against coarseness and bad manners. This was the case with Krupensky. The semblance of friendship with which we had started proved fallacious. We began to hate each other without any real reason. I "saw red" every time he adopted his lordly airs with me, proffering me two fingers of his hand and generally behaving like a bounder.

To this day I do not know what could have been the cause of such a change. It is possible that, having invited me to produce my ballet during Teliakovsky's absence, Krupensky may have been severely reprimanded on his chief's return. As a result, Krupensky probably decided to liquidate the enterprise he had sanctioned, and had found that the best way to do so was to provoke me to some spectacular demonstration. Whatever the reason, I began to avoid all personal contact with Krupensky, addressing myself in all matters to his assistant. I could not risk my cherished progeny being destroyed or compromised.

Apart from Krupensky, I had the full support and sympathy of the entire theatre. The principal scene-shifter Filipov was particularly helpful. He was quite a young man who had only recently taken over this difficult post from the old "fossil" Berger. But he knew his job to perfection and possessed the quality so invaluable in his profession—refusal to admit the impossible. His competence was fully proved at the performance, where everything he had promised took place with faultless accuracy and without a hitch. It was the success of the mechanical side which alone could make the fantastic part *convincing*.

About two months before the first performance, which had been fixed for the beginning of November, Fokine expressed the wish to show me what he had done. I had not asked to see his work before, because, in the first place, I did not consider myself an expert on the technical side of dancing, and secondly, because we had discussed and agreed on nearly everything in our conferences. During these talks it was quite usual for Fokine to display certain steps on my parquet floor or for me to sketch on a piece of paper a "pose" or the group I wanted. . . . These meetings and discussions sometimes took place at Tcherepnine's initiative. After he had composed a scene or a dance, he usually let us know about it so as to play it to us. Being a most accomplished pianist, he succeeded in giving a perfect idea of the sound and colour his music would obtain when orchestrated, especially as he then and there described how the music would be distributed among the instruments. This music, which had just matured and was "served up at once," used to inspire Fokine and me. We were growing to like it more and more, while Tcherepnine himself was completely absorbed in it and was losing his usual somewhat dry manner. . . . Those were indeed very happy times for all three of us!

And then a fresh joy—I was invited by Fokine to be present at a rehearsal.

Chapter XVII

REHEARSALS

A T the present day (thirty years after the period
I am describing) there is nothing unusual in
penetrating into any ballet-school. They have
become so numerous as to be almost ordinary and the
dancers themselves have ceased to be a caste by themselves and have lost the former taint of being "not
quite the thing." Nowadays the strictest bourgeois
mammas dream to see their daughters make a career
in the ballet. Things were quite different in the days
I am describing. In the whole of St. Petersburg
there was but one ballet-school—the Imperial Theatre
School—which was most strictly run. Naturally, no
outsiders were ever allowed within its walls. Being
such forbidden ground, the Imperial School was
even more attractive, especially to the clan of *balletomanes*. It was one thing to make the acquaintance
of a dancer who had already appeared on the public
stage and was leading an independent life; it was
delightful, it had its charm, but there was nothing
so very wonderful in the fact. It was something
quite different to penetrate into the very heart of a
sort of Mahommedan Paradise where, besides the
accomplished artistes, there dwelt so many youthful,
charming, graceful and innocent creatures, whose life
was consecrated to the cult of Terpsichore. . . .
I must confess that when I was taken into the
rehearsal hall of the Theatre School I was almost
dumbfounded. I had often been present at stage

rehearsals and was acquainted with many dancers, and this should have been a guarantee against any surprise. But the sight that now presented itself to my eyes was something entirely unexpected. The daylight, streaming through the tall windows on either side of the hall, seemed to make the sea of tarlatan dresses even more ethereal, transparent, foamy. These young women, maidens and little girls made no use whatsoever of cosmetics, and their youthful bodies and faces were radiant with health and vigour. It made an unusual picture, infinitely more attractive than those which Degas loved to paint. The atmosphere in Degas's ballet pictures is always somewhat gloomy; the dancers, caught unawares during their exercises, which are often far from graceful, seem to be tormented martyrs. Here, on the contrary, everything seemed gay and carefree and, in spite of the masses of people, one breathed freely. The male and female dancers, who sat along the walls in groups or walked about the hall waiting for the rehearsal to begin, did not in the least look like martyrs or "victims of their profession."

Fokine led me in and presented me to the company. My bow was answered by a mass curtsey performed by all the rules of court etiquette. Only after this ritual did I proceed to greet the artists I knew, of whom P. A. Gerdt, M. F. Kshesinskaya and Solianikov were engaged in the principal parts, whereas others like Karsavina, Kyasht, Tchernicheva, Fedorova were performing *variations* in the divertissement of the second picture. Some of them I was seeing for the first time at so close a range and they looked charming in the delightful and becoming costumes, invented during the so-called "Classical" period of 1830, that were compulsory for rehearsals. Kshesinskaya, who did not conform to rules, was the only dancer to appear in a "tu-tu"—much shorter than the regulation ones.

The boys of the school stood in a separate group and they, too, wore their working dresses and ballet shoes. When I passed them they bowed so deeply that I was embarrassed. A youth, or rather a boy, was standing with them. I would not have noticed him had not Fokine presented him to me as the artist for whom he had especially composed the part of Armide's slave, so as to give him a chance to display his remarkable talent. Fokine counted on amazing the public by the unusual height of his *sauts* and *vols*, which the youth performed without any visible effort. I must confess that I was rather surprised when I saw this "wonder" face to face. He was a short, rather thick-set little fellow with the most ordinary, "colourless" face. He was more like a shop assistant than a fairy-tale hero. But this was—Nijinsky! Little did I expect then, as I shook his hand, that in two years' time he was to gain world renown and end his short but entirely fantastic career crowned with the halo of genius.

Soon silence was ordered. Tcherepnine sat down next to the pianist, the artists took their places and the rehearsal began. The rehearsal was that of the second scene—the coming to life of the Gobelins.

It is impossible to describe the excitement which took possession of me. The performance I had invented and dreamed of was unfolding itself to the music which had, so to say, been "made to order" for it, had been composed in accordance with my wishes and been actually sanctioned by me. What happiness it was to see my ideas realised *precisely* as I had wished, clothed in the stylish pomposity with which I had endeavoured to express my infatuation for eighteenth century art, but instinct, at the same time, with the "Hoffmannish" atmosphere of mystery that had delighted me since my youth. On this memorable day I experienced that very rare feeling —not unmixed, somehow, with pain—that occurs

I*

only when something long wished for has at last been accomplished. As I had seen nothing of Fokine's work, I might have feared that he would not succeed in expressing all that was most precious to me. It was possible surely, that this young and inexperienced ballet-master, who, using Isadora Duncan's modern methods, had gained a certain reputation by his production of *Eunice* (a ballet based on Sienkiewicz's novel *Quo Vadis*), would be simply unable to adapt himself to the character of *Le Pavillon d'Armide*, to forget entirely the examples of noble antiquity and revert to the consciously affected, pompous mannerisms of the eighteenth century. What were his qualifications —he, a former pupil of the Imperial Theatre School? Had our preliminary conversations and my explanation of the sketches for the décor and costumes— which, it is true, Fokine took to with avidity—proved sufficient?

During my talks with Fokine I had insisted that he should always bear in mind first-class masterpieces like the scene in the forest and especially the last scene of *La Belle au Bois Dormant*, that contained the Versailles Sarabande and Prince Désiré's wonderful *variation*. But my advice and insistence might have proved futile had the seeds fallen on unreceptive soil. In Fokine's case the soil had been receptive in the highest degree; that was why I was now experiencing such utter happiness. Fokine had managed to satisfy me to such an extent that, without either costumes or décor, my impression of the ballet as a whole was complete. The fancy which had prompted me to create *Le Pavillon d'Armide* was truly being realised.

The faces of the dancers, too, seemed to be shining with happiness. The whole company, with very few exceptions, worshipped Fokine, feeling that in him thay had a leader who would bring them, by a new path, to unparalleled triumphs. . . . *Eunice* had overcome much antagonism and attracted many, but here was something quite different. The production of *Eunice* had been a charming experiment but not a mature work; now a *chef d'œuvre* was being created, and many of the artists knew that *Le Pavillon d'Armide*, though a novelty, was nevertheless asserting and reinforcing the traditions in which they had been brought up and which they loved. The manner was new, but as the work took shape it proved to be an expression of what lay at the foundation of the old school, the "language" that was understood by all, for it was the *native language* of the Russian School of Ballet. N. Legat was an excellent ballet-master, but his faithfulness to traditions savoured of routine; it was academic rather than inspired. In his work one was aware of enslavement—the whole psychology of the slave. The faithfulness to tradition of the daring and fiery Fokine was the result not of strict school training and timid submission, but of free, personal choice. Fokine quite obviously delighted in this evocation of the past.

The rehearsal wound up amid enthusiastic applause from the whole company, in which I joined wholeheartedly. The *corps de ballet* and many of the artists were dismissed and there remained only the performers of the first and last scenes—Gerdt, Solianikov and Grigoriev. I had insisted on the sixty-year-old Pavel Alexandrovitch Gerdt taking the part of my young hero and it had taken much time and persuasion to induce the venerable artist to agree to appear before the public in the part of the twenty-year-old René de Beaugency. He assured me that nothing would come of it and that it would even be slightly ludicrous—pointing with a sad smile to his slightly protruding stomach. I had worshipped Gerdt since my childhood, considering him to be the unique and irreplaceable *jeune premier* of the ballet, and could not contemplate the idea of not having *him* as the hero

of my first ballet. And now I was actually seeing
him perform the part that had been forced on him.

Alas, at the rehearsal I was forced to acknowledge
(without showing it) that he had been right in his
refusal. It was not because he seemed too old as
René; on the contrary, Pavel Alexandrovitch gave
the impression of a man not older than thirty-five;
one could easily imagine that with make-up and wig
he would lose another ten years and be quite near
the age of my hero. What disappointed me was
Gerdt's *acting*, his very definite, dry gesticulations,
his conventional miming. It was all saturated with
school routine. His entrance was too precise to the
music, while the changes of his expression, the
transition from confusion to delight, from fear to
confusion, were almost mechanical. He did not
seem to be *experiencing* anything himself, it was obvious
that he was only carrying out what had been planned.
To make matters worse, his automatic acting was
somehow copied by the cunning, diabolical old
Marquis—the owner of the *pavillon* and father of the
beautiful Armide depicted on the Gobelins. It
seemed to me that Solianikov, whom Fokine had so
warmly recommended to me, had not understood
his part. Directly the rehearsal was over I had a
long talk with the ballet-master, telling him how
disconcerted I felt. I began to beg Fokine to take
on himself the part of René, feeling sure that Gerdt
would willingly cede it to his younger colleague.
But Fokine advised me to wait and see the stage
rehearsals before I made any decision. He proved
to be right. The whole ballet took on a different
aspect on the stage, everything "found its place."

This episode taught me more clearly than anything
else how great an influence school traditions exercise
over artistic expression, and what a store of experience
they have amassed. It is only the experience of
many generations, controlled by actual performances,

that could produce an exact calculation of the effects of distance and thus determine the laws of perspective that are peculiar to miming. Just in the same way, school traditions in decorative art have made it possible for scenic representation of the good old times to become utterly convincing. When seen from near, the painting seems coarse, the colours too bright, the technique too artisan and "calligraphic"; from a distance, the wonderful mirage of the stage gives a complete illusion of reality—an illusion that does not contradict the atmosphere demanded by the subject. I had just such an illusion of reality when watching Gerdt perform, on the stage, the part of René de Beaugency, and Solianikov that of the Marquis. Seen from near in the rehearsal hall their acting and mime seemed poor and helpless; here, before the footlights, everything took the right shape; the precision of the gesture and mime, that I had disapproved of so strongly before, seemed only to make the general effect more convincing. Without it, indeed, there would have been the pettiness, the haphazardness, the "messiness," which is so much in evidence on the ballet-stage of the present day . . . But how can one regain that which is lost? Where now, can ballet-schools be found to teach the traditions of centuries of experience—the traditions that became the real foundations of the art of the Ballet?

After the rehearsal I had no more doubts that fate had brought me together with the very person I needed, and it was natural that my friendship with the young ballet-master should develop quickly. Our meetings became more and more frequent; either it would be he who came to see me and we would sit talking about the most varied subjects till the late hours, or I would go to him, where I was received with the greatest hospitality by his wife, the beautiful dancer, Vera Petrovna (they were a newly-married couple, and their young "romance" was a joy to behold), and by his aged, very pleasant mother. The Fokines lived in a modest but very comfortable little flat near the "Five Corners." It was some distance from our apartment on the Admiralty Canal, but I loved going to see them and used sometimes to return at daybreak, driving home with a sleepy *izvozchik* through the quiet, deserted streets.

All would have been wonderful had it not been for the hostile attitude of the Directorate, which, from the autumn onwards, had begun to take a threatening character. Their hostility was now directed against Fokine as well as me. Two years before, during the revolutionary years of 1905, the young artist had taken sides with his comrades and was one of their delegates to appear before the Director. Since then the odour of subversiveness had clung to him and it is possible that in 1907, when reaction had set in, his attitude had been remembered in high places and, *post factum*, certain displeasure made itself felt—just to discourage him from trying things on again. And now Fokine was making friends with such an enemy of the Directorate as I was considered to be! But Fokine was not at all concerned. He knew perfectly well that they could not do without him and, in any case, being a genuinely talented man, he had no doubt that he would in the end get his own way and would "have the last word."

The hostility towards me became especially obvious at one of the rehearsals of *Le Pavillon*. I had invited Diaghilev to be present as he was "dying of curiosity" to see how my ballet was getting on. He was eager, too, to savour once again the atmosphere of the "theatrical laboratory" in which he had lived for two years and of which he had since been deprived. It never entered my head that the appearance of my friend would be regarded as a lapse in tact, particularly as the presence of other friends of mine, who often came to rehearsals, had never provoked a protest. This time, however, an extremely unpleasant incident occurred, and I am perfectly certain that it was prompted by the wish to annoy me rather than to insult Diaghilev. Diaghilev had been watching the rehearsal for more than half an hour when he was approached by a police officer who politely but firmly requested him to leave the theatre immediately. I tried to protest, but the officer remained unmoved and Diaghilev was obliged to go, feeling almost the same bitterness of disgrace as when he was dismissed. It is possible that Seriozha firmly decided on revenge for all these insults. Certainly he could not have invented a better way than to create his own, world-famous theatre. . . .

Soon after this incident, which had greatly upset me, another occurred, characteristic of what was going on behind the scenes. A week before the performance, our prima ballerina, Kshesinskaya, suddenly refused to go on with her part of Armide. As she gave no satisfactory reasons for her refusal, it seemed rather suspicious. Evidently Matilda Felixovna acted in order to please the Directorate, hoping that her refusal would put a stop to the production. We at any rate took it to be a plot against us and in consequence had some moments of demoralisation. Luckily the crisis did not last long—only about an hour. Pavlova was present at that rehearsal and, hearing about Kshesinskaya's refusal, immediately offered to take her place. We of course were delighted to accept her offer. To this day I can vividly remember the scene. It took place in the Director's box, where Fokine and I had remained after the rehearsal, discussing the crisis. I can see Annushka rushing in, her flushed face and slim figure as she sat on the barrier of the box with her back to the theatre, and the expression of happiness with which she accepted our torrent of thanks.

Fokine immediately set to work to go through the part with her and, sure enough, at the next rehearsal, Anna Pavlovna was *ready*. *Nous de perdions pas au change*. In spite of her exceptional qualities, Matilda Felixovna yielded in some respects to her younger rival, who, besides technical perfection, possessed a natural *port de reine* and a delicate beauty which was then in full bloom.[1]

Though this crisis was so brilliantly resolved, Fokine and I, as the date of the performance approached, became very anxious, expecting, at any moment, something to happen which would finally ruin our enterprise. It was only natural that I should seek sympathy and encouragement in those moments of suspense. I found them in the persons of Prince Argutinsky and S. S. Botkin, who were both most anxious to save *Armide*. I only regretted deeply that their efforts were not united—for those two excellent people had quarrelled and were not on speaking terms. Each of them separately visited me every day and did their utmost to use all social and theatrical connections to prevent our enemies from having their way, but they never came together. Now, from a distance, it all seems rather ludicrous, but at the time we took our anxieties and worries very far from lightly. We were all sick with fear that the performance of *Armide*, which seemed now to have become a common effort, would perish, and we awaited it as a decisive battle which had to be won *at all costs*.

[1] It is curious that at that time I had already painted the "Gobelins" for *Le Pavillon* and had endeavoured to give a resemblance of Kshesinskaya to Armide's features. A photograph of Matilda Felixovna and Gerdt had been especially taken for this middle group, for which they posed in their costumes. The resemblance, however, was not so great as to entail the alteration of the Gobelins after Kshesinskaya's refusal, and it served for Pavlova and all others who succeeded her. After Kshesinskaya's refusal, Gerdt made another attempt to "get out" of his part of René, which he continued to regard as unsuitable for him, and Fokine and I had again to overcome his resistance.

It was at this period that I and N. M. Bezobrazov, who was still considered the king of *balletomanes* and whose influence in the ballet world was enormous, began to find more and more in common. The reader may recollect my story about the performance of *The Hump-backed Horse* when I first "took in" Nikolai Mikhailovitch, who happened to be in the neighbouring box. He had then been a rather stout but still young and healthy man. Now, after twenty years, he had turned into a sad, tired old man. He had become a rather important personality who was never spoken of otherwise than as "General Bezobrazov," although his rank was purely civil, as Nikolai Mikhailovitch had nothing of a soldier in him. It simply meant that he had attained the rank of Privy Councillor, which was equivalent to the military rank of Lieutenant-General, as it was the custom in Russia to address as "General" or "Your Excellency," those who belonged to the "first four ranks" in both services.

In his time Bezobrazov had had innumerable love-affairs in the ballet world, some of which were famous. Now in his old age he had a friendship with the dancer A. G. Vassilieva, who was mediocre as an artist and far from being beautiful, but was a very nice and kind woman. She was also on very friendly terms with my great friend Argutinsky—*honi soit qui mal y pense.*

Bezobrazov and Vassilieva lived *maritalement* in a smallish flat whose walls were covered with ballet souvenirs. Very soon this *nid d'amours séniles*, which was two steps away from the theatre, right opposite the Nikolsky Cathedral, became the place of our gatherings and, so to speak, our headquarters. Several times we were invited to take part in their modest dinner, but we mostly met there for tea. Bezobrazov belonged to the *côterie* which hated Teliakovsky and Krupensky and we often referred to the formula: *ceterum censeo—Teliakovskium delendum esse*! And with it went a whole programme for the future: Diaghilev was to return to the Theatre as Director, while we were all to be his collaborators and the reformers of the Russian Theatre. With such proud aims in view, we had now to *déjouer toutes les intrigues* and ward off every possibility of being defeated.

Chapter XVIII

TRIUMPH OF LE PAVILLON D'ARMIDE

THE decisive moment of our work had at last arrived—we had reached the day of the dress-rehearsal. Every part was ready and had been separately rehearsed and checked. All that was missing was certain properties and details of costume. My only regret was that, in a sudden fit of economy, Krupensky had refused to have the helmets of the knights, imprisoned in Armide's garden, decorated with the enormous plumes of white feathers on which I had especially relied. The great feather fans that were to be carried by the band of little black boys, who were to appear from under the floor, were also missing. I had been told that Krupensky had said: "Benois is quite mad—it is impossible to get such a quantity of feathers in the whole town. I certainly refuse to let him have them." And yet, in the days when I was in his favour, he had been particularly delighted with the knights and their head-dresses, when examining my sketches for the costumes, and had never uttered a word of protest.

The reader may think that all this was a mere trifle and hardly worth while worrying about. But in the theatre it is "trifles" that play an enormous part. The gradation of effects had been arranged by me in such a way as to make the appearance of the foaming cascade of feathers the crowning magnificence of the sumptuous splendour that had gone before. . . . I must add that I was quite ready to have imitation feathers instead of ostrich ones, as I found that these imitations made a far better show on the stage. But even worsted imitations were refused by the Directorate and I was sorry to think how poor and plucked my knights were going to look, and how ineffective the appearance of the black boys. A far greater disappointment was awaiting us at the dress rehearsal.

The dancers had long been fully trained in their parts. They had rehearsed several times on the stage with the décor, but not in costume, as Krupensky did not allow the *corps de ballet* to use the costumes before the dress rehearsal for fear of their getting crumpled and soiled. When the artists now appeared in costumes they had not seen before, with their pompous wigs and complicated head-dresses, there was a great bustle and confusion. The artists could not recognise each other, kept losing their partners and muddling their entries. Fokine was losing his temper. Instead of a beautifully polished performance, worthy of a fête in Versailles, we were watching a chaotic muddle that was strangely reminiscent of Gorsky's hateful productions. . . . We immediately announced to the Director that the performance could not be given without another rehearsal in costumes; otherwise it would be a disgrace. The answer was that this could not be allowed on any account as the programmes for the première had already been printed, giving the date of forty-eight hours hence. We were indignant, too, to discover that our première was to be given *after* the whole of *Le Lac des Cygnes*, which meant that *Le Pavillon* would appear when the public would be tired, less inclined to be benevolent and still less capable of enthusiasm. It was even rumoured that an organised cabal had been formed against us! We were quite justified, it seemed, in expecting a disgraceful fiasco, which would look as if it had been really deserved.

I believe I have already explained that I am an extremely peace-loving person, that I hate any quarrels or rows. I am always ready to give in wherever I can, keeping to the proverb "a bad peace is better than a good quarrel." It is due, no doubt, to my hatred of quarrels, and my consequent affability, that I have had so many quarrels, rows and setbacks in my life. But in the present case it was indispensable to save our progeny *at any price*—or to free ourselves from the responsibility for its failure. I decided to make use of the Press. Bakst's brother, Isaiah Rosenberg, was collaborating in a small way in the daily chronicle column of the *St. Petersburg Gazette*, the most popular and widely-read newspaper in theatrical circles. Before leaving the theatre, I rang him up on the telephone and asked him to "interview" me. Isaiah caught at the idea with delight, but sensibly advised me to write the interview myself. This I hastened to do and, taking my article to him, we went through it together, softening the passages where I had been too ruthless. Krupensky's name was supplanted by a transparent incognito—"someone in brass buttons"; the gist of the interview consisted of a characterisation of the ways of a directorate utterly bound by red tape, showing that such a directorate alone was sufficient to make the complete failure of my work almost inevitable.

The interview appeared the next morning, which was a Saturday, and was a bombshell. Before evening we were informed that the première of *Le Pavillon d'Armide* had been postponed for a whole week. At the same time I received a notification from the directorate signed by G. I. Vuitch, Manager of the office of the Imperial Theatres, who, it seemed, greatly disliked Krupensky, and was probably delighted with what had happened. The note was an invitation to come to *two* extra dress rehearsals, which were to take place within the next few days. I must confess that such a result of my "bombshell" surpassed all my expectations. In lighting the fuse I had never thought that the explosion would have any definite consequences, least of all that the Directorate would acknowledge its mistake—even if indirectly. Now we had the opportunity to improve and arrange everything and to present the performance in a model way. Further, I had received from Vuitch permission to have the feathers about which I was so anxious, and they actually appeared on the helmets and fans at the second of these supplementary rehearsals. There was only one thing the Directorate had not agreed to alter: the première of *Le Pavillon d'Armide* must still come after *Le Lac des Cygnes*, but this did not worry us so much now, for once we were ready there would be nothing to be ashamed of.

Dear Prince Argutinsky had taken measures to secure the good grace of the *Novoye Vremya* and Yuri Beliaev, the most brilliant journalist of that influential paper, had promised to come to the première, to stay till the end, and to treat our ballet with sympathy.

Le grand jour arrived. . . . It was the 25th of November, 1907, and it was truly a great day—for it was a day of the utmost significance in our lives. After two extra rehearsals, where everything had been *mis au point*, we were no longer anxious; we were only sorry that *Le Pavillon* was to begin so late. And sure enough, when the very ordinary performance of *Le Lac des Cygnes* was over and Tcherepnine had mounted the conductor's desk, it was a quarter past eleven.

At the first bang from the orchestra, the stalls and boxes became silent, the curtain rose slowly and the performance began. Behind the glass doors of the darkened *pavillon* appeared the servants of the old Marquis with lanterns, preceding the entrance of the Marquis and the young René. They lit the candles in the chandeliers and the flickering light disclosed the graceful interior of the *pavillon*. The scene un-folded exactly as I had imagined it. The diabolical Marquis was receiving his unexpected guest with refined, old-world courtesy; Gerdt as René seemed younger and more handsome than ever. Oh, how convincing he was in his amazement and admiration of the sinister magnificence of the architecture, how struck he seemed by the beauty of the lady of the Gobelins, about whom the Marquis began at once to relate the most alluring and yet terrifying details! What gladdened me most was the real "Hoffmann" atmosphere that pervaded the whole scene, the ex-pectation of something fatal and supernatural, immi-nent but inevitable.

I shall not describe the whole performance. It passed without a hitch. Even if the public felt a little bewildered by the unusual subject and by the fact that there were no dances in the first and third scenes (except "the March of the Hours") and that the *divertissement* in the second scene was much longer than usual, it showed its approval very distinctly. Frantic applause burst after the Buffoons' Dance, for which Tcherepnine had devised a wonderfully pro-voking rhythm, and where Fokine's talents had been superbly effective.[1] Although it was the Buffoons' Dance that produced the loudest shouts of acclama-tion, all the other numbers were greeted with thun-derous applause and demands of "Encore." At the end of the performance, although the hand of the clock was approaching 1 a.m., we, the three creators of the ballet, were loudly demanded by the public. For the first time in my life, I had the vainglorious pleasure of appearing behind the footlights. Anna Pavlovna, her arms full of the flowers she had just received, kissed me, Fokine and Tcherepnine in front of the public, while Gerdt, deeply moved, kept

[1] The success of the Buffoons' Dance was due, to a great extent, to the leader, the young dancer Rosay.

pressing my hands.   Everyone was happy and pleased.
The Director's box alone remained empty and silent.

It was decided to celebrate our success with a
traditional supper, and my wife and I were taken by
our friends to Medvied.   S. S. Botkin was wreathed
in smiles and expressed his delight by his extraordinarily infectious laughter.   Diaghilev was equally
delighted and pleased.   He had met me in the theatre
with the prophetic sentence: "This must be shown to
Europe," and these words were in full accordance
with the plans for advertising Russian Art which we
had nourished since the Exhibition of 1906.

Chapter XIX

BORIS GODUNOV IN PARIS

IT was not possible immediately to acquaint the public abroad with the Russian Ballet. The enterprise which Diaghilev had long ago planned, and which had begun to take definite shape since 1908, had first to be realised. This enterprise was a series of performances of *Boris Godunov*, which were to be given in Paris. Diaghilev had undertaken this ambitious task with the support of the Grand Duke Vladimir Alexandrovitch, through whom he hoped to get all the necessary funds. He also needed his influence for the forthcoming struggle with the directorate of the Imperial Theatres. Our "madman" Seriozha intended to take the entire cast of the grand opera abroad, beginning with the principal artists, headed by Chaliapin, and ending with the orchestra and choir. The décor and costumes were to be those that Golovin had created for the Moscow theatre. In order to obtain all this it was necessary to have the authority of the Grand Duke. Vladimir Alexandrovitch was, on the whole, favourably inclined towards us. His Imperial Highness had confided the artistic education of his children to Bakst, he was a frequent buyer at our exhibitions, and Diaghilev and I were continually summoned to his presence in order to hear his personal approval of our publications. This encouragement and approbation from "high quarters" was considered by many to be unmerited. Incorrigible conservative elements still looked upon us as decadents, revolutionaries or jesters. The Imperial Academy of Arts was especially indignant that the August President patronised such lovers of unseemliness as we were considered by the old professors and honorary members, who also accused us of throwing over all the statutes of acknowledged Art.

Still, in spite of high patronage, it proved impossible to secure the décor and costumes of *Boris Godunov* for Paris. The Directorate, under some plausible excuse, refused to allow us to use them. We had to think about arranging our own production. The painter Yegorov, who had recently aroused interest by his production of the *Blue Bird* in the Moscow Arts Theatre,[1] was to execute the set designed by Golovin. Seriozha decided to occupy himself with the costumes —for which Bilibin and Steletzky, the two great connoisseurs of ancient Russia, had sketched several examples—in order to help the tailors to create what was needed. Then we scoured the Tartar junk-shops and other special places in the Alexandrovsky and Schukin Market where antique materials were sold, buying up silk and brocade shawls, embroidered collars, head-dresses and so on. In those days things of this kind were still to be had in great profusion and were not very expensive. We were delighted at the thought that Paris would see *de l'authentique*; genuine luxury which was not usually to be seen on the stage. But it was not possible to dress the several hundred people which the coronation scene of *Boris Godunov* demanded, and therefore the greater part of the costumes were made with new materials which had to be dyed. The result was that these new costumes proved to be infinitely more effective than our authentic ones. It would have been better still had our costumes been made according to the

---

[1] The décor of the "Polish" act was mine, and that of Chrom by the Moscow artist C. Yuon.

principle then adopted in Russian theatres—with cheap materials, which were transformed into magnificent brocades of the sixteenth and seventeenth centuries by hand-painting. In our following productions we did not fall again into similar mistakes and confided the work to the artist-dyer Salnikov, who was a genius and a poet in his sphere.

The detailed description of our work on *Boris Godunov* does not enter into the plan of this book, yet I cannot be altogether silent about it. In a way this performance was a sort of general rehearsal for all that was to follow. It was the first time we were appearing in a foreign city with the work we had created in Russia, the first time we had met with masses of financial difficulties and obstacles and faced all sorts of intrigue. There were moments when our performances at the Opéra seemed to us to be a very dangerous adventure which might end badly.

It was among my duties to superintend the lighting and hanging of the sets, to distribute the right costumes and suitable make-up, besides innumerable other jobs in the complicated business of a nomadic camp. Oh, how I cursed the unending stairs and corridors of the Opéra ! . . . One had to manage somehow or other to be everywhere at the same time : in the stores, which had been turned into workrooms for the staff of our St. Petersburg tailor, in the special *atelier* under the very skies where Stelletzky himself superintended the painting of the properties, in the basement where boxes were being unpacked, and in the dressing-rooms, where dirty and smelly rabble (who in those times took the place of permanent "walkers-on") were being transformed into boyars and archimandrites ! In the meanwhile Diaghilev was calling on influential people, canvassing the house for his première, giving lunches and dinners to those whose support he needed, stuffing journalists with the necessary information and even preliminary notices. In those days people had the most fantastic ideas about Russian history, which is hardly known in Europe even to-day. Mussorgsky had barely been heard of and it was only experts like our sympathetic friends, C. Bellaigu, Brussel and Calvocoressi, who really knew anything about us at all. We used to return to the hotel at one o'clock at night, half dead with fatigue; yet we thoroughly enjoyed all this work which was so new to us, and were sad to think that it would soon be over. . . .

What a lot of experience we went through in those days! Experiences that were amusing, alarming, tragi-comic and charming! I cannot think without emotion about our daily meetings which used to take place in the three rooms occupied by Seriozha at the Hôtel de Hollande. Chaliapin was staying at the same hotel and every night he used to descend to Diaghilev's rooms and amuse us with his jokes and tales. It was here that I heard Scriabine playing his piano pieces to Seriozha, but I do not remember what they were, nor why he was playing them. Possibly there was an idea of his creating something for the stage, but nothing ever came of it.

PART III

THE *BALLETS RUSSES*

Chapter I

COLLABORATION WITH FOKINE

OUR activities in Paris in the spring of 1908 must undoubtedly be considered as the prelude to our first Opera and Ballet season of 1909. But there are several events of importance that took place before that date.

The development of my friendship with Fokine seems to me to have been of the highest significance for the future of the *Ballets Russes*. Some weeks after the première of *Boris Godunov* in Paris, our friendship found creative expression in our joint work over a tiny ballet—lasting about fifteen minutes—which we rigged up for the annual students' ball of the Academy of Arts, given in a club on the Vladimirskaya Street.

We had undertaken this trifle solely for our own amusement. After the intense preparations for *Le Pavillon d'Armide*, we greatly missed the excitement of creative work,[1] and here at last was an opportunity. I composed the libretto myself and the simple décor was done from my sketches by a professional. The music consisted of Clementi's Sonatinas—for I fully shared Mozart's tender love for these graceful trifles; they contain more genuine music than many a full-scale, classical symphony . . . The orchestral transcription of the piano pieces was entrusted to the conductor Keller, who had worked for Fokine before and was soon to produce the first orchestration of

[1] I had plenty of other work, but felt irresistibly drawn to return to the ballet.

Chopiniana. We had considerable difficulty in the casting. Only four dancers were required for the parts of Pantaloon, Columbine, Harlequin and Pierrot, but none of Fokine's comrades could respond to our invitation. They were categorically forbidden by the august and frowning Directorate. Even the retired artist Lukyanov refused to take part, fearing to spoil his relations with the authorities. However, several other "veterans" of the ballet were delighted to help us: these were Cecchetti, who took the role of Pantaloon, Marie Petipa, who, alas, thanks to her venerable age, was not very convincing as Columbine, and Bekeffy, who did not lack brilliance as Harlequin.

The performance had little success. The young people who had come to dance could see no point in the "Venetian trifle" that had interrupted their ball at its height. Somewhere, in a Palazzo Rezzonico, in the shape of an intermezzo between two acts of a Goldoni comedy, our Harlequinade might have been considered charming, for Fokine had put his best into it. But here in this club, in front of a public who had no idea either of Venice of the eighteenth century or of the *Commedia dell' Arte*, our performance must have seemed very dull, and certainly out-of-place. The curtain had hardly been lowered over the final group when the voice of the "master of ceremonies" shouted: "*A vos places, Mesdames et Messieurs*" and the opening chords of the Quadrille vibrated through the hall. Nevertheless the curtain had to rise again and Marie Mariusovna received a beautiful bouquet. How this modest ovation differed from her former triumphs! How little this rather heavy and ungraceful lady, crowned with a dishevelled wig, breathless and flushed, resembled the vision who received the passionate kiss of Lukyanov in front of a raving audience and an enamoured boy of thirteen, at the end of the famous "Ukrainian Dance."

Soon after the ball Fokine again distinguished himself in two ballets which were not given as official productions of the Imperial Theatres, but were presented to the public as charity performances. Although the directors were unfavourable towards their young and brilliant ballet-master, still they did not forbid the artists to take part in these performances and even placed the Maryinsky Theatre stage and some of their sets and costumes at his disposal. Who could have thought then that those two modest ballets would soon be world-famous? Fokine himself, in his most ambitious dreams, could hardly have contemplated anything so improbable. But fate had decided that this should happen and one must agree that in this case fate proved to have both taste and judgment.

The two ballets were *Chopiniana*, which afterwards became *Les Sylphides*, and *Une Nuit d'Egypte*, which became *Cléopâtre*. I had been so enchanted by *Chopiniana* and *Une Nuit d'Egypte* when I watched the rehearsals and performances that I there and then resolved to include these masterpieces in our programme should we take the Russian Ballet abroad. My wish was granted next year. *Chopiniana*, transformed, at my instigation, into *Les Sylphides*, was to fill a certain gap by showing what the Russian Ballet could achieve in the romantic style.

There was still more for me to do in the creation of *Une Nuit d'Egypte* (a ballet to the music of Arensky), not, of course, as far as the dancing was concerned, but in the reconstruction of the subject, which both Fokine and I had found to be impossible in its original form. The much-discussed idea of concealing the "love duet" of Cleopatra and the unfortunate Amoûn behind curtains, drawn by women slaves in front of the regal couch, belonged to me. The alterations in the subject were limited to the regrouping of some of the numbers, so as to give the action a

K

logical development; but afterwards, for the Paris performances, I insisted on a radical change, making the final scene of the ballet a tragic one instead of the original "happy ending."

As regards the décor and costumes, the usual limitation of funds, inevitable at charity performances, forced us to take advantage of what was to hand. The costume question in *Chopiniana* was easily solved as all the artistes had white *tu-tus à la Taglioni*. As relics of what seemed, at the time, a forgotten age, they had a particular charm. One of the "fragments" of the panorama for the *La Belle au Bois Dormant* served as the set for *Chopiniana* and I remember how Fokine and I had the whole of it, the length of which measured forty yards, unfurled a day or two before the performance, in order to choose the fragment which would be the most suitable background for the "white" ballet. That was the last time I saw Botcharov's charming picture—the picture that had appeared before the St. Petersburg public eighteen years before and had continued to delight it ever since.

The production of *Une Nuit d'Egypte* presented greater difficulties. It demanded first of all a great number of costumes. It was possible to use some from *Aïda* and *La Fille du Pharaon*; but it proved necessary to have a few perfectly new ones. They were made from the designs by Bakst, and were incomparably more graceful and more in keeping with the dress of ancient Egypt. Levushka was particularly successful with his heavy, pleated brown and blue costumes for the Jewish dance, which, one felt, bore traces of atavistic influence. The décor for *Une Nuit d'Egypte* proved satisfactory. It consisted, if I am not mistaken, of the wings taken from another ballet, to which Allegri had added a palm-tree grove of his own invention. The moonlight produced the required atmosphere of mystery. The part of Cleopatra was taken by Ludmilla Barasch—a beautiful young woman but a poor dancer. She only just managed not to spoil the part.

Fokine deplored the fact that he could not give the part to a private pupil of his—a young society girl to whom he was giving lessons and whom he greatly praised, considering her to be unusually gifted. Bakst, too, was most enthusiastic about this "beautiful genius" whom he had got to know even before Fokine. They both made a great secret of their "discovery," whispering together about her and answering my questions evasively—the young girl was preparing for the theatre without the knowledge of her parents, who were entirely against it, etc. At last the secret was out. The girl's name was Rubinstein, niece of Daniel Rubinstein, a rather exquisite creature and great friend of our acquaintance, Mita Benckendorff, an old patron and "pupil" of Bakst.

The next thing was that Ida Rubinstein was going to appear in public in the part of Salome in Oscar Wilde's famous play, so popular in those days. The actress Vera Komisarjevskaya, who was then at the height of her fame, was also producing *Salomé* the same year. Thus St. Petersburg was to see two different versions of the biblical drama at the same time, and the town was full of all sorts of "exciting" rumours. The appearance on the stage of St. John the Baptist aroused many discussions, as many people considered it sacriligious. But still greater excitement was caused by the rumour that in the dance of the Seven Veils, Salome was gradually to throw off all her coverings and appear completely naked. The news was especially exciting in the case of Ida Rubinstein; it would, after all, be an unusual situation for a young girl belonging to a conventional and well-to-do family. It must be remembered that in those days nudity on the stage was quite inadmissible, and that even Isadora Duncan's bare legs were considered extremely indecent by some people.

Unfortunately the expectations of the St. Petersburg public were to be disappointed. At the very last minute both performances were forbidden by the censor and, in spite of all solicitations, were taken off the stage. The dress rehearsal of Komisarjevskaya's production was attended by "a select few." The final and reprehensible moment of the dance was dissimulated by means of a lighting "trick." I have but a faint recollection of the rehearsal with Ida Rubinstein, and only remember the impression made on me by Glazunov's music which had been especially composed for the occasion. Still, this first appearance of the future celebrity was not without consequence. We had occasion to see what an unusually attractive vision she proved to be on the stage. The enthusiastic praise of Fokine and Bakst was justified and their wish that Ida should be entrusted with the part of Cleopatra, should *Une Nuit d'Egypte* be taken to Paris, met with full sympathy and approval.

Chapter II

PREPARATIONS

OUR plans for the forthcoming Russian Season in Paris began to take a more concrete shape from the beginning of 1909. We had been deeply grieved by the loss of the chief patron of our enterprise, the Grand Duke Vladimir Alexandrovitch, who had done so much for the production of *Boris Godunov* and for our tour abroad. He died suddenly on the 9th February, 1909 (old style). We were, however, reassured by his august widow, the Grand Duchess Marie Pavlovna, who promised to support us in the place of her deceased husband, and her patronage seemed to be entirely reliable.

Diaghilev, in the past, had often been clever in obtaining funds. Once more he decided to resort to a method which, though rather distasteful to his friends—some of us considered it downright dishonest—promised nevertheless the desired results, that is, 100,000 gold roubles or, in contemporary money, about two million francs, a sum which would be sufficient for preliminary expenses. The "method" consisted in helping a manufacturer of goloshes, who had no connection whatsoever with the theatre, in his application for the status of nobility as a reward for his donations to charity. The manufacturer's ambitious dreams had been guessed by Diaghilev's clever but unscrupulous financial adviser D., and Seriozha had no doubts about the support of the Grand Duchess, as the late Grand Duke had known about the plan and had promised to pull strings where necessary. "Let him give the money and I will give my signature at the right time," the Grand Duke used to say.[1]

The preparations and work for our performances were in full swing when the Grand Duchess suddenly refused to give us her support—either because Diaghilev had somehow offended her or because she had listened to the insinuations of his enemies. This unexpected blow caused great consternation and confusion in our camp. The whole enterprise was now hanging by a thread and Diaghilev experienced once again one of the blows of fate he so often suffered. Moreover, it looked very much like a catastrophe. Depending on the 100,000 roubles, we had already spent a great deal of money—artists engaged in St. Petersburg and Moscow, sets and costumes ordered. At last, fearing the repercussions of the coming scandal, the Grand Duchess gave in and signed the necessary paper, but definitely refused any further help.

During our work at the production of *Boris Godunov* in 1908, the stage of the charming, classical Hermitage Theatre, built during the reign of Catherine II, had been placed at our disposal, thanks to the intercession of the Grand Duke Vladimir. It was here, under my supervision, that the artist Lockenberg painted the décor I had sketched for the "Polish Scene" of *Boris Godunov*. Here, too, some of the costumes were made and packed before our departure for Paris. A display of all the costumes was organised on the unusually spacious and well-lighted stage, and the Grand Duke inspected all of them with great attention and interest.

---

[1] One must bear in mind that there was nothing *illegal* in the manufacturer's application. It was a traditional practice to grant the status of nobility to representatives of important old firms. Our point of view was that it was reprehensible as similar affairs usually passed through hands that were not too clean.

During that period I had grown to look upon the Hermitage Theatre, which formed part of the great Winter Palace, as something of "my own," and it gave me enormous pleasure to frequent it. It was entered from the famous Picture Gallery, by crossing the Venetian Bridge over the Winter Canal. As I was almost an *habitué* of the gallery, and was at that time compiling a guide-book of the pictures, I visited it daily. Crossing over, *de plein pied*, from the gallery where I worked as an historian of art, to the delightful rooms where I became a theatrical painter, had a peculiar charm for me. I delighted in the theatre itself—a *chef d'œuvre* of Guarenghi; admiring its ideal proportions, I tried to imagine what it looked like in the days when the great Empress was throned there, surrounded by her magnates and friends.

In 1909 the Hermitage Theatre was again placed at our disposal for the rehearsals of the ballets. This time, instead of being covered with paint pots and stage canvases, the private Imperial stage would be occupied by the ballets we were going to take to Paris—among them a new version of the *Pavillon*. Naturally, when I arrived at the Hermitage Theatre for the first rehearsal, I was filled with agreeable anticipation. The artists were already in their dressing-rooms, the dressers, their arms full of foaming tulle skirts, were hurrying along the labyrinths of corridors, and it looked as if the prologue of the performance I was going to watch was already in full swing. But here I was suddenly accosted by Diaghilev's secretary, M., who imparted to me the astounding news that we were to collect all our belongings and leave the premises immediately, as the permission to work there had been suddenly taken from us! Needless to say, the consternation was extreme. Fortunately, half an hour later M. had comforting news for us: our indefatigable leader had rushed off all over the town to find some suitable rehearsing hall and had already something in view. Shortly after this came a telephone message inviting us all to a certain "Catherine Hall" on the Catherine Canal.

I shall never forget that romantic exodus. M. and I headed the procession in one cab, all our artists, dressers with their baskets and stage hands followed behind in others. The long procession stretched across the whole town. The day was dismal and dull but luckily dry. The atmosphere of adventure—almost of a picnic—seemed to soften our slight feeling of shame at having been "turned out," and when we reached the little-known "Catherine Hall" we liked it so much that our spirits rose immediately. It was the newly-decorated building of a German Club with an impressive entrance and monumental staircase overlooked by an excellent full-sized portrait of Catherine II. This seemed to us to be a good omen. We had just been turned out of *her* Hermitage and here she was meeting us in the new place with her famous gracious smile, full of intelligence and benevolence. . . . The rehearsals started at once and from that moment we had them daily till our departure for Paris.[1]

The rehearsals were a real enchantment. Before one's eyes, as it were, Fokine was ceaselessly giving birth to new and beautiful ideas. There was, from the start, an atmosphere of friendly and eager collaboration. What a charming picture the theatre hall presented when the young people who were not busy on the stage streamed in to watch the performance—sitting in the stalls, in the broad daylight that poured through the tall windows. In many ways it resembled the memorable first rehearsal of *Le Pavillon* in the Imperial School, but here the atmosphere was different. In the Imperial *école de*

[1] I do not remember where the opera rehearsals took place. Possibly not in St. Petersburg at all, as the operas to be produced were all well known to the artistes.

danse there was an air of official severity; all the pupils, boys and girls, had, from their earliest youth, been subject to a strict discipline. Here, in the Catherine Hall, there was no trace of red tape or officialdom; our gatherings were very informal and gay.

This did not prevent the work from being very intensive. Fokine spared neither himself nor others. He could even be abrupt and rude at times; women dancers, occasionally, would weep under the lash of his scolding. But all weariness and bad feelings disappeared when the whole company assembled at the modest but very tasteful meals "supplied by the Directorate." They were served in the theatre buffet on long narrow tables, at which the artistes were joined by Diaghilev, "General" Bezobrazov and our ballet critic Svetlov; sometimes, too, the Tsar's physician, S. S. Botkin, would come, or Prince Argutinsky. Our meal would become almost a family feast.

I think that the happy atmosphere in which we prepared for our first Paris season had much to do with its subsequent success. It gave the whole company fresh vitality. From ballet-master and *premiers danseurs* to the last dancer in the *corps de ballet*, everyone seemed to unfold and become utterly devoted to the art. Of course, Fokine's imagination would have been no less inspired had he worked in different surroundings. But the condition of the "human material" he was working with, which he was "moulding," so to speak, was, on this occasion, particularly apt to his touch. Much of what he was creating was entirely unexpected and new to the company, but it was at once assimilated. The ballet-master's spirit must indeed have been delighted and refreshed by the *happiness* of his contact with the company. Those of us who sat watching the work from the stalls were equally happy; here, we felt something was maturing that would amaze the world.

K*

Chapter III

INVASION OF PARIS

WE really did stagger the world. The Russian Season in Paris, which many of our compatriots considered as nothing more than "a rather successful enterprise," turned out to be something like a "general offensive," arduous, but undertaken with enthusiasm. Possibly some of those taking part were not fully conscious of the significance of the moment, but the entire company seemed to be possessed by a kind of fervour and "every soldier went into battle" feeling that his was a sacred cause . . . While rehearsals in Paris were still in progress on the dimly-lit stage (these rehearsals sometimes ended in quarrels and rows and nervous breakdowns, for the time was short and there was still much to be done), many of those who were watching and especially we, the "directors," had the firm conviction that "Paris had no chance."

The reader knows that I am a Westerner. Everything in Europe lying west of Russia is dear to me and there is no place in the world dearer than Paris, the city of genius, that has been for centuries the fountain and source of vital energy, of beauty, of scientific enlightenment and generous social ideals. Yet, stifling deep in my heart my feeling of resentment at the forthcoming victory of the "barbarians," I felt from the very first days of our work in Paris that the Russian Savages, the Scythians, had brought to the "World Capital," for judgment, the best of art that then existed in the world. A circle of fanatical worshippers—*les fervents des russes*—formed itself round our work, growing wider and wider as time went on. It consisted of French critics, writers and artists who, better than any advertisement or review, announced to the town that in the Châtelet something amazingly beautiful was being prepared. As things promised, the Russian season seemed likely to satisfy not only our "national pride," but the needs of culture in general. Our French friends did nothing but repeat to us: "You have come at the most suitable moment, you are refreshing us, you are leading us to new themes and feelings." I personally felt convinced that the Russian season of 1909 might initiate a new era of the theatre for France and indeed for all Western Europe.[1] My conviction was in fact justified. The influence of the Russian performances, and above all of the Russian Ballet, began to grow and was felt, not only in the theatre, but in wider spheres as well. Later, it is true, the symptoms of recovery weakened and the Western theatre, instead of achieving the full bloom that one could have expected, succumbed to various heresies—sometimes of the most hideous kind. In Paris, particularly, the new cult of snobbery did much to stifle any fresh growth.

The adventurous spirit of the rehearsals in the Catherine Hall was felt again when our company, —our "gipsy camp"—arrived in Paris. Hardly any of the artists had been abroad before. Here they suddenly found themselves on the very banks of the Seine, in beautiful, sunny spring weather. The chief artists of the ballet and opera companies settled in the centre of the town in decent, if not first-class, hotels, but the majority were quartered near the Châtelet. A modest little hotel on the Boulevard

[1] I am quoting here almost the exact words of my article in the *Retch* of 19th June, 1909 (old style).

St. Michel was filled from basement to attics with our "ballet people." One heard them calling out to each other from all the rooms and corridors. It is well known that Russian people, even when they are well-bred, have a certain freedom of manner and difficulty in controlling themselves; even for a simple question or a piece of ordinary news, they express themselves with excessive temperament and in so loud a voice that "Europeans" just shrug their shoulders and murmur: "*Que voulez-vous, ce sont des sauvages!*"

One of the things that greatly surprised us was that the stage of the Châtelet Theatre, famous for its extravagant transformation scenes, was, compared to our own theatres, very primitively equipped. For *Le Pavillon d'Armide* an elaborate and reliable system of hatches and traps and transformation machinery was indispensable. Diaghilev was lucky enough to procure for his "adventure" a first-class stage-mechanic—K. F. Waltz of the Moscow Opera. It was under his management and guidance and with the permission of the directors of the Châtelet that a small party of Russian carpenters altered the whole stage, floor and wings. Their work began immediately after the rehearsals and went on late into the night. This was possible because the Russian theatrical workmen were handsomely rewarded, never grumbled, and gaily carried out all orders.[1]

The Châtelet was practically next door to the Boulevard St. Michel, and the Pont au Change presented a curious sight as crowds of young foreigners, talking loudly, kept crossing it, going to or from the theatre. Those of our ladies who possessed a little

[1] One day I nearly perished because of the whole Châtelet floor being in an upheaval. I stepped on to a sliding plank at the precise moment when it was undergoing a trial. I nearly fell into the abyss which had opened under me, but, straining every muscle, caught hold of the part that was immovable and for an instant found myself hanging in the air.

more money at once bought new hats and smart summer clothes and many of them, who had but lately looked like provincials, soon passed for real *parisiennes*. The men took much longer to become acclimatised.

Our joint lunches were delightful and usually took place in the famous Restaurant Zimmer, actually in the theatre building, or in the nearest Bouillon Duval or Bouillon Boulant. Since 1900 my "residence" in Paris had been the *maison meublée* in the Rue Cambon which is to-day a department of Chanel. I had my meals—when I was not invited *en ville*—at Weber's or in the excellent but now defunct restaurant Tourtel on the Boulevard de la Madeleine. But in the year I am speaking of I was so infatuated with our Bohemian life that I preferred modest meals with our artists in the Quartier Latin. Diaghilev's secretary M. used to join us more and more often; he was extremely attracted by one of the most talented artistes of the company. This led to a real and prolonged affair between them, but M.'s "unfaithfulness" called forth Diaghilev's unbounded rage; he dismissed M. and deprived him forever of his favour.[1]

Even before this happened, Diaghilev had quite openly deserted M., being more and more taken with Nijinsky. Those who were Diaghilev's confidants in his sentimental affairs assured us that Diaghilev's new infatuation had begun in the days of *Le Pavillon d'Armide*. If this story is true, Diaghilev

[1] Diaghilev's morals were no secret to us, and I was therefore extremely surprised by a remark he made one night when we were supping together at the Metropole in Moscow. The huge, newly-decorated restaurant hall had two floors, the second one consisting of separate cabinets like theatre boxes opening into the chief hall. Pointing out a woman who was leaning over the barrier, Seriozha told me that she was O.F., the sister of the famous S.F., and that she was the *only* woman that he could ever fall in love with. It was this same O.F. who three months later caused M. to "betray" Seriozha. Would not this story be an interesting contribution to the theory of *Wahlverwandschaften*?

must have been a perfect virtuoso at dissimulation. I had never seen Diaghilev and Nijinsky together till the days of our rehearsals in the Catherine Hall, and yet I saw Seriozha every day. . . . He sometimes pronounced Nijinsky's name, but only when alluding to him as an artist who deserved particular attention on account of his talent.

In Paris it became plain what an important place Nijinsky was to occupy in all our enterprises and to what an extent the "director" was infatuated with him. Diaghilev at once instituted an advertising campaign for the unknown artist and, before there had been any performance, my Paris friends used to say to me: "Il parait que vous avez parmi vos danseurs un prodige, un garçon d'un talent formidable." This talk was of course about Nijinsky. Nobody asked anything about Pavlova, whose portraits were displayed all over Paris, nor did anyone inquire in the same vein about Fokine.

Certainly Nijinsky justified his advance fame. I shall never forget his "soaring flights" in the *Pavillon d'Armide*. It was a *pas de trois* newly-composed for Paris by Fokine, to the music which originally accompanied the Shadow Dance and the *Enlèvement du Sérail*—two numbers of the *divertissement* that we had decided to omit in Paris so as not unduly to prolong the action. We had seen at the rehearsals how effective Nijinsky's appearance was going to be. He was to be Armide's slave, who accompanied her two confidantes, T. Karsavina and A. Fedorova. But when Vaslav appeared in the white, silver and yellow costume I had designed for him, that harmonised so well with the gold and yellow dresses of his ladies, the effect surpassed everything we had expected. From the moment Nijinsky sprung out of the wings, with his arms charmingly raised and his feet hardly touching the floor, Paris felt the presence of a genius. It is very difficult to define Nijinsky as a person.

In everyday life he was the most ordinary youth. In those days he was almost a boy; indeed he really remained a "boy" until the moment when he was overwhelmed by the insanity that cut short his career. He was of uninteresting appearance, rather short of stature, with a thick neck and large head. His features were almost vulgar, of slightly Mongolian type. He seldom opened his mouth to speak, and when he did, blushed violently, would become muddled, and then silent. What he said did not differ from the usual simple speech that one heard from his comrades. Later on, when, through Diaghilev's jealous guidance, he had collected some general knowledge and ideas on art, he sometimes ventured to air them, but what he said was confused and dull. Diaghilev used to feel embarrassed for his friend, who usually understood that it would be better for him to return to silence.

Nor did anything extraordinary ever happen at rehearsals. Nijinsky performed everything with unfailing precision, but there was something mechanical and automatic in his execution. . . . At the final rehearsals Nijinsky seemed to awaken from a sort of lethargy; he began to think and feel. The final metamorphosis took place when he put on his costume, about which he was always very particular, demanding that it should be an exact copy of the sketch made by the artist. At these moments the usually apathetic Vaslav, became nervous and capricious. Having put on the costume, he gradually began to change into another being, the one he saw in the mirror. He became re-incarnated and actually *entered* into his new existence, as an exceptionally attractive and poetical personality.

The fact that Nijinsky's metamorphosis was predominantly subconscious is in my opinion, the very proof of his genius. Only a genius—that is to say, a phenomenon that has no adequate natural explanation

—could incarnate the "choreographic essence of the rococo period" as did Nijinsky in *Le Pavillon d'Armide* —especially in the Paris version of my ballet. Only a genius could have given so authentic an image of the youth pining for his dead beloved in *Giselle.* His interpretations of the strange being who dances with the Sylphides, of the *Spectre de la Rose,* of the negro in *Schéhérazade* and of Petrouchka were equally manifestations of genius.

It was a great misfortune that Diaghilev, who had fully realised his friend's significance and value as an artist, should have over-estimated his intellect. Diaghilev imagined that he could make that fantastic being, who did not belong to this world and who understood nothing of life, into an active creator. He imagined that Nijinsky, who had no idea of his own, could become his, Diaghilev's "creative agent," thus taking the part that Fokine could not take, because Fokine had his *own* creative ideas. Moreover, Diaghilev, being of a passionate nature, tinged by a certain sentimentality, desired his friend to shine with incomparable brilliance and to "leave his mark in history"—but not *only* as a dancer. This is where the break came. Nijinsky gave in to this suggestion; he began to believe he could be a creator. But in spite of Diaghilev's and Bakst's endeavours to "feed" his efforts, his work was still-born. It is true that his ballets, which had been brought forth with such obvious pain and torment, contained sometimes new and curious details. But novelty and strangeness are not in themselves valuable. That is the real reason why Nijinsky's ballets did not succeed—in spite of the fact that the music for them had been composed by Stravinsky and Debussy. . . .

Chapter IV

OUR FIRST PARIS SEASON

TO our great disappointment, Pavlova could not arrive in time for the first Paris performance, as she was still tied by a previous contract. We had therefore to replace her in the *Pavillon d'Armide* by the Moscow prima ballerina Coralli, a good technician and a very beautiful woman but a pale performer lacking personality. The *premier danseur* of the Moscow ballet, Mordkin, took Gerdt's part as René de Beaugency. He was far too strong and vigorous a dancer for the part and lacked the poetical tenderness which should be the fundamental quality of my hero. But in Paris my ballet gained from the change in the part of the Marquis, which was taken by Bulgakov, in the place of Solianikov. In the latter part of the role, where the ancient Marquis is transformed into the magnificent wizard Hydrao, Bulgakov's interpretation was particularly successful. That Nijinsky was given full scope to distinguish himself was also a great asset. The Parisian public followed his dances with breathless interest and attention. Several successful cuts and re-arrangements of the musical numbers were made in the Paris version of *Le Pavillon*. The cuts shortened the action by at least a quarter of an hour. Lastly I had succeeded in greatly improving the décor and costumes, which had been made especially for the Paris stage. In the St. Petersburg version I had been worried by the neighbourhood of lilac, pink and yellow, and by the somewhat motley details of the décor for the second scene. These defects I now corrected. One of the most effective "improvements" was due to the insistence of our magician Waltz. He introduced two gigantic water pyramids at the end of the second scene instead of the insignificant jet of water in the St. Petersburg version of Armide's gardens. These silvery, foaming cascades made an enchanting and refreshing impression; the sound of their splashing mingled poetically with the music. To me this brought memories of my childhood, when I listened to the Imperial Orchestra in Peterhof playing to the accompaniment of the murmuring waters. . . .

Our first performance, *Le Pavillon d'Armide*, was meant to demonstrate to the French public our understanding and interpretation of that "most French of epochs, the eighteenth century." The result was remarkable. Those who were used to the sickly sweetness invariably used by the Paris theatres to characterise the Rococo epoch (as, for instance, the production of *Manon* in the Opéra Comique) found our colours too vivid and the grace of our dancers too pretentious. But for those who really understood Versailles, the Sèvres china, the tapestries, the gilt apartments of the palaces and the architectural parks, our *Pavillon d'Armide* was a revelation. Among our most enthusiastic friends were Robert de Montesquiou and Henri de Régnier himself.

Le Pavillon d'Armide fulfilled its mission in Paris. The examination had been passed, the reputation made. The "barbarians" had not only proved to be up to standard in their own "barbaric" and wild demonstrations, but had even beaten the "Athenians" themselves on their own ground.

Les Sylphides (as we had re-christened Fokine's *Chopiniana*) was the ballet which stood nearest in spirit to *Le Pavillon*. I had especially insisted on its

DÉCOR FOR THE SECOND SCENE OF *LE PAVILLON D'ARMIDE*
By Alexandre Benois, 1907

Facing p. 292

DÉCOR FOR *LES SYLPHIDES*
By Alexandre Benois, 1909

being included in our programme and had created a décor which was executed for the stage by my friend Yaremitch. In *Sylphides* too we interpreted an epoch common to the whole of Europe, the epoch of "Romanticism." And again we passed the test —in spite of our highly dangerous plan of translating Chopin's dreamy music into dance and transforming his pianoforte compositions by elaborate orchestration.

If the original idea of "expressing Chopin on the stage" belonged to Isadora Duncan, Fokine accomplished a very successful and significant variation of that principle by illustrating this typically 1830 music with a ballet *à la Taglioni*, instead of a classic Greek dance. Our first-class composers Liadov, Glazunov and Tcherepnine had not wished (or had been unable) to preserve Chopin's mood, and in solving the problems of orchestrating piano pieces they stamped them, too obviously, with their own style. They made their orchestral version too complicated and modern, lacking simplicity and airiness. Perhaps it would have been more in harmony to have kept to the piano, increasing its effectiveness here and there by a delicate accompaniment of flutes, violins and bassoons. The sounds should be softened, wrapped, so to speak, in a haze, in order to convey the impression given on the stage—the languid vision of spirits of dead maidens, dancing their dreamy dances among the moonlit ruins and mausoleums.

This was the atmosphere that my décor was calculated to evoke and it was enhanced by Fokine's dances, wonderfully performed by our artistes.[1] This atmosphere became especially tender and convincing when Pavlova (who had arrived for that performance)

[1] How absurd was the novelty introduced in our creation by de Basil when he used the copy of a well-known Corot as back-cloth for *Sylphides*. This error was not corrected by R. Blum when in place of Corot's *Souvenir de Mortefontaine* he used the same artist's *Danse des Nymphes*.

and Nijinsky appeared together on the stage. Their "dance-duet" with its high, noiseless, soaring flights, full of a tender delicate grace, conveyed the impression of a strange romance "beyond the grave," the hopeless love of bodiless spirits, who knew neither fiery embraces nor the sweetness of kisses, for whom all passion is replaced by sad caresses and soft, tremulous flitting . . .

I was not very pleased with the costume I had composed for Nijinsky. It seemed to me to be a trifle comic when I saw it on the stage. It consisted of a black velvet jacket, a collar *à l'enfant*, a light tie, long curls and white legs. And yet, his slightly caricatured appearance made the artist more like a figure from some old beaded *réticule* or painted lampshade. It was just such "funny improbable troubadours" who formed the dreams of our own grandmothers, the creators of the embroidered *réticules* and painted lampshades. In Chopin's music, through the sad tears of a tormented soul, there appears sometimes the strange and yet infinitely touching image of the pale youth who is danced to his death by the spirits of the cemetery . . . In this materialisation of Chopin's dreams, Fokine and his interpreters came much nearer to the illustration of his music than did Isadora Duncan. She danced both mazurka and nocturnes in the manner of an ancient Greek maiden, throwing back her head and clapping her hands, like figures on the vases from the British Museum or the Hermitage. Nevertheless, to Isadora belongs the honour of having first discovered a new principle. It was she who had the courage for the "heroic deed," and I shall not mock at her propaganda for new choreographic beauty—whose fruits have nourished us ever since.

The ballet *Cléopâtre* was far nearer to Isadora's ideas. It was the last ballet to be given during that Paris season, but it was the crowning glory of the whole affair. The reader will remember how delighted I had been with *Une Nuit d'Egypte* and it was I who insisted on this ballet being included in our repertoire. Diaghilev's only objection was Arensky's music, which, though pleasant and even expressive, was nevertheless feeble, somewhat commonplace and too reminiscent of the drawing-room. Seriozha only agreed to include *Une Nuit d'Égypte* when he decided "not to bother about Arensky"—especially as the composer was already in his grave—and to reinforce and ennoble his music with suitable pieces borrowed from the works of other composers. He searched through masses of music and at last the choice fell on the following: Taneyev's Overture to *Oresteia*, Cleopatra's Vision from Rimsky-Korsakov's *Mlada*, the Turkish Dance from Glinka's *Russlan and Ludmilla*, the Persian Dance from Mussorgsky's *Khovantchina* (for the final dance) and lastly *Autumn* from Glazunov's *Les Saisons*.

I cannot refrain from boasting that the last number was my choice. It so happened that I went to see this ballet during the days of preparation for our Paris Season. I had seen it many times before, but on this occasion I especially appreciated the *Autumn Bacchanale*. Pavlova was divine in it; further, it seemed to me that in the literature of choreographic music there were few pieces so exciting as this work of Glazunov's. The music of *Autumn* used in Paris for our version of *Une Nuit d'Egypte* also illustrated a bacchanale, and the success of that number must be attributed chiefly to the alluring rhythm and the intoxicating themes of the music.

Cléopâtre brought the fullest houses. It used to be given after the opera *Pskovitianka* and even then proved a lure to the public. The success of *Cléopâtre* surpassed that of Chaliapin. But it was not in the least due to any "suggestive" qualities. It is true that the Egyptian Queen, in the person of the daring young Ida Rubinstein, gradually discarded all her veils and gave herself up to the ecstasy of love before the eyes of the whole audience. Only at the most critical moment the helpful court ladies—whom we had known in St. Petersburg—surrounded the couch with curtains, and by doing so they really emphasised the point . . . And yet there was nothing in *Cléopâtre* similar to the "gay risky moments" so common in operettes and farces. The disrobing took place to the beautiful but terrifying music of *Mlada.* Slowly, in accordance with the complicated court ritual, one by one, the covers were unwound, disclosing the divine body omnipotent in its beauty. At the end of the ceremony, when the slight figure emerged covered only by the wonderful transparent garment invented by Bakst, one experienced a feeling of awe. Here was not a pretty artiste appearing in frank *déshabille*, but a real, fatal enchantress, in the tradition of the cruel and grasping Astarte . . .

After this scene, the culminating point of Cleopatra's performance was the bacchanale, thus fulfilling my hopes. From the point of view of choreography, this creation of Fokine's must be considered one of his absolute successes on the same plane as the Polovstian Dances from *Prince Igor*, the Buffoons' Dance from *Le Pavillon d'Armide*, the whole of *Carnaval* and *Schéhérazade*.

The bacchanale called forth such enthusiasm in Paris that the conductor was obliged to stop the orchestra for several minutes. If the Polovstian Dances (of which I shall speak later) had succeeded in satisfying the thirst of Parisians for primitive unrestraint, or *Le Pavillon* in pleasing their artistic taste in its love of eighteenth-century refinement, the bacchanale in *Cléopâtre* was a wonderful vision of the radiant beauty of the ancient world. We used to be asked why we had not undertaken to revive something more Hellenic, more frankly classical. The answer was first because at that time, in 1909, there was no such ballet worthy of Paris,[1] and secondly because in *Cléopâtre* the story of the Egypto-Greek, of the most beautiful woman of the ancient world, we were able to display beauty not in traditional draping and *chiton*, but against the vivid, colourful background of ancient Eastern civilisation. We were able to show what had attracted the Greeks and Romans as we are nowadays attracted by sacred India or hieratic China.

The talents of the performers also contributed largely to the success of *Cléopâtre*. They had, so to speak, thrown dust into the eyes of the public by making it believe in the absurd subject, and had quashed the reproaches against Diaghilev's deliberate "vandalism" in making the score of *Cléopâtre* a sort of Russian salad of national composers. It was their talent that created the convincing illusion of a *real* life that could never, in fact, have been led. Egyptian young gentlemen never paid court to the temple slaves and never sent arrows with love-letters to the feet of the Queen. The daughters of Pharaoh would not dream of indulging in love-affairs on the threshold of a temple and never poisoned their temporary favourites in front of the eyes of the people who had come to worship them. Lastly, if Cleopatra did keep Greek dancers, it would not have been in front of the Gods that she would have allowed them to dance the mad bacchanale which roused the usually reserved and correct Paris public to wild enthusiasm and made them shout with delight . . .

Indeed, it would have been difficult to find an assembly of such talented artists as took part in *Cléopâtre*. Everything and everyone was enchanting.

[1] It was only two years later that Diaghilev, Fokine and Bakst created the Hellenic ballet *Narcisse* with music by Tcherepnine and three years later *Daphnis and Chloe* with music by Ravel. *L'Après-Midi d'un Faune*, followed by *Nijinsky*, with Ravel's music.

Bakst's décor alone was outstanding—solemn in its composition, beautiful in its grey-pink and sombre violet! This background, perfectly suggestive of a hot, sultry Eastern evening, was an ideal foil for the purple costumes, the shining gold and the intricately-plaited black hair. How effectively Fokine and Bakst had carried out my conception of Cleopatra's appearance in a kind of sarcophagus adorned with mysterious golden characters! The idea of her being carried in this way instead of in an open litter had come to me while I was listening to the marvellous music of *Mlada*. I suddenly visualised the Queen's journey through the sands of the desert in this closed coffin, and it logically followed that she should be swathed like a mummy to prevent the least grain of sand penetrating through the covering to blemish her divine body.

What a wonderful executive artist Fokine showed himself to be in *Cléopâtre*! This is what I wrote about him and the other performers of *Cléopâtre* in the *Retch*. "In Fokine's interpretation of the past one feels his gift of genuinely experiencing what he is acting. One never ceases to *believe* in him. He is as convincing when playing with his beloved as when swept away by passion—but above all when he throws himself into Cleopatra's fatal embrace and seeks oblivion in her kisses. He is the incarnation of spontaneity, of fiery Southern blood, of heroic youth. Next to this hurricane the image of the tender, flexible young girl created by Pavlova seems still more frail and refined. Nor can I refrain from mentioning Karsavina and Nijinsky, who performed the dance with the veils so gracefully, or Vera Fokina and the two Fedorov sisters, who were such charming and *convincing* bacchantes!"

Next to *Cléopâtre*, the most overwhelming success of our first season fell to the *Polovtsian Camp* from Borodin's *Prince Igor*. Here, too, the enthusiasm for the opera was principally due to the ballet. The chorus sang magnificently. Petrenko was very effective in the part of Konchakovna and the sweet-voiced tenor Smirnov sang his wonderful aria exquisitely. Yet it was not all this that conquered and delighted the audience—it was the *dances*. The décor, too, made an enormous impression. Roehrich had created it as a panorama without side-wings; with a reddish-golden sky extending over the limitless steppes and smoke rising from the motley nomad tents, it was a most apt and poetical setting. The costumes for which Diaghilev had despoiled all the Eastern shops in St. Petersburg were most successful and amazed Paris by the vividness of their colours. Our incomparable ballet artistes had given themselves to their part (one could say that they all had *one* part) with such fire, truly *living* it, that they seemed to have been re-incarnated as ancient heroic savages, sensitive steppe maidens and Hindu *bayadères*. It was impossible not to believe in them. Nevertheless, the fundamental charm of the *Polovtsian Camp* lies, of course, in Borodin's music.[1] The skilful blending of the orchestra with the human voices, the intricate design of Eastern and imaginary themes, the gradual expansion of sound and the wild insistent rhythm— all this is presented in a transparent and simple form, without sophistication but also without a trace of old-fashioned technique. It inspired Fokine and Roehrich; it inspired the dancers at every perform- ance, to yield themselves utterly to the dance.

Our wild Russian primitiveness, our simplicity and naïveté had proved to be more progressive, more

---

[1] I will mention here a curious fact that is characteristic of Diaghilev. In spite of his admiration for Borodin, he cut out from this act the famous aria of Prince Igor "Oh, give me my freedom," when he found that it resembled a popular French march. A year previously Diaghilev had expressed his love for cuts by omitting the tavern scene in *Boris Godunov*, fearing that its coarseness might shock the French!

elaborate and more refined than all that was being created in Paris—the most cultured of cities!

For me, the weeks we spent in Paris were an unending joyful pageant, in spite of many sufferings, anxieties and intrigues. Towards the end of the season, we, the directors, were exhausted; the fact that our financial affairs were in a very critical condition did not refresh our spirits. But the very atmosphere we breathed was *festive*; it was saturated with such a luxury of impressions that for a long time neither Seriozha nor I could collect ourselves. The summer which followed that crazy and stormy spring seemed somehow to be dimmed by the reminiscences of what we had experienced. Roaming through the parks of Peterhof and Oranienbaum, it seemed to me that I could hear in the rustle of the pine-trees the melodies of the "Camp" or the "Enchantment of Armide," and my stories of how the Polovtsian maidens, headed by Sophia Fedorova, dashed like a hurricane about the stage and of the wild leaps of Bolm, the leading archer, so impressed my children that they would try to reproduce it all—and not without success. . . .

My tales were doubly convincing because they were echoed by my dear wife. In spite of our somewhat limited means I had made her come to Paris to join me; I could not bear the whole weight of impressions alone. The theatre was so overcrowded on the day of her arrival that we could get no seats; with Diaghilev and A. Trubnikov we were obliged to sit on the steps of the *corbeille*. Luckily those steps had just been covered with new cloth at Diaghilev's expense. He had been so horrified at the dirt and neglect of the Châtelet Theatre that he had given orders to cover all the corridors, boxes, stairs and parterre with new thick red cloth. It was one of Seriozha's extravagantly "lordly" whims. It caused a monstrous hole in the budget, but added to the brilliance and elegance of our performances.

Chapter V

L'OISEAU DE FEU

BY the autumn of 1909 I was back in the normal round of St. Petersburg life. I had a great deal of work in hand—literary, scientific, theatrical and creatively artistic—and was so engrossed in it all that I remembered the Paris season only when I had to defend it from attacks. That it should frequently have been attacked was very characteristic. Once again it was proved that no one is a prophet in his own country.

During the latter years several changes had occurred in our group. Filosofov had fallen away from us. His estrangement dated from the times of the *World of Art*, for Dima was becoming less and less interested in the plastic arts and, under the influence of his friends, the Merejkovskys, more and more deeply absorbed in questions of religious philosophy. In 1904, when the *World of Art* ceased to exist, Dima finally disappeared from our horizon and settled with the Merejkovskys in Paris, where he spent several years. Nourok too had ceased to frequent Diaghilev's. Nourok's "democratic nature" hated all that was "despotic" and "seignorial" in Seriozha, and as the journal in which he had played a very significant part had ceased to exist, there was no need for him to continue relations with the former editor and publisher. But Nouvel, whose home was nearer to Diaghilev's even than mine, continued to frequent his gatherings with Bakst,

Argutinsky and myself. When the talks about our Paris 1910 Season were seriously renewed, our company was augmented by Fokine and by the still youthful Stravinsky.

All the honour of "discovering" Stravinsky belongs to Diaghilev, who, having heard the young composer's "Firework" Scherzo at a concert, immediately decided that this was the man we wanted. It seems to me that when Stravinsky joined our company he too must have felt that this was the perfect *milieu* for him. Anyway, he was quickly assimilated and our acquaintance began to develop into a kind of friendship, in spite of the difference of age and the fact that he, a beginner, may have felt himself slightly overwhelmed in the society of people as mature and *arrivé* as we already were.

One of the binding links between us, besides music, was Stravinsky's cult of the theatre and his interest in the plastic arts. Unlike most musicians, who are usually quite indifferent to everything that is not within their sphere, Stravinsky was deeply interested in painting, architecture and sculpture. Although he had had no grounding in these subjects, discussion with him was very valuable to us, for he "reacted" to everything for which we lived. In those days he was a very willing and charming "pupil." He thirsted for enlightenment and longed to widen his knowledge. In music we had the same tastes; his favourites, including Tchaikovsky, were our favourites, his antipathies were ours. But what was most valuable in him was the absence of the slightest dogmatism—the dogmatism which, whatever his admirers and adepts may say, later on dried up and froze his creative power. In general, if Stravinsky did sometimes shock us with his "typically Russian" abruptness and a slight tendency to be cynical, he had nevertheless a charming spontaneity and that "sentimental reaction" which is the best source of inspiration. Nowadays, alas, Stravinsky even denies the importance of inspiration for the artist!

We decided at once that it was quite indispensable to make use of Stravinsky for Paris. He himself confided to us that he was busy composing an opera, *Le Rossignol*, whose subject was taken from Andersen's fairy tales, and that the first act was almost ready. But there could be no talk of opera for us; the opera had cost Diaghilev too much and had not justified itself (except for the one act of *Prince Igor*). On the contrary, our triumphs were due principally to the ballet and it was therefore decided that only ballets would be taken to Paris next time. Moreover, Diaghilev's attitude towards his own enterprise had ceased to be that of Olympic objectiveness; thanks to his friendship with Nijinsky, he had become *personally* interested in the success of the ballet.

About a year before, in a "Dialogue on the Ballet" published in a collection of articles on the theatre, I had expressed the wish that the ballet should make use of really Russian—or Slav—mythology. I thought that this would be perfectly feasible because all the elements necessary for a choreographic drama are contained in the "picturesque" and psychological aspects of our ancient legends, folklore and fairy tales. It seemed that one had but to depart from the childish, hackneyed *Koniok Gorbunok* and find a way of transforming these legends and tales for the theatre and musical action, and all the rest would follow of itself. The ancient past of our country, its profound symbolism, were too vivid, too alive, and too attractive not to be used. After the success of our first Paris Season, it had been decided in principle that the moment had come to create a Russian choreographic fairy tale. By joint effort we started to search for the most suitable story, but soon came to the conclusion that no single story existed that was entirely adequate and that one would have to be created by merging several together.

The music was to be composed by Tcherepnine, the dances to be arranged by Fokine; the fundamental elements of the subject were inspired by the young poet Potiomkin. The working out of these elements was undertaken by a sort of conference in which Tcherepnine, Fokine, the painters Steletzky, Golovin and I took part. Our excellent writer Remizov, who was not only a great crank but also a great lover of all things Russian, was carried away with our idea. During the two meetings I had with him, his very tone seemed to give life to our collective work.

But alas, the path leading to the fulfilment of our enterprise was a difficult one and most of those who had taken part in the "conference" gradually fell away. Among them was Tcherepnine, who was prone to inexplicable changes of mood, and whose attitude was in those days cooling towards ballet in general. His dreams about *L'Oiseau de Feu* (our searches had centred around this fairy tale) found expression in a different form—he composed a series of musical pictures, the first of which was very colourful and poetical and was performed at a symphony concert in St. Petersburg during the season of 1909–1910. Having ascertained that Tcherepnine was no longer with us, Diaghilev decided to entrust the music for the "Russian" ballet to Stravinsky. It was one of Seriozha's typically daring decisions. But in this case, when we had become conscious of our new friend's exceptional ability, we realised that the risk was, after all, not so great.

From the first it was clear that Stravinsky would succeed in his task and that his "Russian" ballet would not shame us. If *L'Oiseau de Feu* did not turn out to be exactly what I had dreamed of, the fault does not lie with Stravinsky, for the score is undoubtedly one of his finest creations. It is difficult to imagine music more poetical, more expressive, more fantastic and beautiful. The chief fault of

L'Oiseau de Feu lies in the *fabula*. We tried to get away from *Koniok Gorbunok*, but only succeeded in creating another fairy tale for children—not a fairy tale for grown-ups. The worst of it is that the hero of the ballet, Ivan Tsarevitch (who has penetrated into Köstchei's forbidden garden in persuit of the Fire Bird), and the Beautiful Tsarevna are always remote from the audience. One does not believe in them and therefore it is impossible to suffer with them. The Evil Being in *L'Oiseau de Feu*, incarnated in Köstchei, is more alive and convincing. The music of his part is terrifying and attractively repulsive. But Köstchei appears too late and perishes too quickly. One of the outstanding "conditions" was that the ballet should last not more than an hour and should consist of only one act. The result of this "condition" was a certain acceleration in the working out of the dramatic action. It was then that I demanded of Diaghilev that there should be no "conditions" to cramp our next endeavour, for it was necessary to let the idea ripen fully. He promised, but we never reached a second serious attempt at creating a "ballet on a Russian theme."

At the rehearsals of *L'Oiseau de Feu*, which took place in the early spring of 1910 at the same Catherine Hall, I was delighted with everything Fokine created. The enchanting scene of the Tsarevnas playing with golden apples and the *pas de deux* of the Fire Bird and Ivan Tsarevitch were both excellent. It was all so clever; the struggles of the imprisoned creature of paradise to escape from clinging hands and fly back into its unknown region were expressive in the highest degree. The choreographic problem was particularly difficult: the artist must have full scope to show her capacity for *flying*, but at the same time, her every movement must be tied. Fokine had shown himself to be still more ingenious in devising Köstchei's entrance, which was conceived entirely as a dance, in

the Pagan Dance and in the Berceuse. Had the
horrible Bolebochki and all the vile goblins and
creeping things that Remizov so mysteriously told us
about really existed in the imagination of the people?
Perhaps he improvised them then and there, but in
any case Fokine had believed in the fiction of the
poet and all the horrors that crawled out on the
stage, twirling and jumping, evoked a feeling
of genuine repulsion, even when the artists were
in their working dresses. How Fokine delighted in
creating them! Unfortunately there was neither a
Hieronimus Bosch nor a Breughel among us to make
them really convincing. In former years Somov,
who loved everything eerie, might perhaps have been
attracted by such a problem, but Somov, because of
his keen antipathy to Diaghilev, kept away from our
theatrical enterprises. Nor were Bilibin and Stellet-
zki, our experts on Russian style, suitable for such a
task, as they both were too keen on the ethnological
and archæological side. We had at last to choose
Golovin.

Unfortunately Golovin, a wonderful colourist and
a lover of ancient Russian art, remained true to himself and his work did not harmonise either with
Stravinsky's music or with what Fokine, under its
inspiration, was "modelling" with his dancers. It
must be admitted that Golovin's first sketch for the
décor was, in itself, enchanting. The artist had depicted Köstchei's gardens in the early morning, just
before daybreak, when everything is steeped in a
transparent greyness. A group of poisonous toad-
stools, not unlike Hindu pagodas, symbolised Köstchei's residence; beneath were layers and outlines of
different colours, suggesting overgrowths and thickets
that were soft, green, damp and close. But although
this sketch of Golovin's was indeed a masterpiece, it
was absolutely unsuitable as a décor. The greatest
experts in stage planning could not have made head

or tail of that maze of approximation. It seemed like a huge, chequered carpet, blazing with colour but devoid of any depth. No one could *penetrate* into such a forest—indeed, it seemed scarcely to be a forest at all. Golovin's costumes were still less successful. Taken separately, each of his drawings could have been hung in a museum—best of all in an ethnographic museum, for the colours and designs were remarkable. But these colours and designs did not answer the stage problems. Köstchei's servants and followers were elaborately attired, but they were neither frightening nor repulsive. Golovin had again made the mistake he had made before in his production of the "Tchernomor" act of *Russlan*. The result was that Fokine's choreographic ideas, performed by the artists in working clothes at rehearsals, seemed to be extremely fantastic and eerie, but on the stage everything was submerged in uniform, sumptuous luxury: the Kikimoras looked like page-boys, the Bolebochki like Turkish Janissaries, etc. Even Köstchei himself (in spite of the performer's terrifying gestures and make-up) was hardly frightening, for his costume was reminiscent rather of the traditional attire of "Father Rhine" in German fairy tales. Ivan Tsarevitch would never, as the tale demanded, have spat from sheer disgust in the face of such a Köstchei.

In general, one must admit that the artists fully deserved the success they obtained. Fokine as the Tsarevitch was extremely handsome and heroic "in the Russian way." The Beautiful Tsarevna had all the dignity of a Princess and the modest grace of a young girl. The monster Köstchei was excellent in his part and the two artistes who performed the part of the Fire Bird were perfect. They were Karsavina, who was gradually becoming our prima ballerina, and the still very youthful Lydia Lopokova. The impression of the "flying fairy" as created by

L

Karsavina had something of an Eastern languor. How perfect she was in her moments of suffering, when she endeavoured to free herself from Ivan's imprisoning hands! Lopokova's interpretation was more lively, nervous—even, perhaps, childish. One was a flaming phœnix, the other a delicate humming bird, but both performed with faultless accuracy the complicated choreographic design composed by the "merciless" Fokine—a design as difficult as it was original.

Chapter VI

SCHÉHÉRAZADE

WITH all its shortcomings, *L'Oiseau de Feu* was, nevertheless, an enchanting performance. Our other new collective work, *Schéhérazade*, proved to be a real *chef d'œuvre*. The success of *Schéhérazade* has survived to this day, although Bakst's wonderful décor has been replaced by a poor copy and the costumes—altered and remade no less than thirty times—have lost their magic vividness.

Unfortunately, the performance of *Schéhérazade* in the Paris Season of 1910 had, for me, particularly bitter associations. Both the idea of transforming Rimsky-Korsakov's symphonic poem into choreographic action and the entire stage version of the subject were mine. In arranging it I did not even keep to the author's own programme, but invented something quite different. According to Rimsky-Korsakov, his symphonic poem is meant to describe the adventures of Sinbad the Sailor; I preferred to represent the episode which forms, so to speak, the foreword to the *Thousand and One Nights*, in which the chief figure is Shahryar's unfaithful wife and not the righteous story-teller Schéhérazade. I do not think it necessary to justify myself for having digressed from the author's intention. Many years ago, when I first heard the symphonic poem *Schéhérazade*, I had no idea of the existence of any definite programme; listening [to] the sounds of the music, the picture of the voluptuaries of the harem and their cruel

punishment arose in my imagination. The same
pictures were evoked whenever I heard *Schéhérazade*,
even after I had learnt the author's real programme.
When it was decided that we would take *Schéhérazade*
to Paris, and a pianist, invited by Diaghilev, played
the piano version of the symphony several times to
excite my creative imagination, very naturally the
images evoked were those that possessed me long ago.
Gradually my fancies began to acquire more concrete
form and to fit themselves logically into a theatrical
scheme. From the very beginning it was decided to
omit one part (which afterwards served as an overture) and this made the problem considerably easier:
thanks to these cuts, the action became much more
concentrated. As the ideas came to me, I would
write down the scenes on the score,[1] and that is how
the whole subject of the new ballet was created. All
my directions down to the smallest detail were accepted without any controversy by Diaghilev and
those who happened to be present. Bakst was absent
from nearly all these sessions, and there was no
question of his taking any part in the libretto, but it
was decided from the beginning that the décors and
costumes should be entrusted to him.

How great was my amazement when, having taken
my seat in the stalls of the Paris Opéra, I unfolded my
programme and read under the title *Schéhérazade* the
words "Ballet de L. Bakst." I was so amazed that
I could hardly believe my eyes, but at the first sounds
from the orchestra and the raising of the curtain I

[1] I did this solely to help my memory. One evening, however, as
Argutinsky and I were returning home from one of these creative
evenings I said to him half-jokingly: "This time my notes are in
black and white, which will guarantee that this work will be considered
mine." A year before I had been very hurt that Diaghilev made no
allusion to my creative contribution to the general work of *Cléopâtre*.
The fact that Cleopatra's effective entrance and her equally effective
disrobing were invented by me was never mentioned. What
prompted my friend to act in this way—whether it was due to secret
jealousy or to purely Russian negligence—I have not discovered to
this day.

forgot everything and gave myself up entirely to intense enjoyment of the performance. My enthusiasm was so great that when I went on the stage to embrace Bakst and Diaghilev after the performance, I was quite unconscious of having been hurt by them. It was only after I had re-read the programme in my hotel that I became conscious of the real meaning of the words printed under the title, and my heart was filled with bitterness and indignation. This disappointment of mine had nothing to do with practical considerations; they did not enter my head. In spite of my age—forty years—I was so void of any practical sense that I had only a very vague idea of the existence of "royalties." I had not the least suspicion that I was losing any profit in this case. But I felt indignant that my dearest and oldest friends could have treated me in this way. . . . Next day I was finally flabbergasted by Seriozha's answer to my question as to how this could have happened: "*Que veux-tu?* Bakst had to be given something. You have *Pavillon d'Armide* and he will have *Schéhérazade.*"

I found no answer, but on my return to Lugano, where I was spending the summer, I wrote Diaghilev a letter expressing all my indignation. I told him in my letter that I was "breaking with him for good" and would never again take part in any of his enterprises. . . .

However, the sad story of the wrongs I suffered over *Schéhérazade* has made me anticipate. I have still to relate all that I saw during that Paris Season of 1910 (in which *Giselle* was my only officially acknowledged work), and to describe the preparations for our second season in Paris.

The period of preparation was as full of worries as it had been in 1909. We decided from the very beginning to have no opera, but to confine ourselves to the ballet alone. This considerably lessened our expenses, but even then a gigantic sum was needed, for everything had again to be prepared in St. Petersburg and sent on to Paris. There was no hope whatever of getting any subsidy from the treasury, and poor Seriozha's knocks at innumerable doors only met with refusals. To make matters worse, we had lost S. S. Botkin, one of our most helpful and influential friends, who had connections in the most varied circles. . . . At one time Diaghilev had the idea of arranging performances in England and I tried to make use of my connection with George Edwardes,[1] the well-known theatrical magnate of London, but, thanks to Diaghilev's typically Russian carelessness in his correspondence with George Edwardes, the project fell through.

Meanwhile Diaghilev's financial circumstances became so critical and made him so acutely conscious of his helplessness that, when there was no news for a considerable time from him from Paris, we began to be very anxious about him and thought it possible that he would attempt suicide. . . . Then, as if by a miracle, things righted themselves, the magician in this case being chiefly Gabriel Astruc, and the company with all its productions was able to go off for its second "examination."

The fact that Pavlova had again deceived us had a somewhat demoralising effect on us. *Giselle* was to be produced especially to show Pavlova in the full glory of her talent. The décor and costumes had been carried out from my sketches, when the artist suddenly announced that she could not appear in our ballets. She had to be replaced by Karsavina. I must confess that in those days this seemed to be rather a risk. After a period of a certain indolence (very comprehensible at her young age), Karsavina

---

[1] I have already mentioned that George Edwardes was the brother of my sister's husband. I had only seen him in the days of my youth, but he answered my letter very cordially, and welcomed Diaghilev's proposal to give performances in one of his theatres.

was only just beginning the serious work of perfecting herself and it seemed to us that she was a long way behind Pavlova. Our prejudice was so great that we somehow forgot to consider the enormous success that she had scored during the previous season. However, Karsavina stood the test with the greatest brilliance and from the moment she created the role of Giselle she almost outshone Pavlova. Tatochka now really became one of us; she was the most reliable of our chief artists and one whose entire being was suited to our work. Let us remember that Tamara Platonovna was not only a beautiful woman and a first-class, highly individual artist, but had as well a most attractive personality, was open to varied interests and infinitely more cultured than most of her comrades. . . .

The company, the chief artists and the entire directorate went off to Paris, whereas I remained in St. Petersburg! The reason for this was an accident which nearly caused me to lose the use of my right hand, an accident for which I myself was solely responsible. The spring of 1910 had been exasperating for me. I was tired and worried, and the weather was particularly trying. My state of nervous tension made me react rather painfully to the fact that Diaghilev had not bothered about getting my passport to go abroad. When I visited the passport office, I was told that it could only be ready in two days' time, which deprived me of the pleasure of travelling to Paris with all the company. I returned home feeling very upset; something else happened to put me out still more, and in a fit of temper symbolic of my irritation I banged my fist against the windowpane. Alas, the "symbol" proved to be only too effective. I cut the artery of my right wrist, so badly that the blood spurted out as though from a fountain. The doctor was immediately sent for; he put on the first dressing, after which I was taken to a hospital, where I had some very unpleasant minutes on the operating table.

The result was less tragic than the words of the surgeon led us to expect; still there could be no question of travelling abroad with an arm in plaster, and the anxiety of not knowing if I would retain the use of it. . . . I remained in St. Petersburg in enforced idleness and mentally accompanied my friends on their adventure. I imagined the preliminary rehearsals, the meeting with our French admirers headed by dear Misia Edwardes and the beginning of the exciting, tormenting but infinitely ravishing whirlpool in which I had so delighted a year ago! . . . I also worried about my *Giselle*, till my mind was put at rest by a friendly letter from J. E. Blanche, who took on himself to see that all should be done according to my instructions and wishes.

A month after the "catastrophe," I left St. Petersburg with my family for Lugano, which was only twelve hours away from Paris, but once there I could not make up my mind to go until Seriozha's insistent letters overcame my inertia and made me hurry to Paris with renewed interest in our common work. I was met as was fitting to "a badly wounded hero," and was honoured and spoilt. Misia Edwardes, Dethomas, Sert and J. L. Vaudoyer were touchingly kind to me, and had it not been for the stupid incident of *Schéhérazade* I would have gone back to Lugano feeling happy and rested in spite of having an arm in a sling. But *Schéhérazade*, whose colossal success might have been so soothing and encouraging for me, spoiled everything. This ballet was even more "my child" than *Giselle*, and its production proved infinitely more beautiful than the rehearsals, beautiful as they had appeared to me.

My impression of *Schéhérazade* is best described in the words of my article on the Paris performances, published in *Retch*.

"*Schéhérazade* has for some reason been described as a ballet by Bakst, while the entire libretto with every detail was composed by another person, whose name Diaghilev has not found it necessary to mention. But it is to Bakst that belongs the honour of having created the success of *Schéhérazade* as a spectacle, a production that is really amazing. When the curtain rises over the grandiose green alcove, one seems at once to enter into a world of strange and peculiar sensations—the sensations that are awakened by reading the *Arabian Nights*. The emerald green of the covers, curtains and throne, the blue night of the harem garden streaming in through the ornamented windows, the piles of embroidered cushions —all are absolutely enchanting, and in the midst of these sumptuously intimate surroundings we see half-naked dancers entertaining the Sultan with strictly symmetrical movements of their flexible, graceful bodies. Spicy, sensuous aromas seem to be wafted from the stage, but the soul is filled with foreboding . . . It is difficult to imagine an exposition of drama more sympathetic, more to the point than Bakst's décor.

"And what of Bakst the colourist? Here indeed he has found his real vocation. We see in *Schéhérazade* that Bakst can produce pictures that are truly great— not merely clever graphic art or a kind of illustrated thesis like his picture *Terror Antiquus*. Bakst becomes simple and free on the stage, and acquires *range*— that most valuable artistic quality. His décor is executed (in collaboration with Anisfeld) with a simple and broad virtuosity in the most telling colours; the performers, too, who move against this background in Fokine's amazingly clever combinations, are Bakst's creation, and are in complete harmony with the décor. I don't think I exaggerate when I say I have *never* seen such absolute harmony of colour on the stage.

L*

"*Schéhérazade*, a drama that lasts only about twenty minutes, is performed with incomparable mastery and skill. All the dancers, and especially Fokine, Poliakova and S. Fedorova, are marvellous; as the old eunuch, Ognev is both impressive and repulsive. Kisselev, too, is admirable in the part of the gloomy, disappointed Shah-Zeman. But absolutely inimitable are Zobeida (Madame Rubinstein) in her proud, cunning and unrestrained passion, the noble Shahryar (Bulgakov), a king from head to foot, and, finally, the Negro Favourite (Nijinsky), half-cat, half-snake, fiendishly agile, feminine and yet wholly terrifying.

"The great sin of unfaithfulness in all its enchantment and temptation is committed before the eyes of the public, and is followed by the inevitable punishment and expiation. When the beautiful Zobeida dies at the feet of her husband Shahryar, to whom she had remained faithful in her heart, and Shahryar, the mighty and stern, who loved her so passionately, hardens himself relentlessly to the demands of duty, then weeps over the ruin of his life's happiness—at such a moment one experiences the *beautiful*, heart-rending melancholy that only the rarest work of art can provoke."

Chapter VII

PRODUCTIONS OF 1910

O F the 1910 productions, the sets and costumes of
Giselle were entirely mine, but strangely enough,
though I was given perfect freedom to do exactly as
I wanted, I did not dare to obey in full the demands
of my imagination. I always felt somewhat vexed
when I watched performances of *Giselle* on the
Imperial stage. Although the version used undoubtedly bore the stamp of a certain tradition, it
was far from being in keeping with the style of 1840.
Yet it would, I felt, have been highly interesting to
see this ballet—faded yet eternally fresh—in the form
in which it had been presented to its contemporaries,
Théophile Gautier and Adolphe Adam.

I tried to create something that would answer the
demands of a "sentimental reconstruction," but I
very soon gave up the idea. I succeeded in making
the two décors sufficiently "romantic," but when it
came to the costumes I became suddenly afraid that
my idea of resuscitating old scenic images would be
thought retrogressive and ridiculous, or a proof of
the poverty of my imagination. I therefore decided,
as a compromise, not to make use of the piquant
possibilities of deliberate "lack of taste." Nijinsky's
was the only costume I designed in exactly the correct
style—the so-called troubadour style. And it was
this costume (on what strange things do people's
fate depend!) that was doomed to play a fatal part in
the artist's life. The episode occurred, in the spring

of 1911, in St. Petersburg, where Nijinsky was performing in the traditional ensemble of *Giselle*, still wearing his Paris costume. At the last minute Diaghilev had ordered the already somewhat short *pourpoint* to be shortened another two inches, thus making the rotundity of a certain part of Nijinsky's anatomy—in any case rather prominent—even more noticeable. Our enemy—the same M. Krupensky—chose to regard this as an insult to the Imperial stage, and there was even a rumour that the Dowager Empress had left the theatre, feeling indignant at such indecency. Anyway, Nijinsky was severely reprimanded and fined, whereupon the conceited artist (egged on by Diaghilev) suddenly felt he had been greatly offended and found it necessary to hand in his resignation!

Nijinsky's resignation was welcome to Diaghilev. Vaslav was now entirely at his disposal and under his control. This was important for Diaghilev because he had the intention of *creating his very own* "ballet genius"—in counter-balance to Fokine or any other "outside" ballet-master. I remember how Diaghilev answered me on one occasion when I expressed the fear that we might lose Fokine: "That's not so great a calamity," he said. "What is a ballet-master? I could make a ballet-master out of this ink-stand if I wanted to!" Unfortunately, this was not just bravado on Seriozha's part; he was expressing a genuine conviction. At that time Diaghilev was beginning to feel weighed down by the fact that he took so small a creative part in his own work and longed to show the world all the greatness and variety of his gifts . . .

Frankly, this conceit and wilfulness of Diaghilev's greatly worried me. It was not because I feared he would slip away from my influence (which was still the decisive one) but because I saw in his attitude a great danger for our work. I did not believe in the

COSTUME FOR NIJINSKY IN *GISELLE*, 1910
Sketch by Alexandre Benois

Facing p. 318

SERGEI DIAGHILEV AT A REHEARSAL OF *PETROUCHKA*. ROME, 1911
From a sketch by Alexandre Benois

Facing p. 319

genuineness of his creative talents, and did not even believe in his taste, in so far as his personal taste expressed itself in our common work. I still did not consider that Diaghilev *understood* the ballet. Sometimes we reached passionate disagreement about one question or another, and Diaghilev, though he still attracted me by his energy, his scope and his fearlessness, never succeeded in convincing me.

So it was in the question of the ballet-master. I was fully satisfied with Fokine's wonderful talent and considered that we could not find anyone better suited to realise our ideas. He had, in the 1910 season, given further brilliant proof of his complete sympathy and agreement with us, both by the productions which were entrusted to him as a choreographer and by the gem *Carnaval*, which was entirely his, and can, in its way, be considered as something *absolutely perfect.*

It seems to me that *Carnaval*, which, like his *Une Nuit d'Egypte* and *Chopiniana*, was created quite spontaneously, provides the most vivid proof of Fokine's vocation. Moreover, it is *Carnaval*, first produced at a charity dance in the Pavlova Hall in St. Petersburg, that demonstrates, with particular clarity, how near Fokine was to us and our ideals. The images evoked in his mind by the music were absolutely of the same order as ours. There is nothing surprising in the fact that Bakst, Somov, Lanceray, Dobuzhinsky and I should all have agreed fundamentally, for we all belonged to the same *milieu*, to the same culture, and had received the same education. Fokine had developed in totally different conditions, had associated with different people, had received an education different from ours, and yet it appeared that he nourished the same dreams and ideals as we, and expressed them in the same language. In *Carnaval* the harmony between us was particularly apparent. Schumann's music, that we all loved, was so miraculously interpreted in the poses, movements and moods of the characters that one could only imagine that the soul of the composer had, for the time, been translated to Fokine.

There was not the tiniest fault, not the tiniest *faux-pas*; everything was equally expressive and poetical. Bakst's contribution to the performance—the wonderful costumes and the clever "neutral background" of dark-blue draperies—was a real masterpiece and in full harmony with the music and poetry of *Carnaval*.[1] But what else could one expect from Bakst? Had he not shown in *Die Puppenfee* and *Le Cœur de la Marquise* how sensitive an interpreter he was of bygone days?

Towards the end of the season of 1909–1910, I had another very significant ballet impression. In spite of the hostility of certain members of the Directorate, Fokine's prestige in the Maryinsky Theatre had greatly risen after the enormous success of his productions in Paris, and, consequently, he was given the production of a new version of Venus's grotto in *Tannhäuser*. The young ballet-master achieved a success in this difficult problem as great as the success of his work abroad. The difficulty lay in the extreme length of the choreographic action—the Paris version —which the Directorate of the Imperial Theatres, influenced by Nikisch, had decided to adopt instead of the usual, much shorter, version. But in Fokine's interpretation the "endless performance" did not seem at all endless; on the contrary, our attention was so fixed by the continual change of effects, everything was so wonderfully in keeping with the music, that the great composer himself would surely have been delighted by the way the problem had been

[1] Unfortunately Bakst completely altered his décor when *Carnaval* was transferred to the Maryinsky Theatre. Instead of the neutral background which allowed one to imagine anything one wished, he made a rather ordinary garden, with a bridge. It was absurd that the décor for a Carnival—one of the joys of winter—should be a summer landscape.

solved. Nikisch, who conducted the orchestra at the first night in St. Petersburg, was delighted with the result.

When we gave the *Polovtsian Camp* from *Prince Igor* in Paris, the singers and chorus used to be highly irritated with the ballet, because the famous *Polovtsian Dances* completely outshone the operatic part of the act. It seemed as if all that had happened before the dances had been merely a performance; as soon as the dances began, the performance *came to life*. The chief characters of the opera remained stage figures, in whose reality it was difficult to believe, but when the frenzied Polovtsian Girls, headed by Sophia Fedorova, swept on to the stage, when the savage hero Bolm began to whirl and rave and a ceaseless flow of warriors, boys and maidens joined in the maelstrom of intoxicating dance, dashing, stamping and jumping, the theatre seemed to dissolve and disappear and in its place one felt the vast, limitless, elemental steppe and its genuine, primitive people. The scene was so rousing and inspiring that even the prim, *blasé* European public was transformed into an unruly crowd.

The same effect was achieved when we heard *Tannhäuser* conducted by Nikisch. The strongest impression of that evening was the impression of *life* in the grotto of Venus. Strangely enough, even the old-fashioned, hackneyed German décor, the "boudoir of Venus," ceased to be absurd; everything was transformed into a magic underworld of mysterious galleries and enticing depths. Not for a moment did it enter one's head that this was a stage, that firemen, carpenters and officials were standing behind the wings! The bacchantes and nymphs, in their passionate haste, dashed past in a frenzy of gaiety; everywhere there was laughter and shouting—what genius there is in the eternally youthful themes with which Wagner expresses that ecstasy of laughter and shouting!—one's whole soul was overwhelmed by the magic enchantment.

The fascination of ancient pagan Hellas became so great that it was utterly incomprehensible how Tannhäuser could wish to leave a world so full of real delight for "poetical tournaments" and the love of the virtuous, but rather dull, Elizabeth.

Chapter VIII

PETROUCHKA

I RETURNED to Lugano at the end of June, full of delight at what I had seen in Paris, but feeling, nevertheless, deeply hurt by Diaghilev's and Bakst's betrayal. It was then that I wrote my letter of reproach to Seriozha, in which I announced my refusal to collaborate with him any more. A few weeks later he arrived in person, accompanied by Nijinsky. There was a lot of embracing and even a hint of tears at our meeting. The latter, however, did not impress me at all. Knowing my friend's "incorrigible trickery," I had made up my mind not to expose myself again, and all his persuasion and imploring had no effect on me.

During Diaghilev's stay in Lugano, we met twice a day, but our conversation got no further than stories about what had happened in Paris after my departure and our usual fun-making . . . I cannot deny that I had great difficulty in standing firm to my decision. It is no easy matter to abandon the work to which one is entirely devoted—work which I considered my own. I was firm, however, and as soon as Sergei and Vaslav left for Venice, I resumed my usual occupations.

At that time I was actually returning to "normal life." Thanks to the healing effects of my stay in Lugano, I was gradually beginning to use my hand more freely, and towards the end of the summer I had regained its full use, feeling only a very slight discomfort, which did not in the least interfere with my drawing and painting. I could use my pencils and brushes with the same freedom and confidence as before, and I only lost forever my former technique (which had never been very remarkable) on the piano.

I was back again in St. Petersburg when I received a letter from Diaghilev which greatly perturbed me. Its contents were approximately the following: he did not doubt that my decision was final, and yet, in view of certain *exceptional* circumstances, he addressed me again in the hope that I would forgive the insult I had suffered and once more join my friends. The exceptional circumstances were that, only a few days ago, Stravinsky had composed and played to him a sort of Russian Dance and another piece which he had named *Petrouchka's Cry*, and that both these compositions were, in every sense of the term, works of *genius*. They had both had the idea of using this music for some new ballet, but no story had as yet been devised. They had only conceived the idea of representing the St. Petersburg Carnival and of including in it a performance of Petrouchka, the Russian Punch and Judy show. "Who else but you," wrote Seriozha, "could help us in this problem?" Therefore they had decided to apply to me and Seriozha expressed the assurance that I could not *possibly* refuse.

Seriozha certainly had every foundation for his assurance. Petrouchka, the Russian Guignol or Punch, no less than Harlequin, had been my friend since my earliest childhood. Whenever I heard the loud, nasal cries of the travelling Punch and Judy showman: "Here's Petrouchka! Come, good people, and see the Show!" I would get into a kind of frenzy to see the enchanting performance, which consisted, as did the *balagani* pantomimes, in the endless tricks of an idle loafer, who ends up by being captured by a hairy devil and dragged off to Hell.

As to Petrouchka in person, I immediately had the feeling that "it was a duty I owed to my old friend" to immortalise him on the real stage. I was still more tempted by the idea of depicting the Butter Week Fair on the stage, the dear *balagani* which were the great delight of my childhood, and had been the delight of my father before me. The fact that in 1911 the *balagani* had, for some ten years, ceased to exist, made the idea of building a kind of memorial to them still more tempting. They perished under the onslaught led by Prince A. P. Oldenburg[1] against alcoholism (the common folk certainly gave themselves up to the Russian Vodka-Bacchus at the Butter Week Fair!).

Besides the duty I felt I owed to Petrouchka and my wish to "immortalise" the St. Petersburg Carnival, I had yet another reason for accepting Seriozha's offer —I suddenly *saw* how this ballet ought to be presented. It at once became plain that Guignol-Petrouchka screens were not appropriate to a stage performance. A year before we had tried to arrange a similar Petrouchka performance with real people in the Arts Club, but although Dobuzhinsky had put much of his wit into the production, it turned out to be rather absurd and on the dull side. The effect of big, grown-up people acting with their heads over the edge of a curtain and little wooden legs dangling below, was more pitiful than funny. The effect on the stage of a real theatre would have been still worse; a ballet would have been entirely out of the question, for what could a ballet artist do if he were not allowed to use his "natural" legs? Once the screens were abolished from the stage, they had naturally to be replaced by a small theatre. The

---

[1] The Prince had perhaps a special dislike to the noisy *balagani* because they took place under the windows of his palace. The *balagani* were transferred from the centre of the town—the Tsaritsin Loug—to the Semeonovsky Place, where they soon ceased to exist.

dolls of this theatre would have to come to life without ceasing to be dolls—retaining, so to speak, their doll's nature.

The dolls should come to life at the command of a magician, and their coming to life should be somehow accompanied by suffering. The greater the contrast between the real, live people and the automatons who had just been given life, the sharper the interest of the action would be. It would be necessary to allot a considerable part of the stage to the mass of real people—the "public" at the fair—while there would only be two dolls, the hero of the play, Petrouchka, and his lady.

Soon I decided that there should be a third character—the Blackamoor. In the street performances of Petrouchka there was invariably a separate intermezzo, inserted between the acts: two Blackamoors, dressed in velvet and gold, would appear and start unmercifully hitting each other's wooden heads with sticks. I included a similar Blackamoor among my "chief characters." If Petrouchka were to be taken as the personification of the spiritual and suffering side of humanity—or shall we call it the poetical principle?—his lady Columbine would be the incarnation of the eternal feminine; then the gorgeous Blackamoor would serve as the embodiment of everything senselessly attractive, powerfully masculine and undeservedly triumphant. Having once visualised the complete drama in my mind's eye, and foreseeing what an interesting collision of contrasted elements must inevitably ensue, how could I refuse Seriozha's proposal that I should help to interpret it as a ballet on the stage? I fully believed what Diaghilev had written when he claimed that the *Russian Dance* and *Petrouchka's Cry* were works of genius, and was still further encouraged. How could I maintain my stubbornness and my attitude of "injured pride"? I gave in and informed Seriozha that I accepted his proposal and had forgiven all grievances; I was once more entirely with him and Stravinsky.

Several weeks later Seriozha arrived in St. Petersburg. My scheme was accepted with enthusiasm. We met daily in Diaghilev's flat in Zamiatin Lane where, at the traditional evening tea with *boubliki*, we discussed the "forthcoming" *Petrouchka*. At one time I let loose my imagination and the subject began to swell into something beyond bounds, but gradually *Petrouchka* took shape and fitted ultimately into four, fairly short acts, without any intervals. The first and last acts were to take place at the Carnival Fair; the two middle ones were to show the interior of the Conjuror's theatre. The puppets that had come to life in the first act, under the magic spell of the Conjuror, were to continue living a real life in their own quarters, where a romance was to begin between them. *Petrouchka's Cry*, which Seriozha now described to me in detail, was to fill the first of the two intimate acts; the second was to be devoted to the Blackamoor. The detailed action had not yet been decided.

Stravinsky arrived in December on a short visit to his mother and I was at last able to hear the two fragments which had been the "beginning of everything." Igor played them to me in my little dark-blue drawing-room; the piano was my old, fearfully hard Gentsch, the same instrument (the poor old fellow had since had his abnormally long tail chopped off) on which Albert used to tell me the story of the little boy caught by the devils. What I now heard surpassed my expectations. The *Russian Dance* proved to be really magic music in which infectious, diabolical recklessness alternated with strange digressions into tenderness—then, after a culminating paroxysm, came to an abrupt end. As for *Petrouchka's Cry*, having listened to it about three times, I began to discern in it grief, and rage, and love, as well as the

THE RUSSIAN BALLET

helpless despair that dominated it. Stravinsky accepted my comments, and later on this programme, that was constructed *ex post facto*, was worked out by me in full detail.[1]

To-day, when I listen to the music of this second act of *Petrouchka* and watch what the artist is expressing, more or less successfully, in his gestures and mime—*demonstrating* the absolute co-ordination of action and music—it is difficult even for me to believe that the music was not written to a set programme, instead of the programme being subsequently fitted to the music.

We continued to collaborate, actively and harmoniously, in the creation of the new ballet, in spite of the fact that we did not meet again till the spring of 1911. Stravinsky went back to Switzerland to live with his family while I remained in St. Petersburg,[2] but we kept up a constant interchange of letters. The subject was acquiring definite shape. The dramatic situation produced by the "hopeless love" of the "poet" Petrouchka in the second act was counter-balanced in the third by the undeserved passion awakened in the Ballerina by the foolish Blackamoor. Their personalities began to take definite shape, and when I heard the music of the "Blackamoor's room," I invented his monologue in all its absurd detail: the playing with the cocoanut, the cocoanut's resentment at being chopped open, etc. The Ballerina appears at the moment of the

[1] It was then that I imagined the black room where the wicked conjuror imprisons his puppet—now, alas, fully conscious of its surroundings.

[2] The room I used when working at the composition of the décor and costumes for *Petrouchka* was above the flat occupied by Count Bobrinsky's coachmen, for Count Bobrinsky's house was next door to ours. Unceasing revels and dancing went on there all day long to the sounds of the balalaika and the laughter of gay ladies. At any other time this would have greatly disturbed me, but in the present case all the noise, shouts and stamping only helped to inspire me. It was almost a gift of providence.

Blackamoor's wild, religious ecstasy before the cocoa-nut. At the climax of their love-making, when the enamoured Blackamoor is almost ready to devour his charming visitor, poor Petrouchka, mad with jealousy, rushes in, but, as the curtain falls, the Blackamoor pushes out his ridiculous rival.

The last part of the third act foretells the final *dénouement*. Similar scenes are supposed to go on inside the tiny theatre, passions grow, and at last the pathetic, luckless lover reaches a fatal end. It was essential to carry the finale outside the intimate surroundings of the previous two acts; to set it among the Carnival crowd, at the fair where, in the first act, the puppets had actually been brought to life. I was delighted with Stravinsky's idea of introducing a party of *riageni*[1] into the street crowd. This was a regular feature of the Russian Carnival, which could not do without such a "devil's diversion." All sorts of "creatures of hell" and even the Devil himself were to appear among these masked visitors. At the climax of the drunken revelling, Petrouchka's cries were to be heard coming from the conjuror's theatre. Petrouchka rushes out into the crowd, trying to escape from his infuriated enemy, but the Blackamoor overtakes him and puts an end to his existence with a blow from his curved sword.

This was the general plan of the finale, but we only began working it out when Stravinsky and I met again in Rome. The composer reached the height of tragedy in the final few bars expressing Petrouchka's agony, his piteous goodbye to life. To this day I cannot listen to it without the deepest emotion. The very moment of death—when Petrouchka's soul departs to a better world—is expressed in an unusual and very successful way. A broken sob is heard—produced by the throwing on the floor of a tambourine.

[1] *Riageni* were masked revellers, in traditional dress, who, at times of Festival, enjoyed special privileges.—*Trans.*

This "unmusical" sound seems to destroy the spell, to bring the spectator back to "reality." But the drama of the Conjuror who has dared to put a heart and a soul into his toys does not end so simply. Petrouchka turns out to be immortal, and when the old magician disdainfully drags the broken doll along the snow in order to mend it (and again torment it), the "genuine" Petrouchka suddenly appears in miraculous transformation above the little theatre, and the terrified Conjuror drops the doll and turns to flight.

The finale did not come to Stravinsky at once, and he had to search and use different combinations for it. He finished composing the music only a few weeks before the performance. We were staying at the same hotel in Rome for nearly a month, and every morning I used to hear from my room a confused tangle of sounds, interrupted from time to time by long pauses. This was the maturing of the last bars of the fourth act. . . . When everything was ready, *Petrouchka* was played to Diaghilev and me from beginning to end. Diaghilev was no less delighted with it than I; the only thing he argued about was the "note of interrogation" upon which the ballet score ended. For a long time he would not agree to it, but demanded a more traditional solution—a curious proof of how strongly influenced Diaghilev was by "academic prejudice" even in 1911!

Those were indeed wonderful days for us! Seen from a distance, they seem as radiant as the happy days of my childhood and as the most poetical years of my youth. It was wonderful to be working, in an atmosphere of complete friendship and harmony, on a task of whose significance we were all fully conscious. It was wonderful to bring our work to conclusion in such unfamiliar and beautiful surroundings—in the Eternal City, in rooms overlooking the Barberini Gardens, to the unceasing murmur of

PRINCIPAL DÉCOR FOR *PETROUCHKA*
By Alexandre Benois, 1911

Facing p. 330

ALEXANDRE BENOIS AND IGOR STRAVINSKY,
TIVOLI, MAY, 1911

Facing p. 331

its fountains. It was wonderful, too, for me that my wife had suddenly arrived. Without her I always feel the positive absence of "my better self." She had left the children with friends in Lugano, and had come to join me in Rome. Finally, *comme comble de bonheur*, the Serovs had settled quite near to where the Stravinsky's and we were living. Our three families were inseparable; we roamed about the town, visiting the churches, the museums and the World Exhibition of Art, at which Serov had scored a notable triumph and where we welcomed the King and Queen of Italy when they came to the opening of the Russian section. Sometimes we were joined by Tamara Platonovna Karsavina and her brother, the well-known professor of philosophy; we were gladdened, too, by the sudden appearance of our "domestic imp" Nourok. Our excursions to Tivoli and to Albano I shall never forget. I already knew those places well, but I was in a state of spiritual ecstasy and everything seemed fresh and even more poetical.

The evenings we spent together in the theatre watching our ballets. Diaghilev had been invited to bring his ballets to Rome by the Committee of the World Exhibition of Art, at the head of which stood Count San Martino, who was sympathetically inclined towards us. The managers of the Teatro Costanzi, where our performances took place, were distinctly hostile and gave us a reception which was far from benevolent. Intrigues started from the very first day and at moments almost developed into real obstructions. Our first performance had to be given under very trying and even *dangerous* circumstances, because of the absence of nearly all the technical staff. During the performance of *Le Pavillon d'Armide* I had to stand at the switch-board myself and give the signals for the different changes. I had to press different buttons every minute and heaven knows what would have happened had I made a mistake. At the same time Seriozha, sitting under the stage, was directing the lighting effects, which are also very complicated in this ballet.[1]

The first rehearsals of *Petrouchka* took place in the same Teatro Costanzi. We had to hurry to be in time for Paris and therefore decided to begin the production before the music was quite finished. As the management of the theatre could not find a more suitable building, the rehearsals had to take place in the restaurant of the theatre. The floor was covered with soiled crimson cloth, on which our artists had to dance and sometimes lie. The weather was terribly hot and everybody suffered from it, most of all Fokine, who was always moving, and Stravinsky, who for hours performed the duties of a pianist—for who but the composer himself could read the complicated manuscript or simplify the music to make it comprehensible to the dancers? Even Fokine used at moments to have difficulty in mastering some of the rhythms (which were indeed unusual) and memorising the themes, now so well known and in those days so "daringly original." Seriozha, immaculately dressed from early morning, appeared almost daily at these rehearsals. He looked extremely tired, for the burden he had taken on himself was weighing heavily on

[1] I cannot refrain from relating another curious incident of our tour in Rome. Part of the *corps de ballet* had been promised us by the Teatro Costanzi. Although these twelve ladies were to have small parts, it was impossible to do without them. When Fokine and I arrived about nine o'clock in the morning to inspect the new contingent, we found instead of the charming Italian girls we were expecting, a company of dejected-looking old ladies, whom we took for the *mothers* of the promised dancers. Great therefore was our astonishment when on asking: "Where are the ballerinas?" the theatrical official indicated the old ladies, saying not without irony: "There they are." We were nevertheless obliged to make use of these ladies, but of course we tried to hide them away as far as possible, or to let them appear in half-dark scenes—as, for instance, the "Hours" in *Le Pavillon*. I hasten to add that this is a thing of the distant past and that the ballet now attached to the Opera in Rome is one of the best in Italy.

him and the coming season in Paris would demand a still greater expenditure of energy and strength.

The rehearsals of *Petrouchka* went steadily ahead when we reached Paris. The costumes and décor (perfectly executed from my sketches by Anisfeld) arrived from St. Petersburg, everything was in order, our work progressed at full speed . . . We had now to think of the programme and to decide the question of who was to be considered as the author of the newly-born work.

My enthusiasm for Stravinsky was so great that I was ready to efface myself completely out of reverence for his genius; the initiative of the whole enterprise, indeed, belonged to him—I only helped to endow his enchanting music with tangible, scenic form. The subject of the drama, the characters and development of the action and most of the details were mine, but all this seemed a mere trifle in comparison with the music. So when Stravinsky at one of the last rehearsals asked: "Who is the author of *Petrouchka?*" I answered: "Of course it is you." But Stravinsky would not agree to this and protested energetically, saying that it was I who was the real author. Our *combat de générosité* ended with both of us being named, and here again out of reverence I insisted on his name being placed first. My name appeared a second time in the score, for Stravinsky dedicated *Petrouchka* to me, a fact which touched me deeply.

Unfortunately, there was soon to be a grave misunderstanding. *Petrouchka* re-opened the wound that had hardly healed after the *Schéhérazade* incident. The décor of Petrouchka's room was badly crushed during the journey, and considerable damage was done to the Conjuror's portrait, which occupied the centre of one of the walls. According to my plan, this portrait was to play an important part in the drama: the conjuror had hung it there so that it should constantly remind Petrouchka that he was in his master's power, and must therefore be humble and submissive. But it is just this portrait of his master that arouses Petrouchka's indignation when he finds himself in solitary confinement: he shakes his fists at him and pours on him maledictions and curses. It was indispensable to have the portrait repaired as quickly as possible, but I, unfortunately, had developed an abscess on my elbow and was obliged to sit at home. When Bakst kindly offered to repair the portrait, I gratefully agreed, having no doubt that he would do it perfectly.

How great was my surprise at the dress rehearsal two days later when I saw instead of "my" portrait of the Conjuror a totally different one, showing him in profile, with his eyes looking sideways! Had I been in good health, I would of course have tried to arrange it all in a friendly way; Bakst had probably no evil intentions at all and had only exhibited too much zeal. But I had come to the theatre with a temperature and unbearable pain in my arm, the atmosphere of the rehearsal was tense—in short, I considered the alteration of my portrait an unpardonable outrage against me as an artist, and my whole plan for the ballet. Last year's insult came immediately to my memory. My fury expressed itself in a loud shout across the theatre, filled with a highly select audience: "I shall not allow it! Take it down immediately! I can't bear it!" After which I flung my portfolio full of drawings on the floor and rushed out into the street and home . . .

My state of fury continued for two whole days. It was in vain that Serov immediately offered to give the portrait its original form and executed it with touching diligence; it was in vain that Nouvel kept coming to explain that it had been a misunderstanding and that both Seriozha and Bakst were very sorry about what had occurred. I would not listen, nor

PETROUCHKA'S ROOM

Version made for the Copenhagen production of 1925, from the original décor of 1911

By Alexandre Benois

Facing p. 334

THE BLACKAMOOR'S ROOM IN *PETROUCHKA*

Version made for the Copenhagen production of 1925 from the original décor of 1911

By Alexandre Benois

Facing p. 335

give in. Nor would the pain in my arm stop until the doctor operated on it.

I sent in my resignation to Seriozha, giving up my post of Artistic Director, and announced my refusal to go to London, where the second act of *Le Pavillon d'Armide* was to be given at the gala performance for the coronation of H.M. King George V. My fury became greater still when Serov and Nouvel dared to reproach me. I even began to threaten (without really intending to do so) that I would take Bakst to court. It was not without shame that I remembered this afterwards. I was particularly grieved at having hurt dear Serov's feelings. The kind Antosha wrote me a letter which showed that some words of mine had hurt him personally. I did not reply and, having finished some drawings of costumes specially for the London Coronation performance, I left Paris, thinking that later on I would make it up with my friends. Had I known that I would never see Serov, my best friend, alive again, I would have done *anything* to earn his forgiveness. . . .

I went to see two performances of *Petrouchka* before I left Paris and I must say that I derived considerable pleasure from them. Given in its original form, as something fresh and newly-created, our ballet made a really wonderful impression. Since then Diaghilev's production of *Petrouchka* has become distinctly worn and shabby—which is not surprising, seeing how many years it has been in the repertoire. The ballet has lost its charm for me and I feel sad when I go to see it, for *des ans l'irréparable outrage* seems to have told on everything. Many items have disappeared entirely, as, for instance, the merry-go-round[1] on which children used to have rides and the windmills whose

[1] This merry-go-round was a genuine *manège de chevaux de bois* of the time of Napoleon III which we had contrived to acquire at some fair. The horses and harness were charmingly primitive. Unfortunately the case containing the "museum rareties" of our production slipped off the crane during its unloading in Buenos Aires and sank and was lost in the sea.

multi-coloured, crossed sails waved in the air. The gingerbread and sweetmeat stalls are gone too and the outside steps leading into the huge *balagan*, where the people crowded together, waiting for admittance to the performance. The small table with its enormous steaming samovar where tea was sold is hardly noticeable nowadays. All these things were there in 1911 and they gladdened my eyes, for I had tried to reproduce the picture of our St. Petersburg Butter Week Fair in full detail.

But I was still more grieved by the *disorder* which, in the later productions, reigned on the stage. For the original production every figure had been individually thought out by me. I used to watch carefully during the rehearsals to see that every walker-on fulfilled the part that had been given him. The mixture of various characteristic elements gave the illusion of life. The "people of good society" showed elegant manners, the military men looked like real soldiers and officers of the time of Nicolas I, street-hawkers seemed really to be offering their goods, the peasant men and women looked like real *mouzhiks* and *babas*. I allowed nobody to "improvise" or over-act. Later these instructions were forgotten and improvisation and dilettantism reigned on the stage. People walked about aimlessly from corner to corner, without knowing who they were and what they were to do, trying to cover their "emptiness" by affected gesticulation. I was particularly irritated by the "drunks." In the original production I had insisted that only three tipsy fellows—one of them playing an accordion—should from time to time become noticeable against the background of the more or less "decent and orderly" crowd. Nowadays *everybody* seems to be drunk and the impression is quite false, for although people did drink in Russia, still, the street had its own rules and regulations, its own conception of good behaviour and decency, and it is only thus that the digression from these rules could seem amusing and typical.

Another opportunity wasted nowadays is the entrance of the Bibulous Merchant. The idea of this number had come to me while I was listening to a sort of popular limerick sung by Plevitzkaya, who is now ending her life in prison, but who in those days enchanted everybody, from the monarch to his least distinguished subject, by her typically Russian beauty and the vividness of her talent.

Oukhar-kupets, the Bibulous Merchant, was the name of Plevitzkaya's song, and that was the name I gave to the merchant who appears at the Butter Week Fair accompanied by two gipsies. But now, as everyone is behaving indecorously, there is nothing extraordinary in seeing one more rowdy person. Yet how interesting and full of character this Bibulous Merchant used to be, how typical he was of the old-world Russian merchant from his least attractive but none the less characteristic side! Though the young merchants did not dress in the 1830 fashion in which I attired my *oukhar*, they continued, nevertheless, to behave in the "traditional" way.[1]

I was particularly enchanted with Nijinsky at the first performances of *Petrouchka*. He had not been successful in the part during rehearsals and it seemed as if he did not completely understand what was needed. He even asked me to explain his role to

[1] I had carefully studied the fashions of 1830–1840 for the production of *Petrouchka*, but in later Diaghilev performances they were disgracefully muddled up. I would almost scream from annoyance when I saw them. Every year Seriozha promised me faithfully to restore the original production of *Petrouchka*, but he never managed to do so. After his death, *Petrouchka* was revived by Bronislava Nijinska in 1930 for de Basil's enterprise in Paris. For the décor of this production I returned to one of my old versions and introduced one of the walls of the *balagan* instead of the bright blue "box."

The most carefully executed productions of *Petrouchka* are the ones I undertook for the Maryinsky Theatre in collaboration with the ballet-master Leontiev in 1920 and the one created in Milan in 1929 by **Boris Romanov**.

him, which was very unusual for Nijinsky. But in the end he amazed us as he had in *Pavillon*, *Sylphides*, *Schéhérazade* and *Giselle*. This time also the metamorphosis took place when he put on his costume and covered his face with make-up—and it was even more amazing. I was surprised at the courage Vaslav showed, after all his *jeune premier* successes, in appearing as a horrible half-doll, half-human grotesque. The great difficulty of Petrouchka's part is to express his pitiful oppression and his hopeless efforts to achieve personal dignity *without ceasing to be a puppet*. Both music and libretto are spasmodically interrupted by outbursts of illusive joy and frenzied despair. The artist is not given a single *pas* or a *fioriture* to enable him to be attractive to the public, and one must remember that Nijinsky was then quite a young man and the temptation to "be attractive to the public" must have appealed to him far more strongly than to an older artist.

In her part of the Puppet Ballerina, Karsavina proved once more that for her an artistic problem can always be an adequate substitute for a role full of technical ballet effects. I must add that, in spite of the intentional "silliness" of the Ballerina's part and without making any alteration in the character, Karsavina managed to be both charming and attractive. The amusing costume, which I had copied from a Gardner china statuette, suited her admirably.

The Blackamoor was the character who pleased me least, and that is why I have altered his appearance several times when producing *Petrouchka* on other stages, making his costume sometimes red, light blue or navy. But I think that the first version of 1911 was really the best—a green jacket and trousers made of gold brocade. The excellent artist Orlov, one of our best character dancers, created this part in a masterly way. The chief problem was to give an adequate impression of almost bestial senselessness.

Chapter IX

OTHER NEW BALLETS

PETROUCHKA was undoubtedly the high light of
the 1911 season, but among our other new productions the greatest success was *Le Spectre de la Rose*,
a graceful trifle in the style of the romantic drawing-
room ballads of 1830. The choreography of this
ballet was composed—very rapidly—by Fokine and
exquisitely executed by Karsavina and Nijinsky.
Karsavina created the charming vision of a young
girl, giving herself up to memories of the ball from
which she has just returned; Nijinsky as the Spirit of
the Rose, in spite of the paradox of such a part, was
more enchanting than ever. One watched his flitting
about and the strange "flirtation" of the young girl
and the flower without troubling to think of the *sense*
of the subject—it would have disturbed the pure
pleasure given by their impersonation of Weber's
well-known waltz. The Spirit's final, soaring leap
through the open window must be regarded as one of
the happiest of Fokine's hits, and was invariably
acclaimed by the audience with frenzied delight.

Bakst had been extremely successful in his design
for Nijinsky's costume, which really gave the impression of a perfume, airy and imponderable.
Diaghilev was very anxious that the costume should
correspond exactly to the artist's design, and I cannot forget the amusing scene which I witnessed in the
wings on the first night.

The costume, which had just been brought, was

M

not considered a success and important corrections had to be made there and then. There was no other course but to pin the silk rose petals direct to the flesh-coloured *tricot*. Naturally this could not be done without pin-pricks and scratches, which caused poor Vaslav to squirm and cry out in pain. Diaghilev, in evening dress and top hat, looking very pompous and solemn as he always looked at first nights, stood by, giving directions with growing anxiety, while the role of costumier was being improvised by our stage manager, O. P. Allegri, as the professional costumier seemed to be no good at all. Kneeling on the floor, with his mouth full of pins, Allegri cleverly performed the complicated and responsible operation of "correcting the costume on a living body" just as well as any professional would have done.

The creation of a ballet on a mythological subject presented a far more difficult problem than did *Le Spectre de la Rose*. Our circle had dreamed about such a ballet for a long time, even before we had had any stage experience, when we still contented ourselves with experiments for the puppet-theatre or for *ombres chinoises*. Later on, when we contemplated the production of *Sylvia*, we seemed to have approached the realisation of our dreams, but *Sylvia* proved to be the stumbling-block in Diaghilev's theatrical career, and this catastrophe of 1901 temporarily separated us all from the theatre. Since then Bakst had obtained the reputation of being a kind of expert on the ancient world. His two productions of Greek tragedies at the Alexandryinsky Theatre had proved to be exemplary from the point of view of costume, and the production of *Cléopâtre* finally confirmed his importance as an expert on ancient matters.

After his return from Greece, where he had visited Athens and Crete in company with Serov, Bakst demanded that he should be given the opportunity of expressing all his knowledge of ancient Hellas in

a ballet production. I was somewhat disconcerted
at his choice of *Narcissus and Echo* as a subject, since
it did not seem to me to be at all suitable for choreographic treatment. But Bakst obstinately persisted
in his idea and obtained Fokine's and Tcherepnine's
agreement. He was finally given *carte-blanche* and
several months later the ballet was ready. Nijinsky
was, of course, to take the part of Narcissus, and
Karsavina was to be the nymph Echo. Very soon
Bakst presented sketches of the décor for his ballet
and a series of magnificent drawings of the costumes.
Echo's wonderful dress was designed in violet tints
corresponding admirably with the delicate and poetical music in which Tcherepnine had interpreted the
part. The ballet was rehearsed and produced on the
stage of the Monte Carlo Theatre, where the première
was given in the early spring of 1911.

Generally speaking, the performance of *Narcisse*
proved to be a beautiful and noble spectacle, but it
was not a great success. The reason, I think, was
that the subject is entirely unsuitable for a ballet.
The two characters are the most static in Greek
mythology—Echo is imprisoned in her cave and
Narcissus is immobilised in the contemplation of his
own beauty. I remember how difficult it was for
Fokine to get some variety in Narcissus's interminable
"choreographic soliloquy" in front of his own re-
flection; even Karsavina's beauty and her genuinely
classical poses did not prevent the melancholy mood
demanded by Echo from becoming tedious. Both
dancers seemed to be the "victims" of a strange fancy
and one felt sorry for them. The appearance of the
Bœotian peasants introduced some animation into
the ballet and Bronislava Nijinska was ideal as the
bacchante. The beginning and the end of the act,
representing the forest life of wood-demons and satyrs,
who only risk coming forth from their caves and
burrows when there is no danger of encountering

human beings, was interesting as an idea. There was, however, no cohesion between all these details; they seemed to be artificially strung together, whereas an "ancient" ballet, based on classical mythology, ought to have been an example of clarity and logical sequence.

The most successful part of *Narcisse* is the music—possibly the finest and most inspired work written by Tcherepnine, who is not a fertile composer and has no facility. In *Narcisse* there is not the least sense of effort; everything flows freely, evenly and smoothly. The music seems to express the fantastic and mysterious with the clarity and logic that is so lacking in the ballet action itself. There is almost nothing joyful or light in the score, but that does not prevent *Narcisse* from being beautiful and instinct with the proper atmosphere. When one listens to the music of the ballet without watching the performance, the images which flitted in the composer's imagination are evoked far more convincingly than when one actually *sees* them on the stage. The limitations and conventions of the stage have reduced the composer's images to vague helplessness.

Chapter X

EXPERIMENTS

BECAUSE of that stupid incident of the Conjuror's portrait in *Petrouchka*, the season of 1911—a season of great significance for me—ended in a quarrel. I was so angry that I did not go to London with the company. My being overworked and tired had much to do with the whole affair. During that season I had been officially appointed "Artistic Director" to Diaghilev's company, and although I had occupied that post *de facto* since 1908, my appointment *de jure* compelled me to deal with matters of detail which did not in the least interest me. Such drudgery always has a depressing effect on an artist. Moreover, our tour had been very much prolonged. It began as early as March in Monte Carlo, continued in Rome and reached its climax in Paris during June. That, alone, was sufficient to produce a storm-laden atmosphere.

I have only a faint recollection of my meeting with Sergei in Lugano in the summer of 1911. I am not even certain that he paid us a visit at all that year, on his customary journey to Venice. We met again in February, 1912, in Vienna, where Sergei—by now, in the full sense, a travelling theatrical manager— was on tour at the Opera with his company. He made me come from St. Petersburg to create a ballet to Debussy's music, *Les Fêtes*, and asked me to compose a subject for it. The music was played to me several times as soon as I arrived in Vienna, but, however much I listened to it, it did not suggest to me any definite *story*; its vivid colours only evoked visions of a fête in general. Very soon—perhaps because of my daily visits to the Kunsthistorische Museum, where there is a wonderful collection of Venetian art—this "general fête" began to take a definitely Venetian aspect. Speaking of Venice and its pageantry— what can be more festive and inspiring than the art of Paolo Cagliari? That is why I suddenly conceived the definite desire to create a ballet *à la Veronese*. The décor seemed to come of itself; it was to represent a Palladian Villa somewhere on the Brenta. A sumptuous banquet was to be in progress; the Doge himself was to arrive and be received with unheard-of splendour. Unfortunately the music was too short to produce the final effect. Diaghilev did not doubt that he would be able, without trouble, to get the twenty or thirty bars that were needed from Debussy, but he was mistaken. The composer stubbornly refused to add anything to his music. In consequence Diaghilev suddenly cooled off towards the whole idea, although he was delighted with my designs for the costumes and décor.[1] That is why my "Veronese ballet" never reached the footlights; but the idea of a "Veronese spectacle" was not to be barren. During the two weeks I spent in Vienna, I used, every day, to meet Hugo von Hofmannsthal, who was a great admirer of our ballets and dreamed of creating for us something of his own. In conversation with him I developed my "Veronese ideas" and he greatly encouraged them, hoping to see their fulfilment in Paris. Hofmannsthal *did* see their fulfilment, but in his own ballet, *La Légende de Joseph*, with music by Richard Strauss, for which he demanded a Veronese setting.

[1] The sketches for the décor for *Fêtes* were afterwards acquired by the Tretiakov Museum in Moscow; those for the costumes are in the Russian Museum in St. Petersburg.

For one reason or another, Seriozha did not think of entrusting me with the production and so deprived me of the joy of rendering public homage to one of my favourite artists of the past.

Among my other Viennese impressions of the same year, 1912, I remember several ballets of local make, and a performance of *Le Lac des Cygnes* by our own company. I liked the first for their excellent *ensemble*, clever lighting effects and true Austrian *Gemütlichkeit*. I do not remember what ballets they actually were, but one of them consisted entirely of the music of Schubert and its most successful scene depicted the enthusiastic greeting of victorious troops on their return from the occupation of Paris. The march past of the boys, frantic with patriotic fervour (girls in travesty), took place to the sounds of the famous march, opus 51 no. 1, which never fails to be indescribably stirring.

I was far less pleased by the production of our dear, poetical *Lac des Cygnes*. Seriozha had decided to include this rather sentimental, old-fashioned ballet in his repertoire chiefly to give M. F. Kchesinskaya an opportunity to shine; also because he had a genuine admiration for the sets and *Carpaccio* costumes created by Korovin for the Moscow production. Although it was old and shabby he procured the Moscow setting for Vienna. But Seriozha had little reverence for the ballet itself and even rather disdained it—its "German sentimentality" and romantic *Wehmut* were alien to him. That is why he cut it light-heartedly, without scruples, making two acts out of four and changing about the entries, so that *Le Lac des Cygnes*, which formerly took up an entire evening, could be given between two other ballets. Was such vandalism worth while? I personally have a tender feeling for this early work of Tchaikovsky's, and was grieved, therefore, at the vandalism perpetrated by my friend.

Le Lac des Cygnes is still retained in this mutilated form by various enterprises, heirs to the *Ballets Russes.*

I have no other ballet recollections of 1912 unless I count a ballet with a Hindu subject, *Le Dieu Bleu*, composed for Diaghilev by J. Cocteau and Reynaldo Hahn. I never saw this ballet on the stage, for I did not go to Paris that year and it was not given again after 1912. The only thing I regret is that I never saw the effective décor created by Bakst and his equally effective costumes. I have, nevertheless, the most pleasant memories of the preliminary conversations which took place in St. Petersburg; Reynaldo Hahn, at the piano, played his own and other music, augmenting the effect of the piano by singing the vocal parts, *sotto voce*, with extraordinary distinction. All our circle was delighted with those intimate "auditions." Unfortunately we were far less delighted with the music for Hahn's ballet itself. *C'etait joli*, but did not differ from the pleasant drawing-room compositions characteristic of the post-Massenet generation of composers.

I cannot now explain how it happened that I did not go to Paris in 1912 for our season of ballet. One reason was that I had in fact nothing to do there, since *Les Fêtes* had been cancelled. But it's also true that I was cooling off towards the whole enterprise, chiefly because it was becoming more and more like a touring company. Diaghilev had given up his "general headquarters" and seldom appeared in St. Petersburg, except to stay there for very short periods in a hotel. As a result, the essential character of our preparatory work was altered and everything seemed to hang fire.

However, Seriozha, Nijinsky and Stravinsky visited me in Lugano during the summer of 1912. The new ballet, about which I had heard from Roehrich and

Stravinsky, was now in preparation and Igor played parts of it to me. It was *Sacre du Printemps*, a "primitive" ballet, with no romantic subject, but devoted to the evocation on the stage of certain rituals of the pagan Slavs. The original idea was probably Roehrich's; if, in fact, it came first to Stravinsky it must have been due to the influence of his painter friend. Roehrich was utterly absorbed in dreams of prehistoric, patriarchal and religious life—of the days when the vast, limitless plains of Russia and the shores of her lakes and rivers were peopled with the forefathers of the present inhabitants.

Roehrich's mystic, spiritual experiences made him strangely susceptible to the charm of this ancient world. He felt in it something primordial and weird, something that was intimately linked with nature —with that Northern nature he adored, the inspiration of his finest pictures. Stravinsky was attracted by the idea of "reconstructing the mysterious past" chiefly because it gave him free scope in his search for unusual rhythms and sounds. Naturally nothing was known of the music of those remote days and Stravinsky felt himself free from all constraint and all rules. Diaghilev himself was equally interested in the idea of creating a "primitive" ballet. It satisfied his own "barbarian instincts" (for Seriozha had spent his childhood and youth far from the capital and did not conceal his "Scythian" inclinations) and offered, as he saw, a magnificent opportunity for "shattering" the Parisian audience—better even than *Petrouchka*. In *Petrouchka* one was definitely aware of "the town" and "town culture," for St. Petersburg was half-Russian and half-European. The new ballet was to contain nothing of European or of any known civilisation. If such barbarian rites had ever been practised in Western Europe, thousands of years of culture had eradicated all trace of them.

I was in complete sympathy with the creation of

M*

the ballet. To begin with, I was living through my first years of infatuation for Stravinsky and was full of burning interest for everything he created. Moreover, I was curious to make an excursion on the "wheels of time" into prehistoric centuries, under the enchanting spell of music and painting. The music that Stravinsky played to me in Lugano promised to be something of amazing splendour and originality. The strange, unusual sounds were in themselves indescribably exciting. The only thing that disconcerted me was that the choreography of *Sacre du Printemps* had been entrusted to someone so inexperienced as Nijinsky. But perhaps Seriozha had discovered some new, secret talent in his young friend; Nijinsky's own "primitiveness" might even prove to be an appropriate asset to the experiment.

The winter season of 1912-13 passed without my contributing in any way to what must now be called Diaghilev's enterprise—since my resignation it had ceased to be "ours." I was now taking part in other work, which, for three whole years, occupied and engrossed me even more completely than had our performances abroad. I had been invited by Stanislavsky and Nemirovitch, in the autumn of 1912, to take part in their productions and almost all my activity was now devoted to the famous Moscow Arts Theatre, of which I had been from the beginning an ardent admirer. I was obliged by my new work to spend the winter months in Moscow, and, on the whole, the regime of the Moscow Arts Theatre left little room for independent activities. Even those who have a strong inclination towards individual aloofness (I have this in the highest degree) were unable to resist Stanislavsky's influence when once they get into its orbit. Having been invited in the capacity of a sort of consulting director on all artistic problems in the theatre, and being occupied there with my own productions as well,[1] it was impossible for me to attend to anything else. I was even compelled to neglect my work as a critic and my historical and artistic researches.[2]

And yet, when Seriozha asked me to leave Lugano, where I was spending the summer as usual, and to come to Baden-Baden to discuss the possibility of my taking part in the coming season, I gladly accepted his invitation.

I had dreamt, ever since the days of *Armide*, of seeing on the stage an accurate reconstruction of the luxurious Court Performances of former times. When the Casadesuses brought their ensemble to St. Petersburg in 1909, my dreams began to take more definite shape. I was especially charmed by the music of Monteclair—a forgotten composer of the beginning of the eighteenth century—which they had discovered in the library of Versailles, and I wanted to use it myself. Seriozha entered immediately into negotiations with the brothers Casadesus; they agreed to give the score, but made the condition that they should take part in the performance themselves, with the limited staff of their miniature orchestra of ancient instruments. I was prepared to agree to this, for I was attracted by the idea of hearing something intimate, frail and tender in contrast to the full-sounding orchestras of the present day. It seemed to me that the quiet delicacy of sound would enhance the charm of the vanished epoch. Diaghilev was of a different opinion and the project of a Monteclair ballet was put aside.

But the idea of reconstructing a sumptuous performance with genuine ancient music continued to haunt me—I had recently, in 1913, created something

[1] During my first year in the Moscow Arts Theatre I was busy on two Molière productions, *Le Malade Imaginaire* and *Le Mariage Forcé*, for which I was entirely responsible.

[2] I could relate a great deal about the Moscow Arts Theatre, but it does not enter into the theme of this book.

similar for the Moscow Arts Theatre in the "Ceremony" of *Le Malade Imaginaire*—and I arrived in Baden-Baden with the hope that my wish might at last be realised.

Alas, Monteclair was now entirely out of question. I put forward instead the idea of a Bach ballet. From the point of view of period it would only mean an advance of some thirty years, but from the point of view of variety and richness of sound there could be no comparison between Bach's work and the dainty but very slight music that the Casadesuses had discovered. I did not worry then about the subject, as I knew that it would take shape of itself after I had listened several times to the music. We at once set to work playing through suites, fugues, preludes and other compositions of the great Johann Sebastian, searching for anything that was particularly colourful, sharply defined and unusual. I was concerned to reveal an "unexpected" Bach, not the deep, profound and infinitely elevated genius heard in churches and concerts. I wanted to present an intimate and even "curious" Bach, the Bach who was the father of a large family and who, coming home, would abandon the ceremonial robes of the Cantor of the Thomaskirche for an ample dressing-gown, and start amusing his numerous children with improvisations on the harpsichord. The ballet that interpreted Bach's magical music was to have all the elaborate splendour of Court Festivals of the Rococo period—the splendour of pageants and fireworks and illuminations.

I had ear-marked several pieces some time before, but we made many fresh discoveries in our Baden-Baden "sessions." We ransacked Bach for hours, using the modest hotel piano, played generally by a German specialist in sight-reading. Sometimes dear Valetchka would take his place and the advice and opinions he offered were always listened to with particular attention. Nijinsky used also to be present.

Seriozha had decided to entrust him with my Bach ballet and I did not protest, although I was far from confident that Vaslav possessed the necessary knowledge. All my hopes were centred on the astonishing artistic intuition that he displayed in the creation of his own roles. In any case, Seriozha was preparing to coach his young friend and teach him all he needed to know. The books necessary for his enlightenment were chosen and Seriozha himself was going to take Vaslav to the Cabinet des Estampes and the Correr Gallery. I insisted that Nijinsky should visit baroque palaces and churches in Würzburg, Einsiedeln, Bruchsal—places where eighteenth-century music seemed to have been crystallised in enchanting architectural forms.

In a week's time the music for the Bach ballet had been chosen, and I acquainted Diaghilev with the outline of the subject which had been shaping itself in my mind and which was, to a certain extent, an echo of Bach's comic opera, *Phœbus und Pan.* We decided that during the coming winter I would tear myself away from St. Petersburg (or rather from Moscow) and come to Paris, so as to discuss everything in detail. In the meanwhile we had to part hurriedly because Seriozha and Vaslav were shortly to sail to the Argentine, where Diaghilev's company had been engaged to appear in a series of performances. But man proposes and God disposes.

All who are acquainted with the history of the *Ballets Russes* know the result of that fatal voyage. Diaghilev, who was mortally afraid of sea travel (a gipsy had prophesied that he would die on the water) at the last minute refused to sail, and sent as director in his place his companion, Baron Gunsburg. Before they had reached the shores of South America, the baron took advantage of his position, to marry Nijinsky to Mlle. Romola de Pulszky, who had worshipped Vaslav for several years, and who "happened" to be on the same ship. The explanation of this story is said to be that the ambitious but very unbusinesslike Baron intended Nijinsky to quarrel with Diaghilev, so as to have him at the head of a new ballet enterprise that he was planning himself. Nijinsky, who absolutely lacked will-power, *se laissa faire* and the affair was rushed through. Diaghilev nearly lost his reason when he heard what had happened, partly because he felt insulted in his feelings for Nijinsky, but chiefly because he realised that he had been tricked and deceived.[1]

After this, of course, it was impossible to continue work on the Bach ballet and the idea had to be put away in our archives.[2]

[1] I have related the incident of Nijinsky's marriage exactly as I heard it from Diaghilev.

[2] Nevertheless I did not give up my idea of a Bach ballet and succeeded in achieving it in 1928 in an elaborate production created for Ida Rubinstein in Paris. This time I chose as subject *Les Noces de Psyché*, the part of Psyche being taken by I. Rubinstein and that of Cupid by Vilzak.

My idea of using Monteclair's music for a small ballet was later used by Diaghilev. To my great regret the production of *Les Tentations de la Bergère* was not given to me but to Juan Gris. This happened because I had been stranded in Soviet Russia. I cannot say that the gifted Spanish artist (who died soon after) was very successful in reconstructing on the stage the epoch of *Le Roi Soleil*.

Chapter XI

LE COQ D'OR

I SPENT the whole winter season of 1913–1914 in Moscow, where I was entirely engrossed in my production of Goldoni's *La Locandiera*. This five-act comedy was rehearsed no less than 125 times, as was demanded by the extremely high standard of the Moscow Arts Theatre. The fact that I not only designed the décor but was also producer proves clearly how absorbed I must have been with the work. The result was a great success; but old associations still drew me and, after wavering slightly, I accepted Diaghilev's proposal that I should undertake a new production of Stravinsky's opera, *Le Rossignol*. Seriozha also persuaded me to undertake the production of *Le Coq d'Or*—thus realising an old dream of mine that dated from the days of 1909, when Rimsky-Korsakov's magnificent march was played in the ballet *Le Festin*.[1]

[1] I forgot to mention this ballet—or rather, *divertissement*—in the right place; yet its production gave me great trouble. Not because I designed some of the costumes, but because the *divertissement* was originally my idea. As a matter of fact, that is nothing much to boast about, as the result was something very commonplace—strangely reminiscent of *Koniok Gorbunok*. We resorted to a "Russian Salad" like *Le Festin* only because the production of *Cléopâtre* was not yet ready, and we needed a short ballet of about three-quarters of an hour. I relied chiefly on my favourite finale of Tchaikovsky's Second Symphony which, to this day, I still consider to be sublime ballet music. The development in this magnificent finale of the Ukrainian dance *Zhuravl*, the Crane, produces an ecstasy of dancing fervour that is unparalleled even in the rich musical literature of Russia. The music has an atmosphere of such intoxicating revelry that it is impossible to hear it and not to join in the dance.

[*Footnote continued on next page.*]

I was strongly tempted, too, to fulfil another cherished ambition—to present an opera in which the dramatic action should be entrusted completely to ballet artists, but the vocal element preserved. This risky experiment had been in my mind for a long time. I was not in the least influenced by the desire simply to make a sensation. On the contrary, all through my long artistic career, I have remained innocent in this respect and have never fallen into the temptation to *épater les bourgeois*. What influenced me was my theory that an opera performance is often a very poor spectacle, since there is seldom any artistic justification for the predominance given to the voice. Of course there are exceptions. Chaliapin was always magnificent, diabolically handsome or utterly terrifying, as the occasion demanded. Ershov was excellent as Tannhäuser, Siegfried and Siegmund. Figner was good, too. I could continue with a long list of Russian, French, Italian and German artists, but exceptions only prove the rule, and even these artists had sometimes to sing and act with colleagues whose appearance destroyed every romantic illusion. It is sufficient to bring to memory the wonderful singer Felia Litvin!... How, to be candid, could she impersonate Isolde or Brünnhilde?

Realising that this defect was irreparable, inherent in the nature of opera, I conceived the "criminal" idea of replacing some of the opera artists by a group of performers who would be physically presentable. There can be no obvious monsters in the ballet and a "romance" performed by almost any ballet company can always seem convincing. As a rule, ballet

In spite of the music, our ballet proved, alas, to be somewhat dull and very far indeed from my ideal—chiefly, I think, because of the mixed crowd of sixty dancers who took part in the final ensemble. These sixty dancers had just been performing in the individual numbers of the *divertissement*, the Trepak, Mazurka, Hopak, Lesginka, etcetera. The predominance of the realistic ethnographical element deprived our apotheosis of the fantastical atmosphere inherent in the music (see p. 353).

dancers, if not always beautiful, have, nevertheless, an agreeable appearance. Another defect of the opera is that often the performers taking part in it have no idea of acting, but stalk about like bears and gesticulate aimlessly. What innumerable horrors I have seen at the Italian Opera in the days of my childhood! Sometimes even the greatest opera-fans, hardened as they were to such absurd incongruities, could not restrain their laughter at the extraordinary antics of some famous tenor or soprano!

In the ballet—especially in the good old days when the artists of our ballet company were being educated —the utmost trouble was taken to teach expressive mime. The mere practice of dancing trained young ballet dancers to control their movements, and gave them elegance and flexibility. As occasion demanded, the talented artist could impersonate with success any grotesque or hideous character—one has but to think of Cecchetti in the part of Fairy Carabosse, Bekeffy as Quasimodo, or Gerdt as Bluebeard.

When, therefore, in 1909, I first heard Rimsky-Korsakov's latest work, *Le Coq d'Or*, I decided that it provided an ideal opportunity for me to try the experiment I had planned, with the least risk. It has something of pantomime, something of the puppet theatre. Its symbolism is borrowed from popular imagery, and its meaning is transparently obvious— not in the least dependent on psychological reactions. *Le Coq d'Or* is a very *showy* opera, and consists entirely of action. The chief character, after King Dodon, is the Queen of Shemâkhan, who has to be of enchanting beauty and must walk and dance like a fairy. That is why I had insisted on my experiment with such perseverance. During the years when our company was concerned exclusively with ballet, there was no possibility of producing *Le Coq d'Or*. It only became feasible when Diaghilev returned once more to opera.

Even the fearless Seriozha seemed rather scared

at so dangerous an experiment! *Le Coq d'Or* had to be presented simultaneously in two planes, for it had to be studied by ballet and opera artists both together and separately. The question at once arose as to whether the singers (some of them famous popular favourites) would agree to limit themselves to the part of "orchestral instruments," for their only function would be to "accompany" with their voices the real performance that was taking place on the stage. But I knew that our "Peter the Great" would overcome greater difficulties than these, if he wanted to. One had only to egg him on by pointing out what the difficulties were. This, once more, I succeeded in doing, and Sergei set to work with enthusiasm.

Our first plan was to place all the solo-singers and the chorus in the orchestra, but on second thoughts it was decided to follow my alternative suggestion— to place them on the stage itself and turn their presence to decorative effect. It was necessary to dress them all in the same costumes and dispose them on either side of the stage, leaving the middle free for the action. Unfortunately, I was too busy in the Moscow Arts Theatre (besides my work on *Le Rossignol*) to occupy myself entirely with the décor of *Le Coq d'Or*. In those days I was deeply infatuated with the work of N. S. Gontcharova. After a period of rather absurd experiments of a modernist kind, she had turned with enthusiasm to popular imagery and ancient ikon-painting, and I nominated her my "successor." If she would only agree and fall in with my plan, what a wonderful performance we would show Paris! Great was my joy when I obtained the "Director's" permission to apply to Gontcharova, and greater still when Gontcharova immediately agreed. She believed in my plan, and, seeing its magnificent possibilities, took it at once to heart.

The choreography of *Le Coq d'Or* was allotted to Fokine, who, since 1914, had rejoined Diaghilev.

The chief obstacle to his return—now removed—had been Nijinsky's ballet-mastership. Most wonderful of all, Diaghilev succeeded in persuading the opera artists to accept the sacrifice demanded of them. The production was completely organised in Moscow and St. Petersburg and after that it did not concern me.

I made one condition, to which Seriozha agreed —that my name should appear on the programme as the author of the plan of the production. I attached no small importance to this, as it seemed to me that the example of our *Coq d'Or* might open a new era in opera. Seriozha promised faithfully, but as usual did not keep his word. Instead, he tried to "console" me by sending a newspaper reporter to interview me, who published in a secondary Paris newspaper what should have been officially announced.

I was so accustomed to my ungrateful friend's forgetfulness that it did not even anger me, and my real consolation in this case, as in others, was that my advice and instructions had contributed to the greater success of work that was dear to me.

Chapter XII

THE SEASON OF 1914

THE production of *Le Rossignol* during the season
of 1914 was my personal work.   Strictly speaking,
its story does not belong to reminiscences devoted
exclusively to the ballet, but as my production—
thanks to the style of the opera—acquired, to a great
extent, the character of a ballet, I feel justified in
dwelling on it here, especially as it was the final
chord of the first period of my theatrical activity.
Two months after *Le Rossignol* had seen the footlights
in Paris and in London, the whole of Europe was
blazing with deadly war; together with my family I
left France and the friends who lived there, among
them Seriozha Diaghilev.   We parted for an indefinite
time and were destined to meet again only after nine
years.

I have already said that the opera *Le Rossignol* was
begun by Stravinsky in 1910, when he played me the
music of the recently finished first act.   Being busy
with other problems, he put the opera aside and
returned to it only after he had accomplished the
wonderful journey from *L'Oiseau de Feu* to *Petrouchka*
and from *Petrouchka* to *Sacre du Printemps*.   Naturally
the result was a glaring incongruity between the style
of the first act and the two others.   I remember how
Diaghilev tried to persuade Igor of the necessity of
revising the first act, so that the whole work should
have the same style, but the composer refused and *Le
Rossignol* remained as it was.   The incongruity of the

two musical styles is smoothed over in the performance, which is probably what the composer counted upon. The lyrical quality of the first act, where the courtiers sent by the Emperor come to the seashore to invite the Nightingale to the palace and the Fisherman utters wise Chinese aphorisms, reflects the composer's earlier moods. It serves as an interesting contrast to the two following acts—the pompous court reception of the Japanese Embassy and the contest between Death and the Nightingale at the sick Emperor's bedside.

I was delighted with the final scene of the opera, which is simple and expressive and thoroughly in the style of Andersen's fairy tales. The Mandarins arrive for the funeral ceremony, but, finding their Emperor safe, greet him with a resounding *Zdra-a-stvui-te*—good morning.

How cleverly Stravinsky and Mitousov "fitted in" the fairy tale to the opera libretto! The sea and land-scape of the first act, the throne-room and the golden bedroom in the Emperor's palace, gave me an opportunity to express all my infatuation with Chinese art. At first I hoped to keep to the style of the somewhat ridiculous Chinoiseries fashionable in the eighteenth century, but as the work advanced I became irritated by their insipidity. My love for genuine Chinese Art began more and more to permeate my production. My collection of popular Chinese colour-prints, which had been brought for me from Manchuria, served as valuable material for the costumes. The final result was a Chinoiserie *de ma façon*, far from accurate by pedantic standards and even, in a sense, hybrid, but undoubtedly appropriate to Stravinsky's music. The magnificent march in the second act and the parts of the Nightingale and of Death have a style that is definitely and genuinely Chinese, but the rest of the opera is more "general European" in character.

Only the enormous pleasure I had in working at *Le Rossignol* enabled me to cope with the task, for I had to combine it with strenuous work on *La Locandiera* for the Moscow Arts Theatre. I composed the décor for *Le Rossignol* during my visits to St. Petersburg and made all the sketches on a scale unusual for me. The actual execution of the décor I entrusted to the charming and clever artist Charbé, who brought it and the numerous stage properties to Paris by means of the diplomatic bag. I myself was already in Paris when everything arrived, for our rehearsals had begun.

I remember distinctly my first appearance in 1914 —straight from the train—on the stage of the Opéra at a rehearsal of *La Légende de Joseph.* I can see the fully-illuminated face of Richard Strauss at the conductor's desk, standing out against the dark background of the empty theatre, the group of chosen "friends of the Russian Ballet" sitting on seats placed on the stage itself, and among them dear Misia Edwardes, who greeted me with sincere and noisy delight. Next to her sat her future husband Sert, smiling into his beard as usual. He was the author of the magnificent Veronese décor for *Joseph.* Only Bakst was missing, although he had designed the Veronese costumes for the same ballet. He had had one of his usual quarrels with Diaghilev and had locked himself up at home.

Strenuous preparation for my performance began from the moment of my arrival. I had to be present both at the ballet rehearsals for *Le Coq d'Or* and at the opera and ballet rehearsals for *Le Rossignol.* I was particularly delighted with the presentation of the Chinese March arranged by the ballet-master Romanov, who was just beginning his glorious career; only seven years earlier I had watched him dancing as one of the youthful buffoons in *Le Pavillon d'Armide.* According to my plan, separate links of the long procession were to emerge in strict conformity with the sections of the music. The procession was headed by the dancers of his Chinese Majesty and ended with the appearance of the Emperor himself, surrounded by black-robed Mandarins of the first rank and marching under a gigantic black and mauve umbrella. As the procession of the "Imperial Ballet Company" appeared from the wings, each link made two rounds of the stage and sank down on the floor within the space lit up with lanterns, thus forming a gorgeous and motley carpet of living flowers who emphasised by their movements the principal points of the action. Romanov, with rare sensitivity, understood precisely what I was aiming at and even before the dancers were in costumes the long scene proved wonderfully exciting. But the impression it produced on the night of the performance surpassed all my expectations. In the light of the huge blue lanterns the fantastic costumes stood out vividly against the background of white and blue china columns, and when the Emperor, sparkling with gold and jewels, stepped forward from under his gigantic umbrella and the crowd fell down to worship him, the effect was so great that for the first time in my life I felt genuinely moved by my own creation. I even felt the choking sensation of tears. Misia confessed to me that she actually wept for delight. For some reason she was peculiarly touched by the solitary dancer in black silk who performed his stylised movements in the middle of the stage.

On the whole, I consider *Le Rossignol* one of my most successful productions. It saddens me, therefore, to think that, after only two performances in Paris and four in London,[1] it was buried in the cellars of Drury

[1] Diaghilev succeeded in having the expenses of the luxurious production of *Le Rossignol* paid by the London theatre, Drury Lane. In spite of this, the dress rehearsal and the première were given in the Paris Opéra, thus depriving London of the privilege of a novelty.
[*Footnote continued on next page.*]

362 THE RUSSIAN BALLET

Lane, where half the settings and costumes perished during the years of the War. The disaster came to light in the 1920's, when the Director of the Paris Opéra, Monsieur Rouché, wished to acquire the production of *Le Rossignol* for his theatre. When the calamity was discovered, the matter fell through. In the meanwhile Diaghilev, who had not, during the years of the War, been able to tour with an opera company, ordered a one-act, purely ballet version of *Le Rossignol* from Stravinsky, and, as I was absent, the production was entrusted to Matisse. His costumes were enchanting in colour, but there was none of the sumptuous splendour of the first version, which in 1914, had made *Le Rossignol* a really Grand Spectacle.

I want to add a few words about my impressions of the season of 1914—the last season before the War. My "curious system" in the production of *Le Coq d'Or* created a certain sensation, but it did not provoke as many disputes and discussions as might have been expected. Possibly the public was so enchanted by the spectacle that they hardly noticed the singing, self-effacing crowds, among whom were incomparable singers.

The performance was really stupendous. Fokine had

During the first performance of *Le Rossignol* in London, I had one of my usual quarrels with Diaghilev. Owing to lack of time in Paris, many details of the performance were not yet correct, particularly the complicated, planked footways that supported the platform on which stood the Emperor's throne, amidst a collection of Chinese vases. The court officials, too, were to stand on this platform. As Seriozha vowed and declared that everything would be put right in London, I was lenient towards much that shocked me in Paris. But as usual he did not keep his promise and I was so angry and upset when I saw the same defects at Drury Lane that I began to reprove Seriozha with great violence—loudly enough for my voice to be heard even in the auditorium, in spite of the dropped curtain. The result was a quarrel, but next day Nouvel appeared as peace-maker and we all made it up over a luncheon party at the Savoy. We parted as friends, embracing and kissing each other in the Russian way. Little did we think that nine years were to elapse before we should meet again.

solved the problem magnificently. Karsavina was beautiful in the part of the Queen of Shemâkhan, Bulgakov as King Dodon gave an impressive display of burlesque and Cecchetti had managed to be highly mysterious in the part of the Astrologer. Gontcharova conquered Paris with her colourful décor and costumes. I sat in Misia Edwardes' box at the première. Her box was the focal point of all the principal *amis des russes*, and I remember how every new effect evoked from them a chorus of exclamations. The greatest sensation of all was the appearance of King Dodon's silver steed on wheels. That supreme *arbiter elegantiarum*, Boni de Castellane, fell into a sort of ecstasy, and his fluted "Versailles" voice could be heard throughout the theatre ejaculating "C'est trop joli!" But I was not equally pleased with all Gontcharova's work. It was, I thought, too prominent and seemed even to interfere with the action. I regretted, too, that, in spite of my advice, she had kept to the tradition of depicting the Russian fairy tale in motley, "Asiatic" colours; I would have preferred the amusing, semi-European style of Russian popular prints of the eighteenth century. Rimsky-Korsakov must have had similar pictures in mind when he composed his wonderful march for the soldiers—not *warriors*—of Dodon's army. In general, Gontcharova's interpretation of *Le Coq d'Or* seemed to lack poetry and atmosphere—but that, of course, had no importance for Boni de Castellane and other representatives *du snobisme transcendant*. I was disappointed too in my favourite last act. Gontcharova had succeeded in making the procession amusing and effective, but where was the atmosphere of terror that ought to grow more and more menacing as soon as the sun disappears behind the dark cloud? Alas, the artist had forgotten all about the cloud!

Nevertheless, the production of the *Le Coq d'Or* was one of Diaghilev's great successes. One cannot say as much of *Joseph*, as Strauss's *La Légende de Joseph* was usually called. I am not, on the whole, an admirer of Strauss, and in *Joseph* the author of *Der Rosenkavalier* and *Tyl Eulenspiegel* has failed, even more signally, to conceal his inner emptiness beneath the flash and thunder of his orchestration.[1]

Sert's Veronese setting with its black and gold twisted columns and the Veronese costumes by Bakst were both impressive, but neither décor nor costumes could make the drama convincing. The new *premier danseur* was very handsome, but he did not dance as well as his predecessor, or as he himself did later on. This was Massine, whom Diaghilev had recently discovered in Moscow and who had taken Nijinsky's place. His partner, M. N. Kusnetzova, in spite of her gorgeous dress and train, was helpless and unconvincing as the seductive wife of Potiphar. Finally, the poor planning of the stage prevented Fokine from giving of his best.

Two other novelties of the 1914 season passed almost unnoticed. They were the ballet *Midas* to the music of Stravinsky's friend Steinberg (who was married to Rimsky-Korsakov's daughter) and a tiny ballet to Schumann's music, *Les Papillons*. The latter was, so to speak, a continuation of *Carnaval*. The neglect of both these ballets is undeserved. True, the music of *Midas* is far from a work of genius, but it is never-

---

[1] During one of the last orchestral rehearsals the composer provoked a significant "demonstration" by the tactlessness with which he commented on the absence of some of the musicians. Strauss, infuriated that this should have happened a second time, had allowed himself to comment loudly on the degeneration of the French people. The director of the Opéra, Rouché, managed to smooth things over and to persuade Strauss to apologise.

The incident, which took place in the spring of that fatal year, was the *only* indication of a certain tension between the French and the Germans. The Germans were made much of in Paris in those days and the same Strauss and the charming Count Kessler were fêted enthusiastically. Remember too that in the same season the German Opera was given at the Théâtre des Champs Elysées and that Wagner was sung *in German*—something hitherto unknown.

DÉCOR FOR THE SECOND ACT OF STRAVINSKY'S OPERA *LE ROSSIGNOL*

By Alexandre Benois, 1917

Facing p. 364

MAURICE RAVEL AFTER BATHING, ST. JEAN DE LUZ, 1914
From a sketch by Alexandre Benois

Facing p. 365

theless pleasant and the performance was charming and in excellent taste. Fokine had arranged the dances in a great hurry, but, as often happened with him, the air of improvisation gave the production a particular freshness. Dobuzhinsky's décor, inspired by Mantegna's *Parnassus*, was perfectly enchanting. The décor for *Les Papillons* was also Dobuzhinsky's work. It consisted of two pavilions and a fountain in a moonlit park, and was full of the delicious atmosphere created by the music.

My personal success had never been so great as in that June of 1914, both in Paris and in London. Orders for work were being showered upon me from all sides. The Director of the Opéra, carried away by the success of our ballets, had decided to break the routine of the theatre he managed, by making a sensational experiment. A poem was to be written by Gabriele d'Annunzio, music composed by Reynaldo Hahn, décor, costumes and the general plan of the production entrusted to me. This "miracle" was to be given in the spring of 1915, and I well remember the intimate dinner at Voisin's (now no longer in existence) given to us, the collaborators, by M. Rouché, at which we definitely decided to begin our collective work. Events of infinitely greater significance than the hopes of artists and poets prevented the fulfilment of our dream. I left my colleagues with the intention of meeting them again in two months' time; we could not, at that moment, have supposed that, for some of us, the parting was final, and that the enterprise about which we were so enthusiastic would survive only as a sad and distant memory.

The same fate cut short my plan of collaboration with Ravel. Ravel, a magnificent composer and a charming man, was an ardent admirer of our performances and dreamed of creating a ballet with me. We had not finally agreed on the subject, but it was decided in principle that the action was to take place in Spain. Ravel had a genuine cult for Spain, which I shared. We did not hurry ourselves. We had the whole summer in front of us and decided to spend it together at St. Jean-de-Luz, situated half a mile from Ravel's native place Ciboure. Every day we met on the *plage* and went for long walks together.

In those days Ravel was very gay and fanciful. I remember particularly one occasion during the last days of that happy summer, when dear Maurice, behaving like a mischievous schoolboy, flew in a wide circle and at terrific speed over our heads on a huge merry-go-round at the Ciboure Fair, shouting abrupt greetings to us every time he went past. I also remember our last picnic at Hendaye. Our company was returning in two carriages (it was still the "era of horses") and we were all greatly impressed by the foreboding look of the evening sky, its cumbrous clouds lit up by blood-red rays of the setting sun. Even those of us who were least inclined to mysticism were overwhelmed by the sky's ominous pageantry. The meaning of this tragic apparition of nature was not slow to be revealed; three days after, the tocsin from the church of St. Jean-de-Luz resounded throughout the town and the countryside.

Twenty days later we were hurrying home across seas sown with mines.

EPILOGUE

EPILOGUE

HERE, for the moment, I am cutting short my reminiscences of the ballet. This does not mean that I definitely withdrew from ballet production. On the contrary, my work in Paris for Ida Rubinstein represents in itself a very impressive whole, even without reference to my work in various other cities in Europe. Nevertheless, there can be no comparison between my activity in the sphere of ballet during this later period and what I achieved before the War, when, together with Diaghilev, Bakst and Fokine, I created what was afterwards called the *Ballets Russes*. If I were to continue my narrative, the result would not be in harmony with what has already been related; there would be too much criticism, too many regrets and even, perhaps, "recriminations," addressed, sometimes, to people who were or are very near to me. All this will find its *natural* place in my general memoirs, on which I have been working for many years. There my complaints and my reproaches, reflecting a life's experience, will help me, I have no doubt, to present a many-sided and therefore valuable "human document." In my general memoirs I shall not present myself as one active in ballet work, but as a man of art and a creative artist in the wider sense.

In saying good-bye to my readers, I should like for a moment to look back once again. I shall endeavour to define more precisely what the ballet meant to me, and what, in my opinion, it *should be*. It was my friend (and in some respects my "pupil") who helped my ideals to find creative expression in the ballet. In the second half of his life, having finally freed himself from my influence, he gave the ballet an entirely different direction from what it had taken originally, a direction I cannot help considering to be wrong. Diaghilev's most consistent pupil and follower has gone still further and deeper along the same road. He has gone so far that perhaps Diaghilev himself would have turned away from some of his achievements in despair.

Everything in the world is subject to the law of change, to evolution; "everything flows past," as a Greek Sage enunciated two thousand years ago. There are no breaks and there cannot be. But does it follow that *any* course, at any time, is the right one? Do not some currents encounter rapids, cataracts and deep, still pools on their way? Are there not moments when one feels that the stream has taken a dangerous bend? Is it not then a duty to correct the deviation?

It seems to me that the ultra-progressive ballet has been carried away into a final *cul-de-sac*, and feeling this, I think it is useful to recognise the danger and to try to get out of it.

The time is past when the ballet was something intelligent, poetical and closely linked with the other arts, *principally with music*. In fact ballet can be considered as the plastic crystallisation of music. Nowadays the "progressive" ballet tends to emancipate itself completely even from music, and to become absolutely self-sufficient. The ballet-master, having become "chore-author" and being the sole dictator of the stage, is inclined to discard both pictorial art and music, seeing them perhaps as rivals to his autocratic rule. In Lifar's *Icare*, music is even entirely dispensed with and is replaced by noises.

The ballet is one of the most consistent and complete expressions of the idea of the *Gesamtkunstwerk*, the idea for which our circle was ready to give its soul. It was no accident that what was afterwards known as the *Ballets Russes* was originally conceived not by the professionals of the dance, but by a circle of artists, linked together by the idea of Art as an entity. Everything followed from the common desire of several painters and musicians to see the fulfilment of the theatrical dreams which haunted them; but I emphasise again that there was nothing *specific* or *professional* in their dreams. On the contrary, there was a burning craving for Art in general.

It so happened that we found in Fokine and Stravinsky men who lived with dreams similar to ours. Then came the "miracle" of our meeting, essential to both sides. It also happened that the only member of our circle who was capable of business—Diaghilev —became gradually infected with our common ideals. It was he who made possible the realisation of our ideals—but I must again repeat that our ideals were not limited to the ballet alone, but concerned the whole world of art. *Mir Iskousstva*, the *World of Art*, is the name we gave to our review; it was our first effort to influence society—before we had any connection with theatre or ballet. Later, part of our group seemed to have come to its most complete "agreement" on the subject of ballet, and in consequence we collaborated here with special success.

Unfortunately, the harmony of our collaboration lasted only a few years. External events of a redoubtable character—war and revolution—disunited us. We lost sight of each other for a long period. When circumstances allowed some of the members of our circle to meet again, we discovered that a significant change had taken place in our opinions and tastes. We had ceased to have ideals in common. The future loomed before me like a bad dream.

The mania of "experimenting at any cost," adopted by "professional bold innovators" like Meyerhold,

N

has brought the drama to a monstrous crisis and is to-day to be found in the most advance manifestations of ballet creation. A certain sobering process is apparent in the domain of drama; the heresy is beginning to outlive itself, and this makes me rejoice sincerely. But how much happier I would be to see a similar enlightenment in the region that lies nearest to my heart—in the ballet. How overjoyed I would be to see the ballet emerging from the blind alley into which it has been driven, to the applause of the crowd, by the joint efforts of personal vainglory, inadequately developed taste and a pervading element of coarseness.

Everything flows, everything changes, everything *must* change. Still, through all the vicissitudes of creative activity there flows a life-giving stream— sincerity. Real joy comes to the artist when he realises that his creation—whether a plastic vision expressed in a performance on the stage, or music expressed in sounds, or thoughts in words—is in accordance with what is called his "inspiration." Harmony between inspiration and expression may be more or less complete. When it is lacking the result is *falsehood*. Without inspiration true Art and Beauty cannot be created. Both Art and Beauty disappear and give place to dreary imitation and even, sometimes, to perverted monstrosity when inspiration is supplanted by the vainglorious desire to create a sensation or, worse still, to "follow the fashion."

Monstrosity began to penetrate the closed region of ballet later than any other region of art. When I first knew the ballet, everything about it was stable and quiet, as if it lived in a remote countryside, in the depths of an art province of its own; it enjoyed almost complete freedom from criticism. Russian ballet, when I first became infatuated with it, with all the enthusiasm of my fourteen years, was really in

a state of mummification. It was just this mummification that saved the Russian ballet from the decline
which affected all the other famous ballet-schools of
Europe during the last quarter of the nineteenth
century. In Russia the ballet continued to live its
own life, remote from all disturbances; carried along,
almost, by its own *vis inertiæ*. It was, of course, a
piece of great good fortune that it should have been
in the care of two such excellent artists as Johannsen
and Petipa. Thanks to them, and in spite of the
rigid traditions of the Imperial School, an extraordinary freshness was preserved. And so it remained till Vsevolojsky's directorate, during which,
under his influence, but with the help of Johannsen
and Petipa and above all of the tradition itself, the
Russian ballet blossomed again into unparalleled
splendour.

I consider myself particularly fortunate that at a
time when the soul thirsts for life-giving impressions
in art I should have found our St. Petersburg ballet
at its zenith. Its efflorescence was made possible by
an astonishing combination of elements: Vsevolojsky's
delicate sense of art, Virginia Zucchi's fiery genius,
Petipa's creative imagination, the flourishing state of
the Imperial Theatre School, and lastly the readiness
of a composer like Tchaikovsky to put his genius at
the disposal of the ballet. . . . All this I snatched at,
with the greed of youth, at the very moment of its
origin. After many, many years the delight I then
experienced still has power to stimulate me!

After that "happy period," lasting approximately
from 1884 to 1895, came a time of dreamy lassitude.
Having tasted of those joys, it was painful to watch
Russian ballet drifting into decline. The downward
tendency was emphasised when, after two years of
Prince Volkonsky's timid directorate, Russian theatrical work came under the control of V. A. Teliakovsky, a man somewhat pusillanimous and cold to

poetical feeling, though endowed with great practical sense and even a semblance of taste. My friends and I (being all of us enthusiasts of the theatre in general and of the ballet in particular) found it unbearable to watch the decline that neither the talents of the dancers nor the lavishness of the productions could arrest. We longed to save what was so dear to us, to help it to recover the vitality it was gradually losing. Our circle of the *World of Art* had zest and fervour enough for this work of salvation, but unfortunately general circumstances in Russia in the 1900's were unfavourable.

In the pervading atmosphere of conscious opposition to everything *artistic* my *Pavillon d'Armide* might well have remained a solitary and fruitless experiment and Fokine, for all his talent, have been unable to initiate a new era in ballet. So we decided to create something that would be *our own work*, independent of anybody but ourselves; further, to display our creation elsewhere, in fresh places, to bring it into contact with new masses. What we brought to Paris was not the decadent Imperial Ballet, but something entirely separate— our *own* ballet, a ballet that corresponded with our ideals, that resuscitated the joys of our youth and promised further evolution along the path we had chosen.

The performances of *Le Pavillon d'Armide, Schéhérazade, L'Oiseau de Feu* and *Petrouchka* shown to Europe between 1909 and 1914 were not ballets in the former, narrow sense of the word; rather, a new form of spectacle based on a rejuvenation of the traditions of the St. Petersburg Ballet. We did not aim at astounding the world with sensational innovations; our chief wish was to make the European public participate with us in something that we ourselves loved, something that, before its decline, had delighted and inspired us, something that, with our help, was regaining its original enchantment and vitality. As it was impossible for us to revive our Russian ballet in our own country, we were reviving it, oddly enough, for strangers.

The Russian ballet was not a purely national product; it was something that had been imported and had continued its existence in its new country through foreign talent—Didelot, Saint-Léon, Johannsen, Petipa and many others. The soil of Russia proved more receptive than elsewhere. It has proved so prolific that the ballet has resisted all political storms and catastrophes; at the present day it continues to delight the public in U.S.S.R. in the same way as it delighted the Imperial Court and the faithful subjects of the Russian autocrats.

There is no doubt that had we come to Europe only as representatives of something *exotic*, we would still have created a sensation. But such a success would have been less significant and less stable. The fact that we had shown Europe something *European*, something that had been miraculously preserved in our country and there transfigured and revived, gave our productions a particular significance that contributed largely to their success.

The voices that sang our praises were, alas, mingled with other voices, that demanded something "more modern." Diaghilev was peculiarly susceptible to such demands; they excited and disturbed him to the utmost degree. In general, our indomitably courageous leader was worried only by criticism that accused him of being behind the times or in a backwater. This characteristic of his was well-known to all of us, his nearest friends, who had studied his nature in all its smallest details. The best way to "frighten" Seriozha (and so "force" him to undertake something he preferred to avoid) was to point out to him that he was not keeping pace with the times, that he was falling behind and that he was "a slave to routine."

Bakst and Nouvel often resorted to this kind of blackmail, and I, too, was not entirely innocent. Unfortunately Diaghilev's susceptibility to such influence made him defenceless against our successors— people who made a cult of being "modern," treating it as a *profession de foi*; who considered distortion and extravagance as an indispensable law of artistic creation. From the moment of Diaghilev's "enforced isolation," which began in 1914, there was no one to hold him back, no one to remind him of our chief aim and of the sole, unyielding principle of the *World of Art*, namely "artistic integrity."

The isolated Diaghilev was diverted from the course he had once followed by a tendency typical of the latter part of the nineteenth century, a tendency which later on gained remarkable strength. It is the well-known *snobisme*, in the continental sense of the word. Certainly this tendency always existed in over-refined centres of European culture. Was it not *snobisme* that Molière mocked at in his *Précieuses Ridicules*? But spiritual and physical affectation in the pursuit of *le dernier cri* never achieved such grotesque absurdity as it did in the first years of the twentieth century, and as it continues to do now. It is a period of triumph for all manner of Mascarilles and Jodelets; those who try to unmask these mystifiers risk unpopularity. Diaghilev (especially the "isolated Diaghilev") was not in the least inclined to expose such people; on the contrary, he was tempted to take his usual place and to become their leader. It won for him a halo of a kind; but it produced a fundamental change in the spirit of his work.

Mascarillade does, not of course, exclude "talent." Those who think that the success of modern tendencies is due solely to charlatan methods and artistic jobbing are greatly mistaken. Even the cleverest fakers cannot succeed without making use of the alluring properties of talent. By now the blending of real talent (at times very vivid) with *snobisme* has produced such a monstrous tangle that it is difficult to differentiate between the end of imposture or dilettantism and the beginning of true art. Where is the dividing line between the genuine search for new beauty and mountebank sensationalism? Everything has become involved, and falsehood, whose decay was mourned not so long ago by Oscar Wilde, has once again come into its own and is finding its place in the expression of truth. What a number of sects, formulas and theories have appeared! What clever specialists in doctrine, what brilliant and tortuous sophists, what professionals of paradox! Diaghilev was always inclined towards this creative saturnalia; it is not surprising therefore that he was drawn into the abyss. Torn away from his native soil, deprived forever of the country and the *milieu* in which he had been brought up, feeling forlorn and chronically frightened of this or that, he decided to be the "leader of the movement," to be *plus royaliste que le roi*. It is said that the courage shown by heroes is due sometimes to the fear of cowardice. It was such courage that was the foundation of Diaghilev's character. It helped him to create much that was really beautiful; but it was the same courage that made of him a paladin of modernistic nonsense.

During the nine years of separation from my friend, I had had no proper information as to what he was doing and what was going on in Paris, and when, in 1923, I first saw Diaghilev's new productions, I was highly embarrassed. I could not remain indifferent to what was fascinating and alluring—in other words, to the talent displayed—but that only added to my embarrassment. I was well acquainted with Diaghilev's inclination towards extremes, an inclination that encouraged him to indulge in his favourite "pamps." Formerly there had been many ways of restraining him, chiefly through the "control" of his friends.   Now that all his former friends had disappeared and there remained only Bakst, whose talent he willingly exploited, but whose opinion he did not seriously respect, Diaghilev gave in to his inclination to create a sensation at all costs, and was encouraged to this end by people of the same tendency as himself. This was the "new spirit" in Diaghilev's work, the spirit that surprised me so unexpectedly.   Diaghilev, Stravinsky, the whole company and the *fervents* had become so accustomed to the new atmosphere that they were oblivious to the change and considered everything to be perfectly normal.   When dear Levushka Bakst found that he could not struggle against it any more, he had a final quarrel with Diaghilev, and from that moment ceased to take any part in the work that had lain so close to his heart.   Diaghilev's chief advisers were now the "new friends": Jean Cocteau, who, up till 1914, had been considered by us a sort of *enfant terrible*, but was now occupying the place (vacated by Montesquiou) of arbiter of Parisian elegance, the young Ukrainian poet Boris Kokhno, who became Diaghilev's secretary and, at the same time, his chief theoretician and source of inspiration, and lastly N. Gontcharova's husband, M. F. Larionov, a very gifted artist, but one in whom a strange sterility is combined with a remarkable eagerness to show himself in the foreground.   The "inner emptiness" of the people who now surrounded Seriozha was obvious to me and Seriozha himself could not have found it satisfactory.   However, he was now entirely in their hands and continued to show off his new achievements *de plus en plus fort*, to their unanimous applause.

The first months of my stay in Paris in 1923 passed without my actually seeing the results of this new development, and on the surface everything between us seemed as it used to be.   Diaghilev at once entrusted me with the production of Gounod's operas,

ALEXANDRE BENOIS
From a photograph by Emile Marcovitch, 1939

Facing p. 378

DÉCOR FOR THE THIRD ACT OF GOUNOD'S OPERA *LE MÉDÉCIN MALGRÉ LUI*. Produced by Diaghilev, Monte Carlo, 1924

By Alexandre Benois

Facing p. 379

Le Médecin malgré Lui and *Philémon et Baucis*, which
he was going to give in Monte Carlo in honour of the
centenary of the composer of *Faust*. But from the
moment the ballet rehearsals and performances began
in Monte Carlo, I understood what was up.
Much of it attracted me, and Stravinsky's *Pulcinella*
I found enchanting. The idea of blending Pergolese's
music that he loved with a kind of mockery of it was
supremely successful, and I do not know of any other
work in the literature of music in which a similar
sacrilege has been achieved in a form so damnably
alluring. Perhaps it ought not to have been done,
but the result could in no way be deplored, for it
was musical clowning of *genius*. How like Stravinsky it was—Stravinsky who was still one of my
favourite composers! Picasso's rather absurdly conceived and negligently painted décor, together with
his costumes, reminiscent of street acrobats, was in
full sympathy with the music, and finally, Massine's
choreography[1] was outstandingly successful and marvellously executed.

Les Femmes de Bonne Humeur was another ballet
arranged to old music, but the selection and modern-
isation of Scarlatti was far inferior to the treatment
accorded to Pergolese. Bakst had made charming
costumes (it was before his break with Diaghilev) and
they reminded one of the dresses of old-fashioned
marionettes. The décor, in brownish tones, was in
full harmony with the costumes and only betrayed
the influence of the modern fashion—very naïvely—
by the slight forward tilt of the houses. The marionette character of the choreography openly smacked of
the grotesque, for the interpreters of Goldoni's ballet

---

[1] Later I saw other productions of *Pulcinella* by two very talented
people, Lopukhov in St. Petersburg and Romanov in Monte Carlo.
Both productions, however, destroyed the fragile beauty of this
paradoxical work by complicating and "deepening" the subject
and transforming the transparent design of Massine's dances by all
manner of cunning tricks.

moved about and gesticulated as if pulled by strings. Nevertheless *Les Femmes de Bonne Humeur* made an enchanting impression; it had a charm very similar to the charm of our first ballets—*our* ballets.

Different were the other ballets that went "under the name of Diaghilev." The choreography had been created by Nijinska, an artist of rare talent and wonderful sensibility, and there was much that pleased me in them. I was attracted by the charming and elegant eclecticism of Poulenc's music in *Les Biches*, and by Auric's graceful playfulness in *Les Fâcheux*. It was with delight that I heard once again Monteclair's exquisite score in *Les Tentations de la Bergère*, though it had not gained from having been reinforced in volume. Still, the pervading *snobisme* was too obvious; it gave all these novelties the veneer of passing fashion, a veneer that gives a work of art a temporary success, but makes it fade quickly. The inconsistency and absurdity of the episodes deprived them of any interest; they were nearer "parades at a fair" than real theatrical action. Nor did the décors redeem the emptiness of the action; neither Marie Laurencin's faded pastel colouring, nor Braque's "tasteful muddiness," nor Gris' helpless endeavour to reconstruct the lavishness of the old-fashioned stage, succeeded in compensating for the essential poverty of the productions.

Outwardly my relations with Diaghilev remained the same. There was even an unusual note of tenderness in his attitude towards me. It seemed at times to contain a sort of apology: "Do forgive me my sins," and at others a shade of triumph: "You see, old friend, how far we have gone since we freed ourselves from our provincialism." There could be no talk of my former "guardianship." Seriozha believed in other advisers and considered that he had accurately assessed the real demands of the times—was in advance of the most "advanced." The approval of his young companions encouraged him to new adventures; my remonstrances seemed to him as dull as the nagging of any venerable mentor. A kind of mental coquettishness, an irrepressible desire always to appear young, made him hate everything that seemed to him "sober and reasonable." I was ready to undertake experiments even more risky than those which now occupied Diaghilev, but genuine artistic impulse was still for me the mainspring of creative activity; the wish to perplex or to produce a sensation made me as indignant as ever.

Some of Diaghilev's later ballets I enjoyed, but more often I found in them the conscious attempt to astonish. I was particularly disappointed in the trifling ballet *La Chatte*, which had a great success with the public and even attracted a stream of new admirers to the *Ballets Russes*. The success of *La Chatte* proved that Paris society was demoralised to such a degree that it was ready to reconcile itself to the wildest absurdities provided they were served under the label of *le dernier cri*. *La Chatte* had, however, a certain harmony of its own; the lack of meaning in the subject was in full accord with the drawing-room music, the ugliness of the "constructivist" décor and the lack of colour and sense in the costumes. The result was a wonderful ensemble of ugliness in which the only disharmony was the grace and mastery of the dancers. The artists must surely have felt uncomfortable among what seemed to be a set of glass instruments from a laboratory built by a maniac.

Diaghilev's other ultra-modern and ultra-snobbish ballets, *Le Renard, Les Matelots, Le Train Bleu*, etc., were equally senseless in their ugliness. But they were all surpassed by *Le Pas d'Acier*, which had, apart from its stupidity and affectation, something repulsive in it. The search for novelty and the wish to keep pace with the century had led Seriozha, our "aristocrat" Seriozha, so far as to present on the stage of the Opéra an apotheosis of the Soviet regime. *Le Pas d'Acier* could easily be taken for one of those official glorifications of Industrialism and of the Proletariat in which the U.S.S.R. excels. The cynical zeal of the authors and producers of *Le Pas d'Acier* had actually gone so far as to offset the triumph of the workers by sneers at the defeat of the bourgeoisie. On the stage, among the representatives of the "class that was vanquished," there tramped about unfortunate ladies of society, who, in the days of famine and need, endeavoured to sell at the market those remnants of their belongings that had not yet been stolen by the Bolsheviks! Prokofiev was the author of the imitative music that hissed and whistled like a foundry. After creating this masterpiece, he acted with perfect consistency by returning to the U.S.S.R., where he has continued to prosper to the present day. Curiously enough, Diaghilev cherished the dream of getting into contact with the Soviets and for this purpose even befriended the official poet of New Russia, Mayakovsky.

In time Seriozha grew tired of the world of falsehood into which he had been drawn in his pursuit of *le dernier cri*. I cannot forget the conversation I had with him a year before his death; without any prompting from me, he began to justify himself for the strangeness of some of his actions. It seemed that the burden he had loaded on his shoulders and which he had been carrying for twenty years was getting beyond his strength. His only real joy now was not in the work that glorified him throughout the world, but in collecting ancient books. It was in a way a return to the "beginning of it all," to the impulse that, in 1895, had made him write to me of a "Sergei Diaghilev Museum." He became a bibliophile, a *Russian* bibliophile. Within a few years his library, for which, being homeless, he hired a special apartment, grew to a significant size. Diaghilev spent large sums in satisfying his passion and used to be inexpressibly happy when he had managed to "unearth" some very rare book. His ideal of leisure for the future was *otium cum dignitate*. Diaghilev dreamed of spending his old age in his study, absorbed in the correlation or annotation of ancient texts. Here he would not be ruling over stubborn, vainglorious, irritable people, but would be associating with the finest intellects, the finest manifestations of the past culture of his own country, the country to which there was no returning, but which he never ceased to adore, in spite of all his "Westernisation," in spite of the terrible metamorphosis that had taken place in his fatherland.

Diaghilev died unexpectedly, after a few days' illness. He died, in accordance with the gipsy prophecy that he would "die on the water," not in a ship indeed, but in a hotel on the Lido, whose windows overlooked the Adriatic. For many years he had made a practice of going yearly to Venice to rest after his exhausting seasons and tours. It is there in Venice that he lies buried, in the cemetery of San Michele—Diaghilev, a true Russian.

Our common adoration of Venice was a special link between us, independent of our creative work together or our business relations. Seriozha spoke about Venice with a strange tenderness, rather in the way he talked of the Russian countryside, the birch groves, the sound of the Russian church bells, the unbounded vastness of fields and rivers . . . In common with me, he seemed to feel somehow *related* to Venice. In my case it is undoubtedly atavism, for when I walk along the streets and squares of Venice, mounting and descending the numerous bridges, when I enter the cool darkness of the churches or float along in a gondola, I imagine to myself that these same streets and bridges were crossed by my ancestors, that the gondolier, stånding behind them, called out in the same way at the turnings, that my grandfathers and grandmothers once prayed in the same San Stae and San Moisé. But what was the origin of Seriozha's "mania" for Venice? Why was it that he preferred Venice to any other place in the world? It was not only the natural preference of an enlightened dilettante, nor was it due to the cult of the æsthetic or the cult of fashion; it went far deeper, for it was also a kind of atavism. It is not for nothing that the most celebrated quay in Venice bears the name of *Riva degli Schiavoni*,[1] that the Basilica of San Marco seems a provincial sister to the Byzantine Santa Sophia, and so a distant relation of the Russian Sophias in Novgorod and in Kiev. It was also the artistic side of Venice that satisfied the feeling of restless revolt and the craving for space of Diaghilev's genuine *âme slave*. In the ikoned sanctity of the mosaics, in the unrestrained, almost absurd self-will of Tintoretto, even in the regal grace and limpid solemnity of Tiepolo's ceilings, Diaghilev found an intimate echo that he could find nowhere else.

In the circle of his friends Sergei liked to boast of his descent, *de main gauche*, from Peter the Great. He hardly believed this family legend himself (possibly he had even invented it), but there is no doubt that he actually had in him *something* of Peter. When I was creating pictures and illustrations in which Peter the Great was the central figure, I used involuntarily to imagine Seriozha—*toute proportion gardée*—not so much physically as morally. In Diaghilev there was undoubtedly the inborn love of power, the mind that penetrated to the origin of all things (often without any actual knowledge of them), the capacity to gauge people's weaknesses and play on them, that were fundamental characteristics of the great reformer of Russia. Diaghilev was a born leader and, had it

---

[1] *Schiavoni*, in Venetian, means Slavs, not slaves.—*Trans.*

not happened that life had brought him into contact with artists, he would perhaps have displayed his gift in a wider and more significant sphere than ballet and even than art in general.

However, Diaghilev succeeded in founding a "kingdom" of its kind, and his kingdom did not die with him. It continues to live, handed from one diadoch to another, or even divided between several.

Terpsichore has never held such sway over humanity as she does at the present day. I, who remember the beginning of her triumph in the days of Zucchi and of Vsevolojsky's productions, find it astounding. But I am not gladdened by all the shapes assumed in its triumph by an art I have adored since childhood. I am even, in a way, depressed by the extravagant propagation of ballet, for in it I see the danger of gradual vulgarisation—vulgarisation of what was once highly exclusive, but enchanting and exquisite in its reticence. But such is the order of things and I comfort myself with the thought that throughout the countries of the world, whatever their régime, whatever their race, there *may* be people with natures as sensitive and receptive as were ours when our appreciation of the ballet first began.

To those "chosen few"—our successors, in a certain sense—the ballet, with its thousand and one offshoots of our Russian Ballet, will bring the joy that we once experienced. The ballet will help them—as we were helped by the ballets of our youth—to penetrate the very essence of Art.

INDEX

o

INDEX

Abramtzevo, theatrical experiments in, 197

Academy of Arts, author enters, 103; description of, 103 ff.; uniforms of, 104; cabal against author at, 108; author leaves, 108; author's ambition at, 204; Grand Duke Vladimir, President of, 268; ballet for students' ball of, 273

Adam, Adolphe, music of *Giselle* by, 72, 317

Admiralty Canal, author's apartment on, 256

Aïda, favourite opera of author, 87; costumes of, used for *Nuit d'Egypte*, 276

Albano, expeditions to, 331

Alexander I, lectures on, 155; interest of author's circle in, 183

Alexander III, pleased by Zucchi, 80, 91; portrait by Serov, 191

Alexander III, Museum, 184; author's volume on, 237

Alexandrovsky Market, Tartar junk shops in, 268

Alexandryinsky Theatre, Golovin's production for, 199; articles on, 206, 208; productions by Bakst at, 228; Greek tragedies produced at, 340

Alexandryinsky Theatre Square, Krupensky's office overlooking, 243

Alexei the Meek, Russia under, 152

Alexeyevskaya Street, author's studio in, 243

Algisi, author's prejudice against, 111

Allegri, O. C., pupil of Livogt, 109; studio of, assigned to author, 243; décor for *Nuit d'Egypte* by, 276

Allegri, O.P., Nijinsky's costume in *Spectre de la Rose* corrected by, 340

Alma Tadema, circle's opinion of, 159

Anisfeld, collaboration with Bakst, 315; *Petrouchka* décor executed by, 333

Après-Midi d'un Faune, creation of, 297

A Rebours, prohibited in Russia, 173

Arabian Nights, story of *Schéhérazade* from, 309, 315

Archipov, author's contact with, 176

Architecture of U.S.S.R., 105

Arensky, music of, for *Cléopâtre*, 295

Argentine, tour to, of Diaghilev's company, 351

Argutinsky-Dolgoroukov, Prince V., political tastes of, 183; friend of author's circle, 195; interest of in *Pavillon d'Armide*, 258; friendship of with Vassilieva, 259; secures favour of *Novoye Vremya*, for *Pavillon d' Armide*, 264; at ballet rehearsals, 283; at Diaghilev's gatherings, 302; at creation of *Schéhérazade*, 310

Art Treasures of Russia, author editor of, 206, 219; French edition of, 238

Arts Club, Petrouchka performance at, 325

Astarte, *Cléopâtre* in tradition of, 296

Astruc, Gabriel, support of, 312

Auber, composer, *Fenella la Muette de Portici* by, 94

Aubert, Arthur, sculptor, affected by Zucchi's dancing, 90; author coached by, 103; Birle introduced to author by, 171; joins author in Paris, 180

Auric, *Fâcheux* by, 380

o*